Retelling the Siege of Jerusalem
in Early Modern England

Retelling the Siege of Jerusalem in Early Modern England

Vanita Neelakanta

UNIVERSITY OF DELAWARE PRESS

Newark

Distributed by the University of Virginia Press

University of Delaware Press
© 2019 by Vanita Neelakanta
All rights reserved
Printed in the United States of America on acid-free paper

First published 2019

ISBN 978-1-64453-012-2 (cloth)
ISBN 978-1-64453-013-9 (e-book)
ISBN 978-1-64453-014-6 (paper)

1 3 5 7 9 8 6 4 2

Library of Congress Cataloging-in-Publication Data is available for this title.

Cover art: "Woe, Woe to Ierusalem," from Joseph ben Gorion's *The Wonderful and Most Deplorable History of the Latter Times of the Jews*, 1662. (Reproduced by permission of Henry E. Huntington Library and Art Gallery)

For my parents

Contents

Acknowledgments

This project has been long in the making, and my debts are many and varied. My thanks first to Irven Resnick, Jeremy Cohen, and Martin Goodman who sparked my interest in Josephus at the National Endowment for the Humanities Summer Study, "Holy Land, Holy City in Classical Judaism, Islam and Christianity" (Oxford 2008). I am deeply grateful to Reid Barbour, David Katz, Daniel Woolf, and Beatrice Groves for their generous mentorship, and to Mary Baine Campbell for her excellent advice and encouragement at a tricky stage in the process.

It gives me the greatest pleasure to acknowledge the many mentors, colleagues, and dear friends who read multiple chapter drafts, provided invaluable insights, and nurtured me throughout this process. Rebecca Olson, Rachel Kapelle, Laurel Harris, Terra Joseph, Nowell Marshall, and Matthew Goldie read drafts at various stages of completion, some many times over. Alison Hobgood, Marie Kelleher, Lisa Cooper, Susan McDonough, Aaron Braver, Allan Amanik, and Andrew Albin lent critical eyes and encouraging voices. Megan Titus, Mary Morse, Michael Gordin, Erika Milam, Wendy Belcher, Tom Hare, Cyrus Schayegh and Ioana Patuleanu offered sound advice and warm support. Matt Schario generously shared his technical expertise. My wonderful students Ashley Stenger, Kyle Stenger, Kady Stockman, Michael Boldizar, Rob Stone, Sarah Scarantino, and John Modica helped me enormously by asking perceptive questions. Ted Mills and Henry Vega housed and fed me during my sabbatical. I cannot thank you all enough.

This book was likewise enriched by the feedback and encouragement of fellow participants at numerous conferences and seminars, including those hosted by the Renaissance Society of America, The Society for Renaissance Studies, The Plymouth State University Medieval-Renaissance Forum, The Pacific Northwest Renaissance Conference, and The New England Modern Language Association. I benefitted vastly from my peers in the "Imagining Jerusalem,

1099 to the Present Day" Arts and Humanities Research Council Network, and owe a debt of gratitude to Helen Smith and Abigail Shinn for their interest in my work. Special thanks go to my wonderful cohort at the Folger Institute Faculty Seminar "Pasts in Early Modern Britain" (2017) whose lively discussions helped me pull it all together.

Sincere thanks go to Julia Oestreich at the University of Delaware Press and to Morgan Myers at the University of Virginia Press for their great care in shepherding this project through its many stages. I am deeply grateful to the astute and generous reviewers of the manuscript who gave so willingly of their time and expertise.

Archival research for this project was made possible by generous summer fellowships and a sabbatical courtesy Rider University. I am grateful to the staff at the British, Bodleian, John Rylands, Houghton, Huntington, and Princeton University Libraries whose vast knowledge and efficiency made my work so much easier.

My greatest debt is to my family, particularly my parents, for their unfailing support and faith in me. And to Michael Laffan, whose brilliant mind and unstinting love have enriched this book and my life beyond measure.

An earlier version of chapter 4 was published as "Reading Providence Out of History: The Destruction of Jerusalem in William Heminge's *The Jewes Tragedy*" in *Studies in Philology* 111, no. 1 (2014): 83–109. An earlier version of chapter 5 was published as "Exile and Restoration in John Crowne's *The Destruction of Jerusalem by Titus Vespasian*" which appeared in *Philological Quarterly* 89, nos. 2&3 (Spring and Summer 2010): 185–207.

Retelling the Siege of Jerusalem
in Early Modern England

Introduction

"Hierusalems Destruction: Our Instruction"

It is no exaggeration to say that the Fall of Jerusalem is the most
significant national event in the history of the world.
   —William Knight, *The Arch of Titus and the Spoils of the Temple*

Let us study things that are no more. It is necessary to understand
them, if only to avoid them.
                                      —Victor Hugo, *Les Miserables*

History mattered to the consumers of printed texts and plays in early
modern England and, for some, no history mattered so much as
that of the fall of Jerusalem in 70 C.E. As such, this book focuses on
largely neglected retellings of the Roman siege and the way they informed and
were informed by religious and political shifts across the sixteenth and seventeenth centuries. For decades, the sack of the holy city by Vespasian and his
son, Titus, infused sermons, ballads, plays, histories, and pamphlets. *Retelling
the Siege of Jerusalem in Early Modern England* argues that the story of Jerusalem's devastation functioned as a touchstone for the authors of such texts
who sought to locate their own particular dramas of religious and civil tumult
within a specific post-biblical context.

The story of besieged Jerusalem, first promoted by mid-sixteenth century
preachers anxious to forestall a similarly dire fate for England, gained broader

appeal with the explosion of print culture. Over the seventeenth century, its popularity matched the growing English readership's interest in history. An immensely pliable trope, the siege circulated as a vital form of cultural capital and was deployed in a wide array of contexts intersecting with some of the most urgent religious as well as secular discourses of the day. Given this enduring salience, this book examines early modern England's self-fashioning in the histories translated by Peter Morwen (c.1530–1573) and Thomas Lodge (c.1558–1625), in prose tracts and pamphlets penned by Thomas Nashe (1567–c.1601) and Thomas Dekker (c.1572–1632), and in plays composed by William Heminge (1602–c.1653) and John Crowne (1641–1712). Each chapter examines how these non-canonical but nevertheless influential men of letters reworked the siege narrative to reflect their particular anxieties about subjects as diverse as religious election, divine retribution, providentialism, Catholic resurgence, plague, new world anthropophagy, colonial expansion, civil war, and the trauma of exile. Consequently, I trace the way that the story of Jerusalem's fall transformed depending on genre and audience, variously rendered as salvific knowledge, a modish referent, and an elite scholarly preoccupation.

It is surprising that few scholars have examined the significance of besieged Jerusalem in early modern England. To date, only Beatrice Groves has explored at length the ramifications of this tragic episode. Her distinguished *Destruction of Jerusalem in Early Modern English Literature* (2015) illustrates the narrative shift in the story from the medieval to the early modern period, as well as the story's impact on literary stalwarts such as Shakespeare and Marlowe.[1] But where her center of gravity is located firmly in the 1590s and early 1600s, the bulk of my investigation focuses heavily on the seventeenth century, which saw New World settlement, the build up to the Civil War, and the Restoration. Furthermore, *Retelling the Siege of Jerusalem in Early Modern England* expands our awareness of popular print culture by focusing attention on the beleaguered city's symbolic value to less canonical writers whose labors nevertheless achieved remarkable success in their day. Above all, it charts the changing value of history across the seventeenth century: from requisite knowledge for the elect to a fashionable pursuit for the literate and culturally informed.

As we shall see, few events in Jewish history would prove so eminently evocable in such manifold contexts as the prolonged siege that culminated in the burning of the Temple and the displacement of the Jews. According to the *Jewish War*, Flavius Josephus's famed eyewitness account of 75 C.E., rebellion had been brewing in Roman-occupied Judaea for decades until high taxes levied by the procurators, coupled with their liberal confiscation of large portions of the Temple treasury, produced a violent response from the outraged

Jews. Josephus recounts that a faction he designates "zealots," under the leadership of John of Gishala, instigated a revolt that was answered by an army of nearly sixty thousand, led first by Vespasian, and then—after he had been sent back to Rome to be crowned emperor—by his son Titus. After a deadly siege, during which John and his fellow zealots repeatedly exploited their hapless fellow Jews in the name of resistance, the Roman legions breached the city walls, razed the Temple, and massacred the city's defenders. Jewish hopes were definitively quashed thereafter in 130 C.E. with Hadrian's construction of Aelia Capitolina, a new city atop the ruins, to which the once Chosen People were forbidden access.

Certainly, the most popular source on the siege of 70 C.E was the *Jewish War*. Its author, born Joseph ben Matityahu, was a Temple priest who had surrendered to the Romans following the siege of Jotapata in 67 C.E. Upon casting his lot with the Flavians Vespasian and Titus, who became his patrons, he adopted their *nomen gentilicum* as his patronymic. As may be imagined, Flavius Josephus was a deeply ambivalent figure who at once valorized his Roman overlords, furiously berated the zealots, and deeply mourned the devastation of his people. His popularity among Christians may be attributed, in part, to a section from his *Antiquities* known as the "Testimony of Josephus," which was often taken to confirm the existence of Jesus. At the same time, early Christian writing reconfigured Josephus's tragic account to signify punishment for the Jews' rejection of Christ. Reading against the grain, apologists reworked Josephus's testimony to reaffirm the righteous destruction of his people for deicide. In the process, they cemented the link between scriptural prophecy and the devastation of the Jews.[2] Jerusalem's destruction thus came to be interpreted as a fulfillment of Christ's prediction in Luke 19:41–44:

> And when he [Christ] was come near, he beheld the City, and wept for it,
> Saying, O if thou hadst even known at least in this thy day those things,
>   which *belong* unto thy peace! but now are they hid from thine eyes.
> For the days shall come upon thee, that thine enemies shall cast a trench
>   about thee, and compass thee round, and keep thee in on every side,
> And shall make thee even with the ground, and thy children which are
>   in thee, and they shall not leave in thee a stone upon a stone, because
>   thou knewest not that season of thy visitation.[3]

If Jews would later come back to Jerusalem to mourn its ruin, as Robert Wilken notes, early Christians fired by this providentialist interpretation, "made pilgrimage to the site to see proof of the demise of Judaism with their own eyes."[4]

Centuries later, by contrast, early modern English preachers read Christ's weeping as an implicit warning *to England* to repent for its iniquities. Francis White's Lenten sermon of 1619 implored London, "thou City of God," to be "instructed by Hierusalem, and as thou art to leaue Hierusalems sinne, that thou mayst escape Hierusalems punishment."[5] John Lawrence's 1624 sermon *A Golden Trvmpet* bemoaned that England's sin "drawes teares afresh from the eyes of the Sonne of God, and makes him for want of a *Ierusalem* to weep ouer *London*, as though it would proue a second *Ierusalem*, to crucifie his body againe."[6] Minister Richard Maden, meanwhile, ventured a slightly more sanguine outcome in 1637. Claiming that the fall of Jerusalem prophesied by Christ pertained to all sinners, he suggested that, similarly, "all mankind are capable of salvation, . . . if they repent their of sinnes, and beleeve in Christ."[7]

But by far the dominant tone of such sermons, spread across a century and a half, was one of anxiety for England's divinely mandated future. In 1580, Thomas Cooper's brief exegesis of Matthew 23.37 strategically extended Jesus's warning to his own nation: "And to *England* he now sayeth: 'O *Englande, Englande*, how often times haue I called thee . . .'" To underscore the point, printed marginalia next to the passage dutifully informed the reader "How God calleth England to repentance and without repentance what is like to befall it."[8] John Brinsley's *Tears for Iervsalem* (1656) was dedicated to the "Mourners in Sion" who were sensible of and "cordially affected with the present sad and calamitous condition of the Church of God in the Island of Great *Britain*."[9] Decades later, the author of the significantly titled *Great Britain's Warning-piece; or, Christ's tears over Jerusalem* (1689) still wondered how it "must be no small grief that cou'd draw tears from the Son of God, whose Eyes were dry: under an Agony whose pain was even beyond the expression of Angels," implying, thereby, that England was capable of inflicting just as much pain on the suffering Savior as those events in Jerusalem had.[10] Such anguish echoes Thomas Wilson's 1613 sermon *Christs Farewell to Jerusalem, and last Prophesie*, which, motivated by the same need to save England, likewise fused gospel prophecy with Josephus's history in a familiar sleight of hand: "How this was fulfilled is reported by *Iosephus*, a Iew, himselfe an eye and eare witness of all that horrible calamitie that came vpon Ierusalem, according to this prediction of Christ. Hardly without abundance of teares, can one read the most bitter euils, and perplexed afflictions and shifts . . . they were plunged into."[11] Wilson's sermon obviously recasts Josephus in a Christian mold by making the *Jewish War* into a compendious exegesis of Christ's prophecy in Luke and Matthew. But it is his detail about readers' responses—the "abundance of teares"—generated by the sad spectacle of Jerusalem's annihilation that stands out. Wilson's affective response to

Jewish suffering underscores the markedly different way that early modern England consistently encountered Jerusalem's destruction. Empathy for Jewish pain took the place of jubilation. Christian tears replaced Christian triumph.

Early Christian Reception of the Fall of Jerusalem

The novelty of the Protestant response to Jerusalem's fall is evident from even a cursory overview of the history of the Christian reception of Josephus. The famous bishop and rumored "eunuch," Melito of Sardis (died 180), appears to have been one of the first to work the *Jewish War* into an incendiary sermon, titled *Peri Pasha*, that denounced Jewish reprobation. Although, as M. E. Hardwick admits, we "cannot say with certainty that Josephus' account of the Roman siege of Jerusalem was in Melito's mind, elements in Melito's text reflect the situation in the *Bellum Judaicum* rather than what we find in Scripture."[12] The debt to Josephus is indisputable, however, in the case of Origen (185–254), who made substantial allusions to the *Jewish War* in his *Fragmenta in Lamentationes*. As Wataru Mizugaki argues, such historical incidents as the destruction of the Temple and the fall of Jerusalem were significant to Origen's theology, so much so that his *Contra Celsum* (1:47) takes Josephus to task for not explicitly blaming the destruction of Jerusalem on the Jews' betrayal of Jesus.[13] Origen formulates what Heinz Schrekenberg and Kurt Schubert called a "'punishment theology' postulate." Somewhere along the line, his contention that Josephus's eyewitness narrative *ought* to have established a causal nexus between the Crucifixion and the destruction of the Temple became, instead, an assertion that it *did*—thereby producing "in the interests of apology, a historical hodge-podge."[14]

It was Eusebius, the fourth-century bishop of Caesarea, who may be credited with turning the providentialist interpretation of Jerusalem's devastation into an aphorism. Even Meredith Hanmer's sixteenth-century translation of Eusebius's history of the Church, titled *The Avncient Ecclesiasticall Histories Of The First Six Hundred Years After Christ*, makes it quite clear that the Jews are punished because "besydes the haynous offence committed agaynst *Christ*, [the Jews] had compassed manyfould mischiefes against his Apostles."[15] According to Eusebius's reading of Josephus, the Jews even admit their own culpability:

> *Iosephus* writeth, that vppon the solempne dayes of Easter, there were
> gathered together at Ierusalem, out of all Iudaea, to the number of
> three hundred Millions, and there shutte vp as it were in prison, saying:
> It vvas requisite that destruction due for their desert, dravving nighe,
> by the iust iudgement of God, shoulde apprehende them vpon dayes

(being as it vvere shutte vp in prison) in the vvhich they before, had
dravvne the Sauior and benefactor of al men, the anoynted of God,
vnto his passion.[16]

Recalling Christ's prophecy in light of the subsequent calamities that befell the
Jews, Eusebius marvels at the "prescience of our Sauiour" as "wonderfull, and
passing naturall reason," while at the same time making the Jewish nation the
prototype for all recalcitrant peoples: sinful, proudly unrepentant, the object of
rhadamanthine justice.[17]

Whether early readers of Eusebius had access to a full text of the *Jewish War*
or were even interested in investigating such interpretations is hard to determine. As Honora Howell Chapman notes, Eusebius's investment was in the
"graphic stories, and Josephus provided several . . . which [he] could incorporate
selectively into his overall theological argument for the triumph of the church
over its enemies."[18] This theme of ecclesiastical ascendancy at the cost of Jewish
decline would continue with Basil the Great (330–379), who praised Josephus
as a "diligent" recorder of events; Jerome (347–420), who regarded him as a pre-
eminent Christian author; Isidore of Pelusium (died 450); and even Augustine
(354–430), who was credited with cementing the tradition of reading divine
providence into secular history.[19]

Consistently, their accounts revile the Jews and denounce their impiety. While
they acknowledge some episodes in Josephus's history as tragic, the dominant
mood is exultant. Few tears are shed over Jewish suffering, and nowhere is this
stony attitude more evident than in Pseudo-Hegesippus's virulent *De excidio
urbis Hierosolymitanae* (c.370–75), which narrated Jerusalem's decline from the
revolt of the Maccabees to the fall of Masada. Pseudo-Hegesippus established
a decisive connection between the Crucifixion and the holy city's catastrophic
decline that was readily imported into medieval English accounts of the Roman
siege.[20] Equally popular was Eusebius's presentation of Titus as a virtuous pagan
and the just executor of God's will. The fourteenth-century *Siege of Jerusalem*
perpetrated a similar fiction by portraying Vespasian and his two sons as Christian converts who vowed to besiege Jerusalem in an act of vengeance upon the
people who killed their lord. The trope of Christian ascendancy over Judaism—
enacted in the Roman general's victory over "debased" Jews—similarly animated
the cycle of plays that dramatized divine wrath upon sinful Jerusalem, the subject of Stephen Wright's 1989 study *The Vengeance of the Lord*.[21] Early Tudor
books, such as the one inspired by Jacobus de Voragine's *Golden Legend* and
printed twice by Wynkyn de Worde, likewise made Titus a Christian. In *The
dystruccyon of Iherusalem by Vaspazyan and Tytus* (1510), he proffers just as much

clemency to Jerusalem as "thou had on Ihesu Christe."[22] But the advent of Protestantism in England demanded that the story be told afresh.

Protestantism and Jerusalem

Excellent work on how the Reformation changed English perceptions of Israel and the Jews has already been done by the likes of James Shapiro, Barbara Lewalski, Sharon Achinstein, Elizabeth Sauer, Thomas Luxon, Aschah Guibbory, Stephen G. Burnett, and Eliane Glaser—although none of them focus specifically on the ways the siege story functioned as a mirror to reflect English preoccupations.[23] Instead, their conversations have tended to revolve around representations of Jewry, the millenarian belief in New Jerusalem and, above all, early modern Hebraism. In brief, their work has demonstrated how Protestantism provoked a fresh interest in the Hebrew Bible that can be traced back to Luther's *sola scriptura* dictum—the imperative to understand God's word in its original language.[24] Thus, William Tyndale (1494–1536) celebrated the "properties of the Hebrew tongue [that] agreeth a thousand times more with the English than with the Latin."[25] So committed was he to translating the Hebrew Bible that, even as he languished in prison awaiting execution, he called for "the Hebrew Bible, Hebrew grammar, and Hebrew dictionary" that he might "pass the time in that study."[26] Theologian Hugh Broughton (1549–1612), who believed passionately in the conversion of early modern Jews, advocated that "men of conscience and iudgement" study "Ebrew and Greek for Divinitie" rather than "Latin versions of mans guesse."[27] In the seventeenth century, Broughton's advocacy for Hebrew was carried on by John Selden (1584–1654), the famous antiquarian, historian, and philologist who would lead the way with his knowledge of the Hebrew language, Jewish history, and the Talmud. (Like Tyndale before him, Selden requested that Babylonian and Palestinian Talmudic texts be allowed him while in prison.) The result was a complex construction of kinship between Reformation England and Ancient Israel.

Achsah Guibbory's comprehensive study of the influence of Jewish history on seventeenth-century Christian identity posits that, although English Protestants "remained suspicious of Jews and Judaism," they saw the history of Israel as their very own.[28] Take, for instance, Bishop Joseph Hall's 1628 exaltation of England as an elect nation, a "second Israel," covenanted and holy, "chosen . . . out of all the earth, and divided . . . from the rest of the world, that we might be a singular pattern and strange wonder of his bounty."[29] Similarly, Paul Knell's *Israel and England Paralelled* (1648) articulates a series of equivalencies that climaxes in a triumphant celebration of England as "Happy Nation . . . to have the Lord for our God, to have him as kind and good to us, as he ever was to Israel."[30] But Protestant fascination with Hebrew and post-biblical history did not necessarily translate into an appreciation of the Jews. Bishop Hall's designation of England as "second Israel" already suggests a convenient dichotomy: "Hebraic Israel" as distinct from "Judaic Israel." We recall here Samuel Stollman's cogent formulation in the context of Milton's writing: "Judaic" is the "historical people of Israel, the Jews with their ethnic traits and their history of backsliding." "Hebraic" is the "universal or spiritual Israel, the ideal Nation and Community, . . . Covenant Idea, Holy Community, New Jerusalem."[31] Stollman's distinction is starkly played out when even the Hebraist Broughton scorns "dogge Iewes," and "blasphemous Iewes."[32]

And yet, the popularity of the siege narrative in reformed England suggests the possible deconstruction of this binary as, in James Shapiro's words, "a sense of Jewish history as discontinuous (and in which the experience of the Israelites was viewed as separate from that of modern Jews) was slowly being displaced by a more fluid, continuous narrative of the fate of the Jewish people."[33] Rather than dwell exclusively on mythical Israelites, the emphasis shifted, post-Reformation, to include an understanding of the Jews as a historical people. At the same time, as Alexandra Walsham notes, more and more Protestants were encouraged to see their history as analogous to that of the Jews. They "treated their own nation and the Jews as exact contemporaries, close cousins, even identical twins."[34] Thus, Adam Hill in *The Crie of England* (1595) fears that "if these thinges [sins] be among the people of England, as they were among the Iewes; or rather if England doth iustify Ierusalem, as Ierusalem iustified Sodome and Gomorrah: then no doubt as God spared not the naturall oliue, so hee will not spare the wilde."[35] William Est, who drew on both Josephus and Pseudo-Hegesippus, concurs in his 1613 sermon: "If we compare the sins of *England* at this day, with the sinnes of the *Iewes*, how can we chuse but feare and tremble? Considering that not *Ierusalem* onely, but also *England*, is plunged in as deepe obliuion of the *Time of her Visitation*, as euer that sinfull Citie was."[36] Francis Smith's 1691 denunciation of the swiftness with which the Jews "embrace[d] their own destruction; how swinishly they wallow[ed] in the mire of Sin" is soon followed by the rueful admission, "What Sin was ever committed in *Jerusalem*, that is not also committed in this our Nation?"[37]

Recently, Groves advanced the argument that early modern people embraced the idea of a "continuous" Jewish history by tracing the shift from medieval Catholic to early modern Protestant retellings of the siege.[38] She posits a significant transfer of identification from the victorious Romans to the beleaguered Jews. Where medieval narratives sought to valorize Vespasian and his son in a bid "to depict the Catholic Church as the successor to the Roman Empire," the break with Papal Rome necessitated a reevaluation of affinity. As a consequence, "Josephus's text was read in Protestant England as a document of Jewish, rather than Roman, history. . . . Triumphalism is replaced by an uneasy empathy."[39] I share Groves's assessment, as I do Wright's claim that the "unrestrained violence and brutality" of the medieval siege dramas reflects contemporaneous attitudes toward the Jewish community.[40] To quote Groves again, this "actual violence against Jews indicates the extent to which their audiences were invited to harden themselves against, rather than empathise with, the suffering of Jerusalem."[41] But Protestant England's vexed relationship with Rome no longer made uncomplicated identification with the Roman troops possible. What emerged instead was identification with Jewish tribulation—recall the copious tears that stain Wilson's sermon—that was often as disquieting as it was novel.

To be sure, in the aftermath of the English Reformation, preachers readily adopted the providentialist interpretation of Jerusalem's destruction, laying claim to the status deemed to have been lost by the Jews. Drawing on the biblical rhetoric of covenant, they assigned to England the status of an "elect" nation with all attendant privileges. The classic argument advanced memorably by William Haller in 1963 is of John Foxe's view of England as a "people set apart from all others by a peculiar destiny," chosen to play a special role in God's *theatrum mundi*.[42] Recent scholars have rightly contested Haller's misreading of Foxe's views on divine election and nationalism by showing that Foxe himself understood election in the broader context of an international Protestant Church.[43] Yet, as Jesse M. Lander argues, "meanings unintended by Foxe could be and were made available to a wide range of readers, including, at particular moments, an assertion about England's peculiar, divinely appointed role in world history."[44] More to our purpose, even as Protestants appropriated the rhetoric of election, they were only too aware that they might also inherit Jerusalem's tragic fate. When they fashioned Jerusalem's annihilation as divine judgment on the Jews' sins, they felt impelled to alert England to the responsibilities inherent in the Covenant, as well as the cataclysmic consequences of forsaking it. Knell's *Israel and England Paralelled* is thus forced to change its happy notes to tragic when its author realizes that, "Our sins therefore being as many, nay, more, I doubt, then those of *Israel* . . . without great mercy we must looke yet for greater judgements, at least to have God so threaten us, as here he threatens the people of Israel."[45] The clamorous literature of admonition, other examples of which we have already seen, counseled England to pay close attention to Jerusalem's brutal decline with heightened urgency.

Furthermore—and this cannot be emphasized enough—early modern preachers identified the destruction of Jerusalem as requisite historical knowledge: the one story that virtuous Protestants needed to know for the sake of their souls. One of the earliest to cite the siege in this way was Thomas Becon, who, when faced with the prospect of the Catholic Mary ascending the throne in 1550, immediately thought of Jerusalem's destruction:

> Verely no man, eccepte he be flynte hearted can rede the historye of the destruccyon of Hierusalem, as Josephus doth dyscribe it, wythoute moste large teares. Woulde God it were translated into our Englysh tonge, that all men might rede it and learne to feare God. For if God spared not the natural olyue tree for theyr vnfaythfulness & disobedience, I mean the Jewes, neyther wil he spare the wilde oliue tree, I meane vs that are gentiles, if we commit the like offences.[46]

Becon's empathy, encapsulated in the "moste large teares" that flow freely at the thought of Jerusalem's suffering, severs him from the traditional reception of the story. His newfound if troubled affinity with the Jews who fell foul of God (echoed, as we saw, by Hill's *Crie of England*) demands a fresh telling. It is as if the medieval narrative tradition no longer sufficed. Indeed, to read Becon, one would not think it existed at all. Josephus's history, the source itself, must now be "translated into our Englysh tonge" that "all men might rede it and learne to feare God."

Of course what it meant for "all men" to read Josephus is hard to assess when early modern literacy rates are still in dispute. Stuart Gillespie and Neil Rhodes have argued that, despite the demand for print, a large percentage of the early modern population could not read. David Cressy has suggested that by 1600, literacy rates were only about thirty percent for men and ten percent for women. Adam Fox, on the other hand, reminds us that the term "literacy" is a knotty one. He suggests that many more people "could read than could write" and that some people may have been able to read print when they could not yet decipher various handwriting scripts.[47] Fox's argument supports Margaret Spufford's sharp critique of Cressy's estimates. Although she acknowledges that reading skills cannot be measured in the way that writing abilities can, she estimates that they are likely to have been much more widespread in the sixteenth and seventeenth centuries than hitherto acknowledged. As she notes, "boys below the level of yeomen quite frequently learnt to read, since reading was taught at an age when they could earn little, whereas writing was commonly taught at an age after the meaningful earning lives of such boys had

begun."[48] The point, as I take it, is not so much whether all men could read as
that Becon envisioned an ideal community in which all men anxious to retain
God's grace *did* read about Jerusalem's fall, and took heed.

Becon's prayer for an English translation was answered soon enough by
Peter Morwen, whose religiously inflected adaptation of Josephus, *A compendious and most marueilous Historie of the latter times of the Iewes common
weale* (1558), enjoyed unprecedented popularity, judging by the unusual level of
demand for reprints.[49] Although, as I explain in chapter 1, his source was not
Josephus but a Hebrew abridgement known popularly as the *Josippon*, Morwen successfully introduced Jerusalem's siege to a new and extensive Protestant
readership, teaching them to look to Jewish history to predict a consonant fate
for London.[50] The proliferation of print in the vernacular sparked a familiarity
with Jerusalem's ruin and its relevance to English society as hitherto occasional
admonitory texts—sermons and jeremiads—achieved a longer and more
extensive reach. Acknowledging, in the words of Cambridge vice-chancellor
John Lightfoot (1602–1675), that "this desolation is phrased in Scripture as the
desolating of the whole world," readers rushed to acquaint themselves with this
tragic chapter in Jerusalem's history.[51] Morwen's *A compendious and most marueilous Historie* was reprinted thirteen times between 1558 and 1615 and then a
further twelve times in the form edited by James Howell, historiographer royal
to Charles II. Thomas Lodge's handsome 1602 folio translation of *The Jewish
War and the Antiquities* was meanwhile reprinted fourteen times in the seventeenth century, making it the most frequently reprinted English translation
of any historian of antiquity during the period. Tessa Watts has argued that
books became more affordable over the course of the sixteenth century, not
least because, with wages on the rise, their prices tended to remain fairly steady.
It is no wonder that by 1655, Lightfoot could attest that Josephus was "in every
man's hand."[52]

Lightfoot's testimony anticipates Thomas Hearne's declaration in 1698 that
"this small part of [Josephus's] History being translated into our Language,
is much in the Hands of the very meanest Persons; and by common Experience we find that they are as much affected with the Relations thereof, as
they are with any of the pretty Fictions of Romance and Poetry."[53] Hearne's
declaration is significant for a couple of reasons. It confirms that the history of
Jerusalem's destruction only grew in appeal over the course of the seventeenth
century so that even the "very meanest" were acquainted with its tragic details.
It also underscores that early modern English readers, by and large, continued
to be affected by the story. But Hearne's comparison of Josephus's history to
the "pretty Fictions" of the day also indicates just how far we have come from

Becon's impassioned demand for its translation. No longer was the reception of Josephus's work primarily about the state of the soul or the sinful nation. Rather, Josephus was popular in 1698 because he told an emotionally compelling story. Simply put, the history of the siege had become not so much essential for retaining divine favor, but a fashionable read that even the "meanest" desired to peruse.

Whether as requisite knowledge or cultural cachet, Josephus's text only grew in popularity with the rapidly burgeoning English readership eager to consume historical writing. But though a brief account of the siege by the renowned second-century Roman historian Tacitus (c.56–c.120 C.E) may have been quite neglected, Josephus's relevance never abated. In part, this can be attributed to the "introspective" nature of his work. As Groves suggests, Josephus's appeal lay in "his efforts to understand how God could have allowed the desecration of his dwelling place and his powerful evocation of suffering in which he had, to some extent, shared."[54] It is also true that Josephus's remarkable double perspective as a Romanized Jew granted him a unique status among seventeenth-century readers who, influenced by the humanist values of impartiality and sober judgment, praised his history for its balance.

The Puritan sergeant-at-arms Lodowick Lloyd recalled with some wonder in *The Stratagems of Ierusalem* (1602) that Josephus was a "Tetrarch in *Galiley*, and fought many battels with his countrey against the *Romanes* vntill he was taken by *Titus*, and brought with him to *Rome*, where he wrote of the antiquitie of the *Iewes* twentie bookes in Greeke, & wrote seuen bookes of the Iewish warres, and was . . . much esteemed in *Rome*."[55] In *Of the horyble and woful destruccion of Jerusalem* (1568), John Barker had likewise praised Josephus's history, for "on truth they [his readers] do depend."[56] Thomas Jackson, about whose treatise on chance I shall have more to say in chapter 4, attested not only to the ubiquity of Josephus but also to his supersession of native historians when he observed that English people knew the fall of Jerusalem "so fully and so pathetically related by *Iosephus*" better than their own history. Praising Josephus as one "whom God has appointed as the fittest man to keepe the register" of Jerusalem's fall, Jackson, like so many others we shall encounter in this book, exhorted his fellow compatriots, "At your best leasure without any fee peruse his records, now more common in our English language then the records or Chronicles of our owne nation. And so no doubt it was Gods will to have them, that our Nation might take example, or instructions by them whom they more concerne then they doe any Nation since they were first written by him."[57] Jackson's evaluation of the siege story and its perusal suggests a wonderful combination of divinely directed urgency and leisure that is typical of his historical moment, arrested between the providentialist and the secular. On the one hand, God directs English readers to Josephus so that they may be suitably instructed—which suggests that the siege story remained requisite knowledge, concerning England more than any other country. On the other hand, Jackson emphasizes "best leasure," implying that Josephus had become a fashionable luxury that a large readership could consume for their edification.

Requisite Fashion to Fashionable Requisite

The shift in perception of the siege from requisite knowledge to cultural capital that developed over the course of 150 years constitutes the arc of this book. Here, we shall see Jerusalem's fall in all of its narrative iterations: from Morwen's portable and economical history (black letter, octavo) to Lodge's more expensive folio version, to cheap plague pamphlets, to even cheaper ballads, puppet shows, staged plays, and printed playtexts. This is not to imply that the urgent eschatological and spiritual dimensions that characterized the sermons on Jerusalem's destruction were completely lost by the mid-to-late 1600s. They are very much present in those delivered before the Long Parliament as well as in the millenarianist writings of the late seventeenth century. If the desolation of Jerusalem involved that of the whole world, then the English had as much of a stake in this story as did the hapless Jews. It was their history too.

Thus, in 1682, the Puritan John Flavel still insisted that God "will not favour that in one people, which he hath punished in another: nor bless that in one age, which he hath cursed in another. And therefore that which hath been a sign of Judgment to one, must be so to all."[58] This very sentiment had likewise embroidered John Lawrence's pithy formulation in 1624: "*Hierusalems destruction our instruction.*"[59] In 1691, Francis Smith acknowledged preaching *Jerusalem's Sins, Jerusalem's Destruction* in order "to instruct and inform the Inhabitants thereof in this degenerate and wicked age (wherein all manner of Vices and Sins are most impudently and notoriously committed)," in a bid to lead them back to God.[60] Indeed, Jerusalem's siege continued to be employed in ways that reflected urgent religious concerns. As a powerful narrative of decline and fall that could be alluded to with little explication, it consistently functioned as an important weapon in ideological debates. Church of England stalwarts mapped their anxieties about Catholic resurgence onto the story of Jewish defeat at the hands of Rome. Plague pamphleteers discerned in diseased England the signs of divine wrath that destroyed Ancient Jerusalem. Royalist supporters denigrated the Puritans by comparing them to the bloody-minded zealots who foolishly rebelled against Rome.

However, as the density of printed material grew exponentially, and more and more information proliferated, the reading of histories became primarily fashionable entertainment, the choice of those who wanted to know about the past and who had the leisure to pursue that inclination. For instance, John Crowne, whose dramatic treatment of the siege is the subject of the final chapter of this book, most likely resorted to that story because he was aware of its trendiness. What better way to attract theatergoers than by staging a story as popular as that of the siege, complete with a spectacular burning of the Temple on stage? As I show, Crowne's drama is also a perceptive treatment of exile and dislocation—a topic all too familiar to the restored courtly audience before whom the play was performed, as well as to the Jews recently readmitted to England.[61] Jerusalem's siege remained a prominent story, not least because it continued to be told in a manner that pertained to the present. But it was no longer the only history that all English people needed to read and learn from in order to maintain favor in the eyes of a providentialist deity.

Of course, Thomas Jackson's 1637 advocacy of Jerusalem's tragedy as "example" advances a familiar justification for reading history. In a classic and still thought-provoking assessment, Keith Thomas declared that for early modern English readers:

> The *only* respectable justification for the study of the past was that it
> could be of service to the present . . . The case for recalling the past was
> a practical one. History was a great repository of experience from which
> useful lessons could be drawn. This assumption united the theologians,
> who saw in the past the workings of God, the moralists, who valued
> it for its examples of virtuous conduct, and the 'politic' historians, who
> looked to it as a source for maxims on statecraft.[62]

The siege was one such "great repository" into which early modern preachers and theologians, moralists, and politic historians reached their hands with equal relish. This book studies the diverse ways it functioned as literary shorthand for writers to signal the scale and severity of their religious, cultural, and political concerns. We shall encounter fears of Catholic resurgence; Protestant election and its responsibilities; natural calamities; convictions of an impending apocalypse; a brutal civil war; the exile of the Stuart court; the readmission of the Jews into England in 1655; the Restoration of Charles II; England's burgeoning imperial ambitions; and the exigencies of colonization in the New World. In the process, we shall trace the secularization of the siege narrative as the focus shifted from explicating divine intervention to considering political lessons.

Indeed, the trope's pliability is nothing short of miraculous, which doubtless guaranteed its high value as cultural capital. Daniel Woolf, among others, has demonstrated that over the course of the seventeenth century, history became the "prominent form of cultural currency within the social agora, deployable in multiple contexts, serious or frivolous."[63] Following the publication of Morwen's history, writers of all religious and political persuasions reworked the analog of London as Jerusalem over and again. One might even say that Jerusalem's very history came under siege every time the story of its destruction was retold.

The tumultuous period between the close of Mary Tudor's reign (1558) and the end of the Restoration (1688) is particularly apt for assessing the evolution of the siege narrative, not least because of the remarkable maturation of historical consciousness during those decades. As Woolf argues, one of the great shifts over the course of the early modern period was from a perception of history as analogous or metaphorical to what he terms as "metonymic." The chronological tracks of my book are likewise marked by what he identifies as: "The emergence of a sense of the past as continuous process and the establishment of the primacy of causal relationships between diachronically contiguous or proximate events over exemplary and analogical relationships between temporally remote and disconnected ones."[64] The slow shift away from a strictly providentialist view of history in which God directs outcomes toward a prioritization of causation, contingency, and contiguity are reflected in the siege narratives that unfolded over the course of the seventeenth century, many of which acquired a double signification congruent with England's own fraught political scene. By tracing the stuttering emergence of secular interpretations of Jerusalem's devastation that ran alongside the once-dominant providentialist narratives, I show how Jerusalem was represented both as the covenanted space destroyed for its sins, and as a political realm weakened by civil strife and vulnerable to attack by an imperial power. The buildup to the English Civil War promoted a more nuanced understanding of the civil conflict within Jerusalem and the plight of the besieged Jews, even as England's imperial ambitions would find a burnished reflection in the Roman war machine that had laid waste to the holy city. The result was complex self-fashioning by a nation conscious of itself as at once elect and sinful, politically fractured and imperially ambitious, providentially led and politically motivated, and, by the late seventeenth century, both besieged Jerusalem and triumphant Rome.

Yet, apart from Groves's *Destruction of Jerusalem*, the substantial studies of England's indebtedness to antiquity have tended to focus on Ancient Rome.[65] This book now seeks to redirect the conversation by asking why and how English preachers and writers consistently evoked besieged Jerusalem in their self-fashioning efforts, and offers an original study of the varied connotations of the city's destruction for those who sought to comprehend their troubled times within a larger narrative of divine intervention and/or historical prece-dence. Indeed, this book puts together texts that have never before been read in conjunction, pairing Thomas Lodge's treatment of civil conflict and cannibal-ism during the *Jewish War* with George Percy's devastating account of settler strife and anthropophagy in Jamestown. William Heminge's markedly secular play *The Jewes Tragedy* is here read with popular pamphlets on chance and providence, while John Crowne's *Destruction of Jerusalem* is juxtaposed with diaries and exilic letters by royalists detailing their suffering during the Inter-regnum. Read in this way, Jerusalem's siege narratives not only become crucial intertexts for understanding the crises that beset the early modern English imagination, but they also help us trace the evolution of historical conscious-ness in the period.

Chapter 1 establishes the siege as requisite knowledge by examining Peter Morwen's heavily touted *A compendious and most maruelous Historie of the latter times of the Iewes common weale*. Composed during Mary Tudor's reign, Mor-wen's text is haunted by specters of Catholic culture. The most memorable is the depiction of cannibalism by a Jewish woman named Miriam who, at the height of the siege, kills, consumes, and serves up her only son. Morwen's history imbues the mother's cannibalism with disturbing Eucharistic valences. Miriam, who identifies herself as "handemayde" when she serves up her son to the starv-ing seditionists, becomes the distorted mirror image of the Virgin Mary; but whereas the sacrifice of the Son of God grants eternal life, her consumption of the son brings only damnation. Subsequent narratives inspired by Morwen's history, such as Nashe's *Christ's Teares over Iervsalem* (1593) and Heminge's *The Jewes Tragedy* (c.1628–30), become further charged with anxiety when consid-ered in the context of the anti-Catholic, anti-transubstantiation discourses influ-enced by Protestant reformers such as John Calvin, Huldrych Zwingli, and Jean de Léry, that continued to circulate in post-Reformation England. The chapter ends with an examination of the English enthusiasm for corpse pharmacology, or the consumption of mummified flesh ("mummy") as a nostrum. Drawing on Nashe's avowed hope that his *Christs Teares* would prove just as palliative to his English readership as a piece of Jerusalem's "mummianized earth," my chapter argues for the impossibility of any simple repudiation of Miriam's cannibalism as "other" given the popularity of mummy as a secular substitute for the con-sumption for Christ's healing flesh in the Eucharist. In so doing, it underscores the vexed identification between Protestant and Jew that made the siege narra-tive requisite—if unsettling—reading to a newly elect people.

Chapter 2 demonstrates the pervasiveness of the siege narrative, and specifically its providentialist interpretation, by returning to Nashe's *Christs Teares* and reading it alongside other plague pamphlets and medical literature produced during the late sixteenth and early seventeenth centuries, most notably Thomas Dekker's *The Wonderfull Yeare* (1603). The chapter argues for the way that plague becomes an instrument of divine vengeance that makes London's suffering akin to Jerusalem's. Interestingly, this vengeance is presented in a striking *political* analogy between the plague's violent effect on human bodies and the disruption to civic life caused by the seditionists who led the rebellion against Rome. Plague, figured as an invader in medical tracts by William Bullein (1515–1576), is explicitly linked to the figures of the zealots Jehochannan, Eleazar, and Simeon in Dekker's *The Wonderfull Yeare* in a laconic reference that belied the need for further elaboration, so familiar had the story become. Indeed, the link between the plague victim's wrecked body and the damaged body politic is reinforced in numerous other pamphlets, suggesting the siege's growing value as cultural capital. Plague literature, though heavily providentialist, thus becomes a useful site in which to discern anxieties over civic disruption that would assume a dominant focus in the more secular accounts of Jerusalem's destruction in the mid-to-late seventeenth century.

Chapter 3 introduces the secular and primarily political focus of Thomas Lodge's comprehensive translation of the works of Josephus (1602) by revisiting Miriam's cannibalism in the context of the infamous Jamestown "Starving Time." Lodge's translation, which strikingly collapses the civilization-barbarism binary through graphic descriptions of the degeneration of Jewish *civitas*, coincides with stories of similar descent in Jamestown where, driven by extreme famine, New World settlers were believed to have killed and cannibalized their own. The writings of Lodge and of settlers such as George Percy, when read together, expose the porosity of the boundary between civilization and savagery. Furthermore, Lodge's translation, in the manner of Michel de Montaigne's famous essay on cannibals, presents a striking value system wherein the actual consumption of human flesh is less reprehensible than the metaphorical cannibalism of those who tear whole communities apart in savage greed. The eating of human flesh by other humans, generally presumed to be the ultimate manifestation of intra-species violence, has its more damning figurative extension in acts of internecine brutality, exploitation, and torture—all hallmarks of colonial encounters. To move, therefore, from Morwen's history of Miriam's cannibalism to Lodge's edition is to move from a distinctly Protestant interpretation of the episode to a reevaluation of seemingly stable secular categories such as culture and barbarism.

Chapter 4 continues to trace the secular arc by revisiting Heminge's *The Jewes Tragedy*, a somewhat disparaged play composed during the tumultuous exordium to the English Civil War, and recuperating its critical importance in the contemporary discourse that predicted Jerusalem's dire fate for London. Heminge, who had an eye for the popular, relied on the siege's value as cultural capital but deviated from his contemporaries by eschewing the conventional Christian moral and its accompanying providentialist rhetoric in favor of a thoughtful political analysis of events that was closer to the secular temper of Lodge than to that of his source, Morwen. Rather than focus on supernatural punishment, *The Jewes Tragedy* exposes the heavy price of imperial ambition when provoked by territorial unrest. My chapter examines Heminge's focus in the context of the fraught political and religious climate of the mid-to-late 1620s (when the play was probably composed), as well as of the Restoration (during which it was first published). Specifically, it investigates Heminge's contentious interrogation of providentialism and the corresponding shift in the seventeenth century away from a deterministic worldview in which God assigns outcomes, to a more secularized conception of history focused on human interventions. The chapter concludes with a brief consideration of the way that *The Jewes Tragedy* at once presents the Jews as tragic victims of internecine conflict and valorizes Titus Vespasian—thereby appealing both to the more moderate supporters of the Jewish presence in post-Restoration England as well as to the court in its Augustan self-fashioning and imperial ambitions.

The final chapter underscores the degree to which the siege narrative became fashionable coin by examining an immensely popular and extravagant late Restoration dramatization that spoke directly to the vexed issue of Christian-Jewish identification. John Crowne's *The Destruction of Jerusalem by Titus Vespasian* (1677) powerfully articulates the nightmare of exile and dislocation endured not only by the Jews recently readmitted to England but also by the Restoration court, whose members would most likely have comprised the audience at the Theatre Royal. Where, previously, devastated Jerusalem served as a stern warning to sinful London, the new correspondence Crowne implicitly established between exiled/restored aristocracy and exiled/restored Jews resists the ready and uncomplicated vilification of the Jewish nation that permeated many early modern sermons. Crowne's meticulous focus on rootlessness and dislocation in besieged Jerusalem, and his presentation of sundered love as a type of exile, assumes significance in the contexts of the English court's attempts to reconstitute its own checkered history of banishment and restitution; its policy of toleration of the recently readmitted Jews; and the contemporaneous millennarianist discourse that called for the restoration of those Jews to Israel. This chapter closes with an analysis of the evolving presentation of the Jews who, though frequently berated for their sinfulness and obduracy, were increasingly presented as hapless victims of political greed and ambition. Though not fully philosemitic, the texts I examine in this chapter lend a dimension and depth to the perception of the Jews and their history that complements the rise of English philosemitism as identified by scholars such as David Katz.

To ignore the salience of besieged Jerusalem to early modern England is thus to miss a critical aspect of English self-fashioning. Whether viewed as requisite knowledge or fashionable history, the fall of Jerusalem remained extraordinarily relevant to English preoccupations in the century and a half covered by this book. This narrative was dynamic and evolving, consistently freighted with the political, religious, and cultural preoccupations of the historical moment in which it was retold. If we wish to chart the growth of early modern secularism, or an incipient philosemitism, if we are interested in Protestant anxiety over Catholicism or fears of election gone wrong, and if our subject is civil strife or the vicissitudes of empire-building, then besieged Jerusalem is the site for tracing all of these various and often interconnected concerns.

CHAPTER I

Unholy Ghosts

In 1584, the Puritan preacher and schoolmaster John Stockwood published *A very fruitfull and necessarye Sermon of the moste lamemtable destruction of Ierusalem, and the heauy iudgements of God, executed vppon that people for their sinne and disobedience*. This was nothing less than an anxious diatribe directed against the Jews overcome by the Roman legions in 70 C.E., which predicted a consonant dire fate for the English should they fail to live up to the promises of the newly reformed Protestant Church. In it, the plain-speaking Stockwood advocated passionately for a book "which . . . in english, I wold wish euery man to buie, that reading in him the most fearfull examples of God his wrath upon the people for their sinnes, they may for feare at least, of like punishments be moued to repentaunce. . . ."[1] The book Stockwood identified as crucial to the retention of divine favor was Peter Morwen's (or Morwyng's) *A compendious and most marueilous Historie of the latter times of the Iewes common weale, begynnyng where the Bible or Scriptures leaue, and continuing to the vtter subuertion and last destruction of that countrey and people*.

Morwen, a Protestant theologian at Magdalen College at Oxford, and later Canon at Lichfield, composed *A compendious and most marueilous Historie* while in Germany to escape the persecutions of the Catholic Mary Tudor. So ardently did Morwen support the Protestant cause that he was even expelled from Magdalen for his convictions by Bishop Stephen Gardiner. Living out Mary's reign on the Continent, Morwen was one of the first to return to England with Elizabeth's accession in 1558. Published that same year, his history would become one of the most popular, if not definitive, English renditions of Jerusalem's destruction that allowed Protestants to at once reframe the fall of God's Chosen People as giving way to the triumphant rise of the English Reformed Church as well as caution the latter of a similar decline should they fail to live up to their new covenanted status. Like his more famous counterpart, John Foxe—a fellow at Magdalen who also fled to Germany to compile his magisterial account of Protestant persecution, *Actes and Monuments* (1563)—Morwen employed the argument that God sometimes elevates idolators (the Romans/the Catholic Church) in order to punish the sins of his Chosen People (the Jews/the Protestants). In so doing, he cemented a critical, often unsettling identification between Ancient Jews and reformed Christians, both, in their own way, under threat from Rome.[2]

Morwen's prefatory "Epistle to the Reader" assigned the impetus for his vernacular translation to Richard Jugge, "a certaine honest man, a Printer of London, studious in his vocation of the commoditie of this our countrey."[3] Jugge, printer to Queen Elizabeth, whose shop could be found "at the signe of the Bible," was energetic in that trade. Not only was he licensed to produce an edition of William Tyndale's New Testament, but he also published the first edition of the Bishops' Bible in the vernacular a decade after printing *A compendious and most marueilous Historie.*[4] Jugge's investment in England's "commoditie," here understood as spiritual advantage or profit, established his commitment to advancing English interests. Indeed, Morwen evinced a similar altruism when he offered his translation as a warning to his countrymen and women: "As when thou seeest the Iewes here afflicted with diuers kindes of miserie, because they fell from GOD: then maiest thou be admonished hereby, to see the better to thyne owne wayes, lest the lyke calamities lyght vpon thee."[5] As Morwen elaborates, it was imperative that "an vnderstanding and declaration to all menne in the Englishe tongue, as wel as in other, of the destruction of so famous a common weale" be accessible to the English people for their "inestimable profit."[6]

Jacob Reiner has suggested that Jugge, "a most enterprising businessman with much foresight," had "capitalized upon this prevalent interest in the Jews, and the numerous republications of this volume evidence the success of his venture."[7] But even the most cursory perusal of Morwen's preface reveals a far more principled and urgent commitment. Although he strategically employed the justification for producing secular history, attractive both for the "pleasauntnesse of the matter" and to satisfy the curiosity of those "delighted and desirous to vnderstande the ende," this was not his primary motivation in translating the narrative of Jerusalem's destruction.[8] Rather, Morwen's effort was "most marueilous," not least because it was full of "inestimable profit" given the author's

meticulous attention to England's "commoditie." Just as Stockwood's own sermon was "fruitfull and necessarye," so was the history he so passionately advocated. Simply put, this was not merely casual entertainment proffered to an
increasingly literate people hankering after the latest fashion in print. Rather,
as per Stockwood's advertisement, this was the one "book in English" that every
God-fearing Protestant had to know in order to secure their nation's continued
well-being before God.

The value of Morwen's admonitory history is clear not just from the extravagant praise it drew from the likes of Stockwood but also from its impressive
number of reprints in a short span of time, appearing in 1558, 1561, 1567, 1575,
1579, 1593, 1596, 1602, 1608, and 1615. Louis Feldman's bibliography on the *Josippon*, Morwen's source, lists thirteen editions between 1558 and 1602 that include
a staggering four reprints in 1579 alone. In 1652, the translation was republished
with a new title—*The Wonderful and Most Deplorable History of the Latter
Times of the Jews*—and would become an important polemical weapon in the
bitter controversy over the readmission of the Jews into England. *A compendious and most marueilous Historie* and its mid-seventeenth-century editions
alike served as the source and inspiration for countless narratives of Jerusalem's
fall, including poems like T.D.'s *Canaan's Calamitie* (1618), prose tracts such as
Thomas Nashe's *Christs Teares over Iervsalem* (1593), as well as plays such as
William Heminge's *The Jewes Tragedy* (composed c.1626, published 1662), and
John Crowne's *The Destruction of Jerusalem by Titus Vespasian* (1677). If the
story of the siege was begging to be introduced to a newly reformed readership,
then Morwen, it would seem, hit upon just the right way to tell it.

Despite its claims of authenticity, Morwen's translation was not actually
based on the revered eyewitness account of Jerusalem's devastation—Flavius
Josephus's *Jewish War* of 75 C.E. Although his title claims the veracity of one
*"who saw the most thinges him selfe, and was aucthor and doer of a great part
of the same,"* the author of Morwen's original source was, rather, the tenth-
century writer Joseph ben Gorion. Morwen introduced ben Gorion to his early
modern English readers as Josephus by the simple expedient of claiming that
"Joseph ben Gorion" was Josephus's name rendered in Hebrew—a belief that
had gained popularity in medieval Europe.[9] Yet, ben Gorion was actually the
author of the *Josippon* (or *Sefer Josippon*), a Hebrew chronicle derived from a
Latin abridgement of Josephus that had been heavily Christianized. Even so,
the popular notion prevailed that *Josippon* was the original Hebrew version of
the *Jewish War* that Josephus alluded to having written in his "owne language."[10]

Modern scholarship suggests that Morwen's history was even further
removed from the source, being based on Sebastian Munster's Latin version of

Abraham ibn Daud's twelfth-century abstract of the *Josippon*.[11] Despite its tangled antecedents, Morwen's text was often regarded as the authoritative version of the siege until Thomas Lodge brought out his "authentic" translation of Josephus's complete works in 1602. Though the cleric Samuel Purchas (1575–1626) in *Purchas His Pilgrimage* (1626) recommended both the *Jewish War* and *Josippon* for a comprehensive account of Jerusalem's destruction, earlier preachers such as Stockwood made no distinction between the two texts. Even after the publication of Lodge's scrupulous edition, Morwen's translation remained the favored account—one that not only answered the early Protestant demand for Ancient Hebrew texts but, relatedly, also affirmed the explicit and unambiguous link between Ancient Jerusalem and the early modern Reformed Church. As Beatrice Groves observes, the second part of Morwen's title ("*begynnynge where the Bible or Scriptures leaue, and continuing to the vtter subuertion and last destruction of that countrey and people*") suggests one reason for this version's popularity given that it "explicitly presents the text as a continuation of scriptural history."[12] Erin E. Kelly, affirming that English Protestants used Josephus's history of Jewish decline to justify "the recent triumph of the true—English Protestant—church," notes that Morwen's translation "combines, condenses, and edits the many versions of the same events presented in Josephus's texts into one linear Protestant narrative of world history," which he advances "as a lesson in proper behavior for his Protestant readers." Citing implicit parallels between the oppression of the sinful Jews by the idolatrous Romans and the oppression of the true Church by Catholics, Kelly suggests that Morwen makes "the history of humanity since the time of Christ comprehensible as a Protestant narrative."[13]

I would argue that there is a specific and highly influential aspect of this requisite history that merits even closer attention: namely, the way that descriptions of ruined and famished Jerusalem function as allegories for the scarred religious landscape of post-Reformation England. Seen in this light, *A compendious and most marueilous Historie* is interesting as a Protestant narrative not just for its providentialist view of history, nor even for the analogous relationship it reinforces between Jerusalem and reformed England. Rather, the text is singularly Protestant because of the complex ways it is both haunted by and resists the specter of Catholic ritual/theology, recently reanimated under Mary Tudor. The most obvious instance of this is the Catholic symbolism that pervades one of the most notorious episodes of the history: the killing and consumption of a little boy by his mother at the height of the famine provoked by the siege. As Josephus had it, the gruesome instance of cannibalism was perpetrated by a widow, Mary (or Miriam or Mariam), who—trapped within the city walls—killed, ate, and served up her own son.

As may be imagined, this story exerted a perverse fascination upon centuries of readers familiar with Josephus's history, and heavily Christianized
versions of the *Jewish War* (that interpreted Jerusalem's destruction as divine
vengeance for the Jews' rejection of Christ) inevitably identified Mary's actions
as precipitating the city's final devastation. As Groves also observes, Jerusalem's
extreme suffering was "encapsulated by this act which simultaneously broke
the ultimate taboo of eating human flesh and the closest human bond." Miriam's act thereby became an "enduring image of the unimaginable horror of
life trapped within the city."[14] I further agree with her claim that, in a striking
appropriation of Josephus/*Josippon*, Morwen's history and the adaptations it
inspired through the sixteenth and seventeenth centuries freight Miriam's cannibalism with disturbing Eucharistic implications.[15] Miriam's son offers up his
flesh and blood to save his mother but he is also served by her in turn to other
members of the community. Miriam thus becomes the distorted mirror image
of her Virgin namesake—a point also noted by Merrall Llewellyn Price.[16] If the
sacrifice of the Son of God grants eternal life, then Miriam's consumption of
her son brings only death and damnation.

Yet I would hold that the retelling of Miriam's story by Morwen and his
emulators reveals something more—namely, the degree to which this episode
and its buildup are imbued with both the trauma of Henry VIII's split with
Rome and the anxiety occasioned by the return of the repressed faith under
his daughter. Though the cannibalism is most clearly charged with perverse
Eucharistic valences, images of the upheaval caused by the Reformation are
summoned up even in the passages that anticipate the grisly episode: from
descriptions of destroyed "goodly buyldynges" that evoke the ruined and defaced
religious architecture of England to the obsession with monumentality and
tombs in the absence of Catholic sacramental machinery for the afterlife. Texts
inspired by Morwen's history such as Thomas Nashe's flamboyant *Christs Teares
over Iervsalem* of 1593 are more attuned to the Eucharistic adumbrations imma-
nent in Miriam's consumption of her son. Indeed, Nashe goes even further
by hinting at a residual Protestant hunger for salvific flesh and blood in the
absence of the transubstantiated body and blood of Christ.

Miriam's flesh eating certainly incarnates the disquietude English Protestants felt regarding the comestible divine body, though I suggest that the der-
ogation of Catholicism in these accounts is more complex than has hitherto
been acknowledged. While Kelly is right to highlight Morwen's connection
between the Roman triumph over the Jews who fell away from God and the
Catholic threat to the Protestant Church under Mary Tudor, his framing of the
Jewish mother's anthropophagy within a larger narrative of desolation and loss

suggests the painful nature of the rupture with the Church of Rome, and the degree to which the English Protestant world remained haunted by Catholic culture even as it resisted its resurgence.[17]

Uncanny Catholicism

The Catholic phantoms that trouble Morwen's history are manifest in the palpable tension between the just ruin of Jewish civilization as Morwen understood it, and the poignancy and tragedy of that destruction. The history he relates is unrelenting in its description of the atrocities visited upon the Jews as penalty for their "doggidnesse and intestiue hatred."[18] Jerusalem is a place of topsy-turvy as the "exceeding riche men" filch meat from one another so that "where was woont to be the dwellyng place of most wyse and prudent menne: nowe is it made a common hostry of wicked murderers and theeues."[19] The degradation brought on by the collapse of Jewish civilization is presented as fitting punishment for forsaking the law of God and transgressing the Covenant. When "dearth" and "famine" falls in the "meane season," the Jews are forced to make their way down the food chain, consuming not just animals such as horses, cats, and rats, but also mice, serpents, worms, and every creeping thing from spiders to newts to weasels.[20] Rather than recoil from such comestibles, they are said to rejoice upon finding them: "Whosoeuer at that time coulde get any hearbes or rootes, myce, serpentes, or other creepyng woormes what so euer they were to eate, he was counted happy, because he had founde meate to sustayne and saue his lyfe withal."[21] What should be repellent ("doung and very mans excrementes") becomes a desirable, even luxurious, means to prolong life. As such, Miriam's consumption of her son's corpse, which, rather than revolting her, is "sweeter . . . then hony," becomes the most extreme instance of this subversion.[22]

That said, Morwen's elaborately detailed account of Miriam's anthropophagy—which I shall turn to below—draws its power from the widow's pitiful adherence to the civilized norms and values, either decaying or absent, that contrast starkly with the savagery that mires her. As we shall see, it is in these passages, reeking of decay, that the traumatic haunting of the English Church's break with Rome is most discernible. The cannibal episode is framed by a report of the ruin of civilization in Jerusalem that is signaled partly by the destruction of "faire houses, and goodly buyldynges, that there shoulde be no monument of any noble house left to any of the citezens of Hierusalem." It must be noted here that Morwen's narrative is particularly scrupulous in detailing architectural destruction. To the "foure" kinds of plague—sword, pestilence, hunger, and fire—that the Lord visits upon the recalcitrant Jews he adds a fifth, namely, "the ruine and decay of all beautifull and gorgeous buyldinges."[23]

Such detail would have resonated in a singular way with the Protestant readership over the years. Reformed England had witnessed more than its fair share of the ruin and defacement of priories, parish churches, monasteries, nunneries, and wayside chapels. As Gary Waller notes, at the end of the sixteenth century, "wrecked or abandoned religious buildings had become a striking presence in the English landscape," creating a vista "of devastation and ruin, not unlike the aftermath of a war."[24] Margaret Aston agrees that, for succeeding generations, these ruins must have appeared like "the gashes in an urban landscape continuing long after the Second World War."[25] As early as 1536, Thomas Starkey had similarly deplored the destroyed property and, in an appeal to Henry VIII, expressed what a great "pity it were that so much fair housing and goodly building . . . should be let fall to ruin and decay, whereby our country might appear so to be defaced as [if] it had been lately overrun with enemies in time of war."[26] Philip Schwyzer suggests that, for at least a century after the dissolution of the monasteries, "almost no one saw anything beautiful or sublime in the shattered husks of the religious houses."[27] In the mid-seventeenth century, Sir John Denham still lamented the "dismal heaps" that were ruins of Chertsey Abbey,[28] even as chroniclers such as William Lambarde praised God's hand "that hath thus mercifully in our age delivered us, disclosed Satan, unmasked these Idoles . . . and raced to the grounde all Monuments of building erected to superstition and ungodlynesse."[29] The devoutly Protestant Morwen attributes the devastation of Jerusalem's buildings and monuments ("brente euerye one sticke and stone") to divine wrath. But if the likes of Lambarde appear unabashed in their appreciation of destroyed Catholic places of worship, Morwen's text also strikes a strangely plaintive note for the ruined buildings that presaged the end of Jerusalem's superior culture.

The dirge for civilization's end is continued memorably by Miriam herself, who recounts a litany of woe: famine, devastation by the sword, an encroaching enemy, bloodthirsty seditionists, "fyres, burnynges, and ruines of houses, famine, pestilence, spoyling, and destroying."[30] Confronted with such vicious and incontestable destruction of society, Miriam shares with her doomed son her expectation of a cultured future that he will never have: "I hoped once, that when thou shouldest come to mans state, thou shouldest haue susteyned myne age with meate, drynke, and cloth, and after when I shoulde dye, to burie me honorablie, lyke as I was mynded to burie thee, if thou shouldest haue died before me."[31] Here, Miriam contemplates the fit order of things; her son, when come to man's estate, should have taken care of his aged mother and provided her not just with life's necessities but, significantly, also with an important marker of elite society—a noble tomb.

By evoking the tomb that is denied her and her son, Miriam signals a serious breach in the social fabric. As Nigel Llewellyn notes in his influential study of English funeral monuments, the chief function of tombs was to substitute monumental bodies that would maintain cultural unity and social continuity for the natural and social bodies of the dead, thereby bridging and negating the rupture caused by death.[32] Peter Sherlock concurs, arguing that monuments have "one primary task: to attract visitors and make them remember the dead . . . They recreate the culture and society of the people who produced them, communicating everything from social, political, and religious ideals, to the nature of gender relations and the shape of creation itself."[33] Such "self-proclaimed voices" of the dead, then, bridge past communities with those of the future. Seen in this way, Miriam's rueful acknowledgment that she has no "good nor honorable tombe" does more than just acknowledge the danger of desecration after death; it also effectively negates the possibility of a posthumous life.

Miriam's decision to consume her son, motivated partly by an inverted desire to reinstitute the norms and conventions that govern civil society, finds troubling expression in her decision to offer up her body as a monument:

> Wherefore I haue thoughte good to chose thee a sepulchre, euen mine owne body, lest thou shouldest dye, & dogs eate thee in the streets. I wil therefore be thy graue, and thou shalt be my foode. And for that, that if thou hadst lyued and growen to mans state, thou oughtest by ryght to haue nourished me: nowe feede me with thy fleshe, and with it susteyne myne age, before that famine deuour thee, and thy body be consumed. Render therefore vnto thy mother that which she gaue vnto thee, for thou camest of her, and thou shalt returne into her.[34]

In making her own body her son's fleshly sepulcher, Miriam enacts a horrific parody of the relationship of reciprocity ("graue" for "foode") that ought to govern society. With civilization gutted, she has to reinstate it in this perverse incorporation. In a proleptic gesture, she grants her boy the future that he has been denied—the role of the dutiful and caring son. She may fail to feed him in the present ("she began to scrape in the chaffe and duste for bealtes doung, but coulde finde none"), but her failure ought not to preclude his prospective success.[35] "By right" he ought to have nourished her, and it is a right now that she, his loving mother, will not deny him: "my welbeloued sonne, whom I haue loued alwayes with al my strength, be therefore meate for thy mother."[36]

That Miriam also announces to her son, yet living, her determination to become his tomb is a striking detail that would have resonated in a distinctly uncomfortable fashion with Protestant readers, especially in the seventeenth century. The memorable yoking together of cannibalism and the funeral monument may be read, retrospectively, as a disquieting commentary on the contemporary preoccupation with posthumous life and memorialization. Even if Protestant culture purportedly severed the commemorative connections to the dead that were redolent of the former faith, the early seventeenth century witnessed a remarkable increase in the building of funeral monuments, over one-third of which were commissioned and built while the subjects they depicted were still alive.[37] As John Weever acknowledged in his *Ancient Funerall Monuments* (1631), there was historical precedent for such a practice:

> It was vsuall in ancient times, and so it is in these our dayes, for persons of especiall ranke and qualitie to make their own Tombes and Monuments in their life-time; partly for that they might haue a certain house to put their head in (as the old saying is) whensoeuer they should bee taken away by death, out of this their Tenement, the world; and partly to please themselues, in the beholding of their dead countenance in marble. But most especially because thereby they thought to preserue their memories from obliuion.[38]

Jude Jones notes that monumentalizing one's tomb in the post-medieval period was an entirely elite preoccupation "which achieved considerable popularity given the possibilities for increased upward social mobility which occurred from the sixteenth century onward."[39] Weever's mention of persons of "especiall ranke and qualities" further resonates with longstanding descriptions of Miriam as "a notable ryche woman," and connects her desire for a fitting tomb for her son to that of the upwardly mobile and elite of the early modern period. Miriam's determination for a tomb, furthermore, links her with women (often widows) in the seventeenth century who were so industrious in the commissioning and overseeing of tombs for their beloved deceased.[40]

But by offering her son her own body, Miriam affords him a tomb like no other, for it is the place from whence he came: the "selfe same shoppe, in the whiche the breath of lyfe was breathed into thy nosethrylles."[41] In an uncanny twist, then, her son not only has the dubious privilege of seeing his tomb fully finished in his own lifetime, but he also actually advances its longevity through his own body ("feede me with thy fleshe").[42] As flesh of her flesh, Miriam's boy gets to behold his dead countenance not in stone but in his mother's living visage. Though the sepulcher of her body cannot outlive marble or the gilded monuments of men, Miriam nevertheless anticipates the imminent preservation of her son's memory from oblivion. As Sherlock reminds us, monuments "tell posterity what should be known about the past" and "early modern memorials should be analysed as sites that strove to change the memory of their subjects, as well as objects that created continuity."[43] As her son's living tomb, Miriam proclaims his epitaph in no uncertain terms: "thy lotte be in the garden of Eden and Paradise: be thou meate for me, and a rebuke and shame to the seditious, that they may be compelled to say, *Loe, a woman hath killed her sonne, and hath eaten hym.*"[44]

Miriam's pronouncement, furthermore, combines the two most common types of epitaphs in Protestant churchyards: "prospective" and "retrospective," to borrow Erwin Panofsky's terms.[45] On the one hand, it anticipates and advances the hope of a future existence ("thy lotte be in the garden of Eden and Paradise"); on the other, it sums up and preserves for imagined future generations the deceased's achievements on earth ("meate" for his mother). In Sherlock's phrase, then, it sends "deliberate messages from the past to posterity"—a "rebuke and shame to the seditious"; "an ignominie and reproach to the seditious, that by violence haue taken away our foode."[46]

The transience of Miriam's world, emphasized by the destroyed buildings that surround her, only intensifies her desire for existence beyond the ephemeral by means of the tomb. It is the very fragility of stone that evokes a paradoxical desire for its imputed permanence. But the fact that the tomb is supplied by the attenuated flesh of her own emaciated body also exposes the myth of posthumous existence through the monument. Thus, in Morwen's text survival beyond death—the persistence of that which has been eradicated—links the tomb with the ruin, and both, in uncomfortable and undeniable ways, with the phantom of Catholic culture that manifests palpably in the cannibalism of the little boy. In a disconcerting turn, the very history designated essential for the prosperity of the English commonweal represents futurity as phantasmic—*unheimlich* incarnate in the womb-as-tomb.

The Eucharistic Feast

Miriam's ghastly attempts at reinstating a crumbling culture do not end with the transformation of her own body into her son's funeral monument. She follows that up by replicating the other great symbol of community and social ties: the banquet. When "the sauour of the fleshe rosted" wafts into the streets and brings the ravenous seditionists to her door, Morwen has Miriam answer their rough summons with excruciating politeness:

Be not displeased, I beseeche you, with your handemayde for this, for
you shall see I haue reserued part for you. Syt you downe therefore, and
I wyl bryng it you, that ye may taste thereof, for it is very good meate.
And by and by she layde the table, and set before them part of the
chyldes fleshe, saying, Eate, I pray you, here is a childes hande, see here
his foote and other partes, and neuer report that it is any other womans
child, but myne own only sonne that ye knewe with me, him I bare, and
also haue eaten part, and part I haue kepte for you.[47]

Miriam's feast is in striking contrast to previous descriptions of desperate scav-
enging in the text. Morwen tells us that when any "chaunced to finde any dead
horse or other beast in the towne, a man shoulde see many Israelites striue &
fight for it, in all pointes like to famished Rauens lighting vpon a dead carkasse,
so that in suche contentions very many were slayne."[48] But as the self-professed
"handemayde," Miriam is scrupulous about not only cooking her son's flesh
but also laying the table, serving the dish, and inviting her guests with utmost
courtesy to partake of the delicacy. The perfect hostess, she further takes care
to assure her guests of its provenance. In a scene that provokes equal parts pity
and horror, a weeping Miriam proceeds to thank her son for not just preserv-
ing her life but also endearing her to erstwhile enemies: "thou hast defended
me from the wrath of the seditious." In a chilling mockery of fellowship, the
seditionists become Miriam's "freendes" for "they sitte at my table, and I haue
made them a feast with thy flesh."[49]

Miriam's "feast" is thus the ersatz distorted version of community fellowship
around the table that typifies her cankered society. Significantly, Miriam's self-
appellation of "handemayde" invites a perverse association with serious religious implications: that of the Virgin Mother, the self-professed "handmaid of
the Lord" in Luke 1:38, translated in Miles Coverdale's 1537 New Testament as,
"Here I am the handemayde of the Lorde; bee it vnto me, as thou haste sayd."[50]
Such symbolic resonance was commonly exploited in the literature of the time,
a notable example being John Heywood's allegorical tale of 1556, *The Spider and
the Fly*, which represents Mary Tudor as a handmaid sweeping away the foul spider of Protestantism with her broom. Heywood's identification of the ardently
Catholic queen as a maid with a "brome not sword of rigor (doble edged blade)
/ But the branche of mercie" links her with the Virgin Mary, as Sara Duncan
notes, in her intercessory role with God for the salvation of human souls.[51]

As we can already see from Morwen's history, the association of the handmaid with the Virgin Mary was by no means restricted to Catholic texts.
Elizabeth I famously cast herself as God's handmaid in *Christian Prayers and*

Miriam serving her son to the seditionists in R.D.'s *The strange and prodigious religions, customs, and manners, of sundry nations*, 1688. (Reproduced by permission of the Houghton Library, Harvard University)

Meditations in English, French, Italian, Spanish, Greek and Latin (1569), pur-
ported to be a collection of her private devotions. In a Latin prayer, Elizabeth
refers to herself as *ancilla* (handmaid), a direct echo of Mary's presentation of
herself in the Vulgate Magnificat, and significant as an early instance of Elizabeth's purposeful appropriation of Mariological tropes and images.[52] By likewise identifying Miriam, a *mater dolorous* in her own right, as a "handemayde,"
Morwen exploits an explicit connection with the suffering Virgin even as his
Jewish mother transforms the significance of the name "Mary" or "Miriam"
(Maria in the medieval *Siege of Jerusalem*) from the bearer and nurturer of the
Son of God into a desperate cannibal.

Merrall Llewellyn Price has likewise argued that the cannibal-mother first
introduced by Josephus was transmitted down the ages as "the mirror image of
the blessed Virgin, the bad woman damned rather than redeemed by the body
of her son, the Law-less Mary reproved rather than revered by the paternal
Joseph, the Jew condemned through her own body rather than being saved
by her avoidance of its pleasures."[53] Yet, while I agree with Price's assessment,
I would also note that the distinction between Morwen's telling and the later
translation of Josephus by Thomas Lodge is worth bearing in mind. Where
Lodge's identification of Miriam's son's death as a "sacrifice" clearly echoes a
Greek tragic heroine such as Medea, the same ascription is charged with dis-
turbingly religious resonances in Morwen's text, in no small part due to Miriam's designation as a "handemayde." In this context, the seditionists' refusal to
eat of her "sacrifice" parodies the behavior of reprobates who refuse to sit down
at the heavenly banquet.

The hint that Miriam's son and Jesus also function as inverted images of
one another is magnified in the many texts inspired by Morwen's history, most
notably Nashe's *Christs Teares Over Iervsalem* and William Heminge's *Jewes
Tragedy*. The latter explicitly posits the analogy. Far from being the babe in
arms of Josephus's *Jewish War*, in Heminge's play Miriam's son is an articulate
little boy whose aghast realization "I hope you do not mean to kill me mother"
provokes the telling response: "Yes, my sweet Lamb, look; here is the knife
prepar'd."[54]

Miriam's apostrophe of her son as a "sweet Lamb" made ready for the
"knife prepar'd" would have conjured up images of the Binding of Isaac as
well as the *agnus dei*. As Kenneth Stow notes, the "Eucharistic host was often
visualized not only as Jesus incarnate but also as a child, and sometimes as
Isaac, the perfect sacrifice."[55] But if the interrupted sacrifice of Isaac was
done in willing obedience to God and the sacrifice of Christ was the ultimate expression of divine grace and the expiation of sin, then Miriam's boy

can only interpret his imminent slaughter as a punishment for wrongdoing: "Alass what have I done, what deed so foul / To make you so unkinde?"[56] Heminge's stage directions have the boy kneeling before his mother promising her duty and obedience if she will only spare his life: a visual echo of the agony in Gethsemane. But though he may promise, "My duty shall observe ye ten times more / Then ever my obedience did before," he is no Christ praying for the cup to pass. When he dies it is in terror and darkness unrelieved by the prospect of salvation.

Despite mining the Christological resonances of the scene, Heminge, as I argue in chapter 4, largely refrains from the stock etiological explanation for the boy's destruction (divine punishment for sin) and allows the child's question "alass what have I done" to linger unanswered. Christian interpreters of Jerusalem's devastation had plenty to say about the "deed so foul" that makes Miriam's son the scapegoat for an entire community, but Heminge teases his readers with nothing more than the brief unglossed analog of Christ and the cannibalized boy.

Morwen's other imitators, by contrast, were far less restrained about portraying either Miriam as the inverted image of the Virgin Mother or her crime as a savage Eucharistic feast involving her degenerate countrymen. As such, they effectively linked her story to libelous allegations against medieval Jews for the ritual murder of Christian children, about which I shall say more later. To be sure, the supposed depravity of the Ancient Jews is on full display in Nashe's *Christs Teares Over Iervsalem*, a florid piece of denunciatory prose composed during the plague that ravaged London in 1593, and reprinted in 1594 and 1616. Nashe's entire text is littered with moldering reprobate bodies that are the direct consequence of the Chosen People's rejection of the law of God and of Christ. As Nashe fulminates:

> It is not vnknown, by how many and sundry waies GOD spake by Visions, Dreames, Prophecies, and Wonders, to his chosen *Ierusa-lem*, onely to moue his chosen *Ierusalem* wholie to cleaue vnto him. Visions, Dreames, Prophecies, and Wonders, were in vaine: This gorgious strumpet *Ierusalem*, too-to much presuming of the promises of old, went a whoring after her own inuentions; She thought the Lord vnseparately tyde to his Temple, & that he could neuer be diuorced from the Arke of his Couenant; that, hauing bound himself with an oth to *Abraham*, he could not (though he would) remoue the Lawe out of *Iuda*, or his Iudgement-seate from *Mount Silo*. They erred most temptingly & contemptuously.[57]

In Nashe's text, the Jews' arrogant presumptions upon "the promises of old" deaden them to the glory of the Incarnation. Imagining that God was bound inextricably by His promise to Abraham, they willfully ignore Christ's tearful entreaties to repent. In a curious move, Nashe emphasizes the so-called folly of the Jews by comparing them to the intransigent armies that attempted to resist Tamburlaine. As legend has it, the Scythian conqueror would first fly a white flag and then a red, before finally hoisting the black flag portending the doom of his enemies. Nashe's Jews likewise spurn Christ's "White-flagge of forguie-nesse and remission, and the Red-flag of shedding his Blood for them," until their "obduration" earns them the same "Black-flagge of confusion and desola-tion."[58] Their misery culminates at the perverse banquet hosted by the cannibal widow—the feast of her only begotten son.

Modeled on Morwen's Miriam, Nashe's self-professed "Monarch-monster of Mothers" even invites the shocked onlookers to relish the prospect of her cannibalism:

> Eate, I pray you, heere is good meate, be not afrayd, it is flesh of my flesh, I bare it, I nurst it, I suckled it. Loe, heere is the head, the handes, and the feete. It was myne owne onely sonne, I tell you. Sweet was he to mee in his life, but neuer so sweet as in his death. Beholde his pale perboyld visage, how pretie-pitteous it lookes. His pure snow-moulded soft fleshe will melt of it selfe in your mouthes: who can abstaine from these two round teat-like cheeks? Be not dainty to cut them vp; the rest of his body haue I cutte vp to your hands.[59]

Miriam's calculated gesturing to the head, hands, and feet reinforces the hor-rible equivalence between her son and Christ with his iconic wounds, which Nashe takes a step further when he accentuates the similarity between the "tender-starued Mother to kill and eate her onely sonne" and God's "owne onely child, *Christ Iesus* (as deere to him as thou to mee, my sonne) he sent into the World to be crucified."[60] But in *Christs Teares*, eternal life is replaced with the awful stench of mortality.

Part of Nashe's literary effect is derived from the way that he systemati-cally elides traditionally eschatological symbols of all salvific promise, as is clear from his reworking of the pelican—popular in Protestant iconography as a symbol of Christ—to connote civil discord. The bird that pierces her own breast to feed her young was traditionally equated with Christ's life-conferring sacrifice, but in Nashe's text, Jerusalem is "the Pellican in the Wildernesse" that "(by thine owne progenie) [has] thy bowels torne out: by ciuill warres [shall be]

more wasted then outwarde annoyance." Repudiating any possibility of symbiotic love, Nashe's Christ informs the beleaguered city that, "Those whom thou
most expectest loue of shall be most vnnaturall to thee."[61] There are no intima-
tions of immortality.

The Catholic Host

The oppositional resonances in *Christs Teares* between the sacred sacrifice
of the Son of God and its profane counterpart in Miriam's cannibalism are
ineluctable despite (or, perhaps, because of) the medieval European tradition
that made the Virgin Mother actively complicit in preparing her Son for sacrifice.[62] In the fifteenth-century lyric "The firste day when Crist was born," Mary
is responsible for not only Jesus's birth but also his Passion: the description
of the brutal suffering of the Savior is punctuated with a fervent "I thonke a
mayden everydel."[63] Her role was rendered equally prominent in religious art:
a Swabian "Hostienmühle" or "host-mill" centerpiece that dates from the same
century, now in the Ulmer Museum, clearly shows Mary pouring flour into the
mill that produces the holy wafer.

The "contaminated Eucharistic structure" (to borrow Alex Mueller's words)
of Miriam's preparation of her son's body for the feast is particularly fraught,
and suggests that the sacrifice of the Mass was dangerously open to imputations
of cannibalism.[64] The Fourth Lateran Council of 1215 had declared transubstantiation (whereby the bread and wine on the altar was transformed into the
body and blood of Christ) to be true doctrine, though it only gained credence
and philosophical authority later in the thirteenth century, when Aristotelian
theory came to dominate scholarly discussions of material form and material
change.[65] The Council of Trent formulated a non-contingent, non-arbitrary
relationship of absolute identity between the signifier (the consecrated host)
and the signified (the body of Christ) so that Christ is "truly, really, and sub-
stantially contained in the august sacrament of the Holy Eucharist under the
appearance of those sensible things."[66] In Julia Houston's summation then, "The
host is not a type similar to the body of Christ or a reproduction of Christ or
a dimensionally limited appearance by Christ. It is Christ."[67] St. Thomas Aquinas (1225–1274), the principal philosopher of the Eucharist, insisted that "we
have under this sacrament . . . not only the flesh, but the whole body of Christ,
that is the bones and nerves and all the rest," and that "the complete substance
of this is changed into the complete substance of that."[68]

For other medieval Aristotelians, however, the Eucharist posed a conun-
drum: what the priest consecrated at the altar had to transform from the

substantial forms of bread and wine into the substantial form of the body and blood of Christ, while yet retaining the "accidents" of bread and wine (taste, smell, and color) so as not to repulse the faithful with the prospect of cannibalizing Christ.[69] Aquinas himself was alert to possible imputations of cannibalism in the Eucharist when he averred that the invisibility of Christ's presence in the host meant that we must not rely on our senses:

> We could never know by our senses that the real body of Christ and his
> blood are in this sacrament, but only by our faith . . . Divine providence
> very wisely arranged for this. First of all, people have not the custom
> of eating human flesh and drinking human blood; indeed, the thought
> revolts them. And so the flesh and blood of Christ are given to us to be
> taken under the appearance of things in common human use, namely
> bread and wine.[70]

Aquinas admits concern that "this sacrament should be an object of contempt for unbelievers, if we were to eat our Lord under his human appearance."[71] The anxiety over cannibalism that imbues Aquinas's discourse was a familiar one and had been acknowledged by, among others, the early Christian apologist Tertullian (c.160–c.225 C.E.). Tertullian advanced the possibility that eating God in the Eucharist and truly feeding on His flesh and blood might be viewed, not as cannibalism, but as a "paradoxical redemption of that most horrible of consumptions," to quote Carolyn Walker Bynum's paraphrase.[72] But sanguine as his declaration purports to be, it reveals the strain of attempting to banish the specter of anthropophagy in the "paradoxical redemption" of ghastly consumption. To that end, we must now consider Protestant repudiation of the same.

Transubstantiation as Cannibalism

In order to fully appreciate the disturbing Eucharistic potential of the Miriam episode, it is helpful to briefly review the history of Protestant associations of cannibalism with the Eucharist—a bias that would have been all too familiar to Morwen and Nashe's readers. During the Reformation, the doctrine of transubstantiation was roundly abjured by the likes of Huldrych Zwingli (1484–1531), Jean Calvin (1509–1564), and Jean de Léry (1536–1613) who, determined to construe Eucharistic eating as depraved and barbaric, drew overt parallels between Catholics and cannibals.[73] As Maggie Kilgour observes, "In order to delineate themselves as one religious body against another, the Reformers defined themselves in terms of eating, as those who ate spiritually in opposition

to the others who ate God literally."[74] Christ, Calvin insisted, was not "put there
to be touched by the hands, to be chewed by the teeth and to be swallowed by
the mouth." For Calvin, the Mass was a "horrid abomination" inspired by Satan
to "adulterate and envelope the sacred supper of Christ with thick darkness."[75]
As George Hoffman argues, for many sixteenth century Christians "the Roman
altar began . . . to resemble more the site of holocausts than the convivial table
around which the apostles gathered . . . and the priest appeared more like those
high priests who had conspired to execute the savior than like Jesus."[76]

The war against Catholic ritual was aided by a rather creative use of ethno-
graphic materials as pamphleteers accompanied denunciations of the Mass as
a demonically inspired bloodbath with images of New World cannibalism and
human sacrifice, to which we shall return in chapter 3. Transubstantiation, in
Zwingli's view, made the Mass a cannibalistic ritual and therefore "monstrous,
unless perhaps one is living among the Anthropophagi."[77] The same connection
between the Catholic and the barbaric other was pronounced by the Calvinist de Léry: "They [Catholics] not only wanted to eat the flesh and blood of
Jesus Christ grossly rather than spiritually, but what was worse, like the savages
named Ouetaca [of Brazil], of whom I have already spoken, they wanted to
chew and swallow raw."[78]

For Thomas Cranmer (1489–1556), the challenge was to stress the significance of the Eucharist while yet retaining some intimation of the sensual
aspects of the feast. Christ, he admitted, "ordained sensible signs and tokens,
whereby to allure and draw us to more strength and more constant faith in him.
So that the eating of the sacramental bread and wine is, *as it were*, a showing
of Christ before our eyes, a smelling of him with our noses, a feeling and grop-
ing of him with our hands, and an eating, chewing, digesting and feeding upon
him to our spiritual strength and perfection."[79] Though Cranmer and his fellow
Church of England stalwart Richard Hooker (1554–1600) sought to strike a
balance between the extremes of Catholic transubstantiation and the Zwin-
glian position, more radical Protestants were vociferous in their denunciation
of the Eucharist. Thomas Becon (1511–1567), who in 1550 passionately pleaded
for the history of the Jews' destruction to be translated into English, denounced
transubstantiation in his pamphlet *Against the gross and fantastical opinion of
the Papists, which affirm that Christ's natural body and blood is carnally eaten and
drunken in the Lord's Supper*, and castigated the cannibalistic priest who "doth
only with his greasy fingers touch and handle that very self-same body, but . . .
doth also break it, crush it asunder with his teeth, eat it, swallow it down, &c."[80]

In Becon's language, the priest is a "greasy massmonger" and "always desirous
to shed blood."[81] Thomas Turke's "The Holy Eucharist and the Popish Breaden

God" (1625) compared the Catholic consumption of Christ's body and blood in the Eucharist to both the whale swallowing up Jonah as well as men eating oysters: "so on Him they feed; / Whole and alive, raw and yet not bleed." Turke was particularly aghast that "This cooker, void of humanity, / Is held in Rome for sound divinity."[82] Perhaps most famous in this vein is Edmund Spenser's (1552–1599) scathing portrayal of the cannibal priests in Book 6 of the *Faerie Queene*, at whose bloody Mass the lovely Serena is forced into the role of "host"—the degenerate version of the sacrament. In an elaborate but unmistakable parody of the Eucharist, "the saluage nation" determines to present her "blood" to God as sacrifice and then to "make a common feast, and feed with gurmandize" on her flesh. Miriam's grim blazon of her son's body in Morwen's history ("here is a childes hande, see here his foote") finds parallel in the visual dismemberment of Serena by the cannibals: "Some with their eyes the daintest morsels chose; / Some praise her paps, some praise her lips and nose" (6.8.38–39).

That anti-papal writings continued to be a major feature of the seventeenth century is evident from Anthony Milton's estimate that some five hundred such works or more were published between 1605 and 1625, by no less than 150 different authors, all of which dealt with controversies between the Church of England and Rome.[83] Later in the seventeenth century, fears that the doctrine of transubstantiation would be reintroduced by Charles I's Archbishop Laud (1573–1645) and his supporters (alleged Catholic sympathizers) prompted a fresh wave of revulsion among Puritans that endured for decades. The New England divine Edward Taylor (1642–1729), for instance, damned "feed[ing] on Humane Flesh and Blood" a "Strange mess!" and of such "Barbarousness" that even Nature must recoil. "Can Bread and Wine by words be Carnifi'de?" he asks, and "manifestly bread and Wine abide?"[84] Transubstantiation's embrace of metamorphosis proves too disagreeable for Taylor, who shies away from the incipient barbarity of consuming flesh and blood and, instead, takes refuge in metaphor. Taylor's distaste is mirrored in John Milton's trenchant equivalence of transubstantiation with cannibal bestiality in a visceral account of the chewing and digestion of the host. In *De Doctrina Christiana*, Milton inveighs against the Mass and the way it "brings down Christ's body from its supreme exaltation at the right hand of God. It drags it back to the earth, though it has suffered every pain and hardship already, to a state of humiliation even more wretched and degrading than before: to be broken once more and crushed and ground, even by the fangs of brutes."[85] As Milton avers, one needs "not teeth but faith" to eat Christ's flesh.[86]

Early modern Protestants were thus expected to imagine the rending of Christ's body in the breaking of bread but not to think that they were consuming that broken body when eating the bread. It was a delicate balancing act. As Gary Taylor reminds us, though the table had been substituted for the altar, the Eucharist was still a very important custom, even for the Puritans who preferred to sit rather than kneel to receive communion.[87] Miriam's invitation to her neighbors as well as the seditionists to sit at her table and eat her only begotten son would have stirred not only associations with the Eucharist but also, equally, the allegations of cannibalism leveled against it. It is of note that the committed Protestant Morwen has Miriam exhort the seditionists to "Taste & see howe sweete my sonnes fleshe is" and "Beholde, I haue prepared a fayre table for you."[88] Her lines carry distinct biblical echoes of Psalm 34:8, "Taste and see that the Lord is good," and 23:5, "You prepare a table before me in the presence of my enemies," respectively—lines of tremendous significance to the Eucharistic liturgy.

Beyond this, her cataloging of the various items on the dish "here is a childes hand, see here his foote, and other partes" travesties some medieval accounts of the manifestation of the Christ child in the Eucharist—notable among which was the fifteenth-century narrative of Colette of Corbie, a Franciscan nun who had a vision of Christ in the form of a serving dish filled with the body of a child, dismembered into fragments of bloody meat. The seditionist "freendes" who sit at Miriam's "table," those whom she encourages to "eate, and satisfie themselues," become thereby dark simulacra of early modern communicants. Nashe, who satirized Catholics, Jews, and Presbyterians alike in *The Unfortunate Traveller*, was clearly more ambivalent in his religious denunciations than was Morwen, but he too played up the specter of Catholicism inherent in Miriam's bloody banquet. His robust condemnation of those who "grosslie palpabrize and feele God with their bodily fingers" was directed not only toward atheists, who need such tangible proof but also, implicitly, Catholics, who insist on the fleshy manifestation of Christ in the host.[89]

Transference of Anxiety: The Jewish Cannibal

There is another crucial element to consider in the Catholic haunting of the narratives of Morwen and his imitators, and that is the medieval allegation of the Jewish blood libel. Recent scholarship has made a strong case for the way that medieval narratives, recognizing that the Catholic doctrine of transubstantiation was dangerously vulnerable to cannibalist accusations, consciously displaced those accusations onto non-Catholic targets, predominantly Jews, regularly associated with child-killing and infanticide. Miri Rubin opines that the Jew came to "carry all the pent up anxiety, shame, and fear which Christians harboured about themselves, their bodies, their God, their doubts, their desires."[90] Resonances of anthropophagy embedded in the Eucharistic sacrifice were projected outward even as the belief in Real Presence was underscored by widespread accounts of the physical manifestation of the infant Christ in the host (thereby linking the Nativity to the Passion).[91] Jews thus figure prominently in the Eucharistic exempla that feature bloody and dismembered Christ figures.[92] Price's study of cannibalism in *Consuming Passions* draws critical attention to the "sermo de corpore Christi," where a Jew looking for a Christian traveling companion enters a church and sees a priest holding aloft the "ffeir child, I-wounded sore / in foot and hond." The child is divided and the congregation receives individual replicas of his body, which, to the Jew's horror, they proceed to devour. Interestingly, as Price notes, this gory vision is explained away as the Jew's inheritance of the sins of his ancestors: "And thy kun made him dye / Therefore al blodi thou hym seye."[93]

Even as the marvelous appearance of the child in the host realized the miracle of transubstantiation for the faithful, it also produced the phantasm of murder and cannibalism that had to be exorcised.[94] The Eucharist, suggests Francesca Matteoni, "becomes the place of fantasies in which Christians confronted their own feelings of sorrow, guilt, and revulsion at the awful spectre of infanticide. The symbolism of the bleeding host was powerful and frightening; projected onto the Jews it was evidence of fears and concepts that were entangled with Christian sensibility."[95] In 1205, Pope Innocent III declared that Jews feared the blood and flesh of Christ embodied in the host, which in turn spawned allegations of host desecration.[96]

Such charges leveled against the Jews became entangled with those of child-killing to produce a discourse of horrific infanticidal cannibalism that parodied the Mass. In point of fact, the allegations of child-killing were ancient, voiced memorably in John Chrysostom's *First Homily Against the Jews*: "What tragedy, what kind of wickedness, did they not outstrip in their bloodlust? . . . Wild beasts often lay down their lives, disregarding their own safety in order to protect their young; but the Jews, without any necessity whatever, slaughtered their progeny with their own hands to serve the accursed demons, who are enemies of our life."[97] The idea that took root, inspired by polemicists like Chrysostom, was that there was no limit to the atrocities that could be performed by a race of people capable of deicide. Thus we hear of the 1329 case where a Savoy Jew admitted under torture to a "confused fantasy" of selling Christian children to be killed and converted into "a salve or food" that would then be distributed among members of his community who "eat of this food at every Passover instead of a sacrifice."[98] Protestant accounts of cannibalism in besieged Jerusalem cannot be read entirely independently of either tran-substantiation or the related anti-Semitic imputations of somatic incorpora-tion.[99] That said, the cautionary tone of the siege narratives was predicated upon a relationship of correspondence and potential equivalence between besieged Jerusalem and contemporary England that is echoed, interestingly, in Nashe's determination to "write something of mourning, for *London* to harken counsaile of her great Grand-mother, *Ierusalem*."[100] The admonitory quality of Nashe's history and, more so, Morwen's—both avowing a diachronic equiva-lence between London and Jerusalem (and therefore between Christian and Jew)—complicate any simple anti-Semitic shading of Miriam's cannibalism. With the overt disavowal of the doctrine of transubstantiation in Reforma-tion England, the charge habitually leveled against the Jews rebounds on the original levelers. Where medieval Catholic narratives customarily projected the cannibalistic nuances implicit in the Eucharistic sacrifice of the Mass outward onto the Jews, early modern accounts of Mary's "sacrifice" advance the possibil-ity of the return of the relegated Catholic sacrament should Protestantism fail to live up to its promise.

Despite the involved Jewish-Catholic resonances, and notwithstanding the fact that Miriam's transgression represents the ultimate horror in the mythol-ogy of cannibalism (the devouring of one family member by another), the early modern texts that narrate Miriam's story refrain from vilifying her in simple terms. This is partly because they retain the *Josippon's* attitude of pity and hor-ror and partly because they frustrate simple polarities. Though Nashe decries Miriam's act as emblematic of Jerusalem's moral aberrance, he is also unexpect-edly attuned to the anguish that generated it. Miriam's suffering may make her a distorted image of the *mater dolorous*, but her agony is no less real for that. She is not dismissed as a symbol of absolute alterity (the savage "other" as opposed to the civilized "self"). Rather, by establishing a congruent relation-ship between besieged Jerusalem and Catholic-vitiated London, texts such as Morwen's history and its derivatives, especially *Christs Teares*, effectively com-plicate the binaries of self and other, sacred and profane, and even Christian and Jewish, revealing instead a crucial overlap between anti-Catholicism and anti-Semitism.

Protestant Cannibalism: Mummy as Salve

In a curious move that confounds any simple repudiation of either cannibal-ism or the Catholic Eucharist, Nashe describes his work in the preface to the 1616 edition dedicated to Elizabeth Cary, Viscountess Falkland, as a "handfull of *Ierusalem's* mummianized earth (in a few sheets of wast paper enwrapped)." Mummy was a substance "prepared for medicinal use from mummified [usually human] flesh," thereby suggesting that Nashe's grisly alimentary Jerusalem with its maternal cannibal functions, first and foremost, was a cure.[101] Certainly, six-teenth- and seventeenth-century pharmacopeias are replete with references to mummy. It even appears that the practice of consuming the flesh of mummified corpses operated on the assumption that the human body contained a myste-rious healing power that could be transmitted by ingestion. In early Islamic medicine, the name "mumiya" was assigned to a natural mineral pitch ("mum" or wax) that was found solidified on mountainsides in Persia, and it was only in the eleventh century that the term came to be associated with ancient Egyptian corpses.[102] In Simon Corda's Latin translation of the Arab physician Ibn Sera-pion the Younger (c.1070) "mumia of the sepulchers" is a substance of "aloes and myrrh mixed with liquid of the human body."[103]

During the early modern period, mummy was used in Europe to cure a plethora of ailments including gout, fever, diarrhea, ulcers, hemorrhoids, epi-lepsy, and convulsions. Applied externally, the oil of human fat treated rheuma-tism, nervous disorders, aches, pains, and melancholy, and was even believed to promote the growth of flesh. Although the use of mummy really only gained popularity in the seventeenth century when it was used as a general cure-all by persons as eminent as Charles II, it nonetheless finds mention in John Hall's 1565 edition of Lanfranc's *A Most Excellent and Learned Work of Chirurgery*, where it is described as "among our apothecaries extant" and "the very flesh of man's body, as it were burned to a coal."[104] Mummy also features in William Bullein's *Bullein's Bulwarke of defense agaynst all Sicknes* (1562) and, in 1575, John Bannister, the queen's physician, recorded both a water of rhubarb and mummy to be drunk to cure ulcers of the breast, as well as a mummy plas-ter to be used for a tumorous ulcer. In 1589, he expanded his list of uses for mummy in the *Antidotary Chirurgical* to include numerous balms, plasters, drinks, powders, and oils.[105] In 1595, Nashe himself wrote that while "mummy is somewhat obscure," for physicians and their "confectioners [it is] . . . as famil-iar as mumchance [a card game] among pages."[106] Richard Sugg speculates that Nashe was probably responding to complaints that he had coined words in his bombastic *Christs Teares*. He certainly appears to have come up with the word "mummianized," and Sugg suggests that criticism of Nashe's term may reflect the relative novelty of corpse medicine at the time.[107] Nashe probably learned about mummy from Bullein and, given his love for all things startling and novel, would have hastened to use the term. Focusing on the significance of "mummianized earth," Groves suggests that Nashe was also influenced by the belief that Jerusalem's soil conferred spiritual and physical benefits. As she observes, pilgrims had frequently returned from the Holy Land with handfuls of earth or "blessings" that were believed to possess prophylactic or medicinal powers.[108] Nashe's text as "mummianized earth" would thus function as a metaphorical parallel to the pilgrim bringing his ampulla of holy earth back from Jerusalem.[109] Nashe himself appears to play with this allusion when he describes the devastation of Jerusalem's soil as punishment for Jewish sinfulness. "The Earth left to be so fruitfull as it wont. No season but it exceeded hys stinted temperature" carries the implication that Jerusalem's once sanctified earth is now tainted and unnatural.[110] A few pages earlier, he ghoulishly literalizes the "mummianized earth" of the preface when he describes bodies left in the ground to molder, again a consequence of Jewish miscreancy: "olde Sages and Gouernours strowe the streetes with theyr white hayres like strawes"; their "withered dead-bodies serue to mende High-waies with, and turne standing Quagmyres to firme ground."[111]

It is as if the palliative and salutary qualities that belonged to Jerusalem's once sacred soil transfer to Nashe's text, which must be chewed and digested by sinful Londoners if they are to be cured of their iniquity. Furthermore, by elevating his own writing as a cure (mummy), Nashe in his preface anticipates and parodies the link between the dreadful consumption of Miriam's son and early modern medical practice. Louise Noble informs us that the most highly prized mummy in early modern England was that from a fresh corpse, preferably of a youth who had died a sudden and violent death, because of the widespread belief that a "swift death captured the body's healing life force, while a slow death depleted it."[112] One might argue that Nashe's tract supplies the superior potent mummy that Miriam's act fails to achieve, since her poor son dies a slow and protracted death, starving by degrees until she finally stabs him. Indeed, Nashe arrogates a superior palliative power to his text when he implies, to quote Groves, "that the somatic force of his prose and its fleshly excesses—the huge heaps of dead, the grotesque descriptions of bodies, and the maternal cannibal—may themselves be part of its curative effect."[113] As she goes on to note, *Christs Teares* is presented as fashionable medicine wrapped in waste paper, akin to the drugs pharmacists wrapped in recycled pamphlets.

Nashe's equation of his text with mummy takes on additional significance when we recall that corpse pharmacology was mobilized as an important polemical weapon in the virulent debates over transubstantiation in early modern England. The Catholic convert Richard Smith, later Bishop of Chalcedon (1558–1655), suggested in his 1612 dispute with Daniel Featly (1582–1645) that "it was no horrible, nor wicked thing to eat man's flesh, since we usually eat it in mummy."[114] The equivalence Smith establishes between transubstantiation and mummy is the subject of Noble's study, in which she draws attention to the "uncanny parallel . . . between the medical ingestion of corpses in Protestant England and the religious ingestion of transubstantiated divine flesh in the disputed Catholic Eucharist."[115] Given that Catholic theology deems Christ's flesh a healing sacramental food, Noble suggests that the "post-Reformation cultural fantasies of consuming medicinal flesh . . . invert to representations of the Catholic sacrament."[116] In her *Medicinal Cannibalism in Early Modern English Literature and Culture*, Noble discerns a "discursive overlap" between the medical ingestion of corpses and the "denial of the Eucharist as corporeal matter that reveals a residual Protestant hunger for the real flesh and blood of Christ."[117] She postulates that:

> As the Protestant Eucharist was emptied of the consumable body of Christ, the ingestible medical corpse rose to darken the Protestant doorstep. The close parallel between religious reform, which ultimately denied the role of the natural body in sacramental eating, and medical reform, which advanced the pharmacological ingestion of corpses, raises the intriguing possibility of the medical corpse as uncannily appeasing a residual Protestant hunger.[118]

Noble's intriguing thesis is supported by Karen Gordon-Grube who likewise discerns an equivalence between the functions of mummy and the Catholic host: "Perhaps for Protestants of this period, healing with mummy and blood on some level fulfilled a substitute function to that of the transubstantiated flesh and blood."[119]

It is evident that the revulsion produced by the consumption of Christ's real body in the Eucharist did not translate to mummy. Thus, Edward Taylor, who denigrated the Catholic Eucharist, had few qualms about prescribing mummy as a remedy.[120] In 1638, Featley would attempt to explain his repugnance toward transubstantiation (and preference for mummy) by offering that "it is not the disregard of the countenance of man, or the disfiguring his shape, which makes anthropophagy or man eating so horrible a sin: but the making the flesh of one man the food of another, and the belly a sepulchre." A few lines later he insists, "For our question is not of the medicinal use of man's flesh, altered by art, but whether it be not a sin, and that a horrible one, to eat with the mouth and teeth the flesh of a known man, nay of the Son of God."[121] As Sugg speculates, corpse medicine may have been preferable for the likes of Featly because it typically involved the body of an unknown person.[122]

Still, that the consumption of mummy by early modern Protestants gestured uncomfortably not just to the much-maligned Catholic sacrament but also to the popular perception of Jews as consumers of human flesh, is suggested by Nashe himself in yet another extravagant prose work, *The Unfortunate Traveller*. In particular, the text plays with and interrogates the conventional stereotypes of Jews as cannibalistic procurers and traders of corpses for mummy in the interactions between the protagonist Jack and the Jewish surgeon Dr. Zachary. Jack has a morbid fear of being killed and processed into mummy by Zachary, but as Noble points out, the fiction, far from being ratified by the text, is actually destabilized within it.[123] Jack's capture and imminent dissection by his Jewish jailer are consistent with the usual charges of Jews abducting and killing children, and partaking in ritual murder and cannibalism.[124] At the same time, as Noble also notes, Nashe leaves us in little doubt that medicinal cannibalism and the attendant commercialization of Jack's body is an English practice.[125]

Indeed, the so-called anti-Semitism of *The Unfortunate Traveller* is extremely ambivalent, a point also made by Matthew Martin. He rightly posits that "the excessive, phantasmagorical nature of the work's construction of Jewishness betrays the anxiety and insecurity at the heart of its construction of Englishness."[126] But I maintain that the destabilization of the seemingly anchored categories of "Jew" and "Englishman" is both more unsettling and more effectively achieved in *Christs Teares over Iervsalem*, where the boast of prized mummianized earth rests uneasily cheek by jowl with the Jewish cannibal mother.

Conclusion

Miriam's anthropophagy as narrated by Morwen and emulators such as Nashe shows how Catholic figurations shadowed early modern Protestant narratives of Jewish antiquity—so much so that Morwen's avidly consumed history of decline and fall reveals spectral traces of that which is lost but never entirely gone: the gorgeous building now ruined, the once pulsating body immured, and, in the Jewish mother's act of eating and serving up her only begotten son, the suppressed religion reinstituted. Nashe similarly admits the return of the repressed in his Eucharistic-heavy depiction of Miriam's cannibalism, and further intensifies it by presenting his text as "mummy," thereby reasserting a deeper equivalence not just between sinful Jerusalem and reformed England but also between Catholic practice and English Protestant culture. Morwen's history, Nashe's *Christs Teares*, and the texts of their ilk functioned within a powerful literature of apocalypse that was hyperalert to discern signs of the inimical fate that befell Jerusalem in the raging political and religious furor of their day. Morbidly enticing as Miriam's cannibalism was, it dispenses a pointed moral to the tenuously covenanted English Protestant nation, that "God grant us and all Christians to take example least following them in the like sinne, we feele the like smart."

CHAPTER 2

Bodies Besieged

On September 8, 2016, London's *Telegraph* ran an article confirming the presence of *Yersina pestis* (*Y Pestis*) bacteria in skeletons dating from the Great Plague of 1665. These remains had been uncovered during a dig at London's Liverpool Street the previous year. Quoting Richard Stabler, Associate Professor at the London School of Tropical Medicine, the article informed its twenty-first-century readers that there was "always debate around whether the great plague was actually 'plague.' The discovery of this bacteria puts such controversy to rest."[1] Recalling the dire trifecta of plague, fire, and war that made 1666 London's *annus horribilis*, the report concluded by reassuring its readers still reeling from the Brexit vote to leave the European Union that the plague bacteria extracted from the site did not survive in the ground—implying that they, at least, had one less thing to fear.

It is now commonplace to identify rodents as the primary vector of the *Y Pestis* bacteria. But in the sixteenth and seventeenth centuries, plague was commonly understood as divine punishment for sins that were often social in nature; from thieving and gambling to drunkenness, prostitution, and usury.[2] Dr. Cogan's *Haven of health* (1584), for instance, explains the dreaded disease as "the wrath of God for sin, for so God threateneth, that he will send sickness and disease to those that will not hear His word and disobey His commandments."[3] "Our sinnes have made this breach with God" is likewise the message of the 1641 plague pamphlet *Londons lamentation, Or a fit admonishment for city and countrey*. An earlier plague pamphlet from 1577 even incriminates the theater in a sly bit of syllogistic reasoning, claiming that "the cause of plagues is sin, if you look to it well; and the cause of sin are plays, therefore the cause of plagues are plays."[4]

Hardly surprising, then, that plague literature of the early modern period was imbued with a fierce reforming zeal that often manifested as gloomy delight, especially when establishing a grim cause-and-effect relationship between iniquity/impiety and natural disaster. Under the ferociously Catholic Queen Mary (1516–1558), plague was repeatedly offered as punishment for the Protestant policies of the previous era. Then, the outbreak of 1563 under Elizabeth was duly blamed on residual Catholicism. By 1636, the culprit for the "plague of God" had become religious conformity—the "new mixture of religion that is commanded in churches"—imposed by Archbishop Laud.[5] As Alan D. Dyer observes, "the possibility of less abstract causation" such as stagnant water, polluted air, overcrowding, and vermin was noted in such literature but was "presented as merely the agencies used by God in carrying out His will."[6] Instead, popular plague texts, partly motivated by the conviction that Final Judgment was a burning brothel away, emphasized blasphemy, heresy, "filthy drunkenness, abominable whoredoms, open profanation of the sabbath, unlawful pastimes, with infinite many more" causes of plague.[7]

If the causes listed above look strangely familiar, it is because they also feature prominently in the popular literature of admonition that cautioned sinful England against declining in the same manner as Jerusalem of 70 C.E. It strikes me that the story of besieged Jerusalem not only lent to early modern plague literature an explanation for malady—devastation as divine retribution—but also shared a valuable rhetoric that rendered the diseased body a besieged space. Certainly, the plague literature discussed in this chapter is characterized by violence and the total ruination associated with military siege. Plague becomes a tyrant, a conqueror at the head of a marauding army, attacking the body with relentless brutality. The beleaguered body, like sacked Jerusalem torn apart by the seditionists within and the Romans without, is ravaged as its internal organs revolt against one other. Implicitly drawing on the etymology of plague as "stroke" or "wound" (from the Greek *plaga*), the plague texts with which I am concerned emphasize the brutality of the disease, all the while linking the afflicted body with the disordered body politic. Ernest B. Gilman has argued that "in the early modern formation of an English national consciousness . . . the vulnerability of the kingdom as a single victim—its constitution as a suffering individual—serves as a means of conceiving the state as such, and of symbolizing the forces that threaten it."[8] In this context, I further contend that the fevered and contagious plague-ridden body functioned as sinful London mapped onto besieged Jerusalem, wracked by moral and political transgression.

There is no denying that early modern plague literature is an excellent index for measuring the popularity of the siege trope, and its circulation as cultural currency. While several ruined cities such as Sodom, Gomorrah, and Nineveh feature in plague literature as examples of God's anger, references to Jerusalem's downfall far outweigh them in such pamphlets as those penned by popular writers like Thomas Dekker and Thomas Nashe. This suggests how readily Peter Morwen's *A compendious and most marueilous Historie* had captured the public imagination. As this chapter shows, plague writers were clearly confident that their allusions to the siege would resonate with readers. I also reveal the wide applicability of the trope of besieged Jerusalem as a metaphor for unimaginable horror catalyzed by human sinfulness.

The most prolific writer to make sense of the plague by relying on Morwen's history was undoubtedly Dekker (1572–1632), whose *The Wonderfull Yeare* (1603), *Newes from Hell* (1604), *A Rod for Run-awaies* (1625), and *London Looke Back at that Yeare of Yeares 1625* (1630) drew heavily on the image of Jewish suffering to explain English pain. Likewise, Nashe's *Christs Teares over Iervsalem* (1593)—discussed in the previous chapter—and the similarly titled anonymous ballad (1640) explain England's woes in the context of Jewish sinfulness in order to exhort their compatriots to atone. Indeed, throughout the late sixteenth and seventeenth centuries, much popular plague literature, whether delivered from the pulpit or sung as ballads in the street, took recourse to Jerusalem's devastation to comprehend victimization at the hands of this deadly disease.

Even where Jerusalem is not explicitly cited, echoes of the holy city's horrific destruction reverberate. The same writers often discoursed on siege and plague alike, most notably Thomas Lodge, who followed his monumental translation of Josephus's complete works in 1602 with another erudite translation titled *Treatise of the Plague* (1603). Whether laconic or elaborate, references to the siege in Adam Hill's *The Crie of England* (1593), Lancelot Dawes's *God's Mercies and Iervasalem's Miseries* (1609), George Wither's *Britain's Remembrancer* (1628), William Hampton's *A Proclamation of Warre from the Lord of Hosts* (1626), *A Warning or lanthorn to London by the doleful destruction of faire Jerusalem* (c.1658), and Daniel Defoe's *Journal of the Plague Year* (1722) attest to the enduring popularity and relevance of the story as a way to inform current crises.

In some instances, Jerusalem's devastation functions as the primary framework for addressing issues involving the plague in England. *Christs Teares over Iervsalem*, *God's Mercies and Jerusalem's Miseries*, *Londons VVarning by Jervsalem* (1619), and *A bottle of holy tears, or, Jeremies threnes and lamentations for Israel's misery and Ierusalems woefull desperation* (1645) all rely exclusively on

Jewish miseries to supply the template for English woes. For example, in *Londons VVarning, by Jervsalem*, Francis White establishes an unambiguous equivalence between the besieged Jews and London's plague-ridden denizens, who similarly inhabit "a dead world, a dead time." Alluding to the widely read Bills of Mortality—the weekly printed broadsides that listed all the local deaths from plague—he expresses the desire for bills that could similarly indicate the deadening of the soul:

> And could you but euery weeke haue bils brought you in, to signifie within the City liberties, and without, how many soules dye in a weeke; some of a surfet of drunkennesse, some of a swelling tympany of pride, some of the burning feauer of malice, some of the dropsie of couetousnesse, some of one or other disease of the soule; you would blesse your selues, to see most mens bodies to be but liuing Sepulchres for dead soules.[9]

In equating diseased London with besieged Jerusalem, White delivers to his parishioners a somber acknowledgment of what Beatrice Groves calls "the shared sinfulness and vulnerability of humankind."[10]

Immoral Equivalencies

Indeed, some of the most widely circulated plague texts were characterized by the discomfiting equivalency between Ancient Jew and English Protestant first established by sixteenth-century preachers such as Thomas Becon and John Stockwood, who so passionately demanded the reintroduction of Jerusalem's tragic history to a faltering reformed readership. This shared iniquity is memorably captured in a sermon on divine justice appended to the widely circulated volume of plague prayers issued by the Church of England in the mid-sixteenth century. In the aftermath of the Reformation, the Church intensified its efforts to provide succor during plague times and combated each outbreak with prayer schedules, public fasts, and communal acts of thanksgiving. In 1563, under the auspices of the Elizabethan government, the Church created the first nationwide schedule of prayer and fasting: *A Form to be Used in Common Prayer*. The chosen sermon for the volume, titled *An Homily concerning the Justice of God in punishing of impenitent sinners and of his mercies towards all such as in their afflictions unfeignedly turn unto him*, maintains the providentialist reading of plague as chastisement for sin and draws upon the popular analogy between England and sinful Jerusalem to emphasize the peoples' culpability in their own misery:

"Let us not (O dearly beloved) fall into the uttermost of all mischiefs, that we should be incorrigible with punishment also, and worse under the scourge, as were those stiff-necked Jews, who when first after threatening and then after plagues of war, famine, and pestilence, they remained indurate and incorrigible."[11] It is worth noting that this homily, with its didactic explication of Jerusalem's miseries as meted out by "our heavenly schoolemaster," was printed by the same Richard Jugge who had published Morwen's influential history. Clearly relying upon its readers' familiarity with *A compendious and most marueilous Historie*, the plague sermon alludes explicitly to the total devastation of the Roman siege, a devastation believed to have been predicted by Christ according to the gospels of Matthew and Luke:

> Yea, and when all this [extreme famines, horrible wars and captivities, and dreadful plagues] could not amend them but that they waxed worse under the rod and correction did he not at last, which is most horrible, utterly destroy them with famine, war, and pestilence, and carried the rest into captivity and destroyed utterly their Cities and countries, according to the prophecy of Isaiah, and as our savior Christ likewise in the Gospel foreshoweth of the miserable destruction and ruin of their Cities and temple, so horrible that one stone should not be left upon other?[12]

The wages of sin is death: bloody siege and destruction for Jerusalem, plague and pestilence for England. *An Homily concerning the Justice of God* concludes with a hope that its readers will give up wickedness "now at the last when we are in most greatest danger to give over ourselves . . . turn unto the Lord our God and call for help and mercy." As encouragement, it proffers the figure of Job, "the blessed man of God" and the embodiment of faith in times of tribulation. But even Job's benign presence fails to vanquish the specter of the iniquitous Jews—"a people ever stiff necked and rebellious"—and their destroyed homeland.[13]

To emphasize the degree to which London paralleled Jerusalem in despising God's grace, several plague writers plucked out the omens and portents that crowded Jerusalem's fraught skies on the eve of its destruction and hung them over their own blasé metropolis. The use of omens to signify a transcendental dimension to the plague was, admittedly, not a new literary device. Both Livy and Dionysus of Halicarnassus reveled in descriptions of supernatural apparitions. But the specific phenomena mentioned in English plague narratives were clearly drawn from popular accounts of besieged Jerusalem.

The implication was that early modern Londoners were impervious to heavenly admonition just like the Ancient Jews who failed to recognize the import of phantasmagoria such as a sword-shaped comet or spectral armies in the heavens. The frontispiece to George Wither's *Britains Remembrancer* (1628), for instance, depicts aerial troops similar to the ones Josephus describes with "iron chariots all ouer the countrie, and an army in battell aray passing along in the clowds, and begirting the citie."[14] The imminent desolation of plague-beset London is starkly real for Wither precisely because Londoners were receiving the same warnings that manifested to the "stubborn unbelieving *Jews*," and similarly ignoring them:

> And we
> Are doubtlesse blind, unlesse confest it be,
> That at this houre, upon this Kingdome here,
> These marks of Desolation viewed are.[15]

Repeatedly, diseased Londoners are reproved for not taking notice of the many warnings to repent in language that echoes similar complaints about the obduracy of the sinful Jews on the eve of their destruction. The ballad *Christs Teares over Jersusalem, Or, A Caveat for England to call to God for Mercy* similarly cautions its readers that God has

> sent strange tokens in the ayre,
> to make thee understand:
> He is offended fore
> at thy great wickednesse
> And that except thou dost repent,
> thy plagues shall he expresse.[16]

Dekker's *A Rod for Run-Awaies* recalls how "The Gospell (and Gods Heralds, Preachers) haue a long time cryed out against our iniquities, but we are deafe, sleepy and sluggish." Now the English must be shaken from their sinful somnolence for "Thunder speakes from Heauen to wake vs."[17] Equally, Richard Milton in *London's Misery* (1625) confesses that

> we have sinned and done amiss;
> Wherefore thine [God's] anger fiercely kindled is.
> Upon this city, vengeance thou hast pour'd,
> And we like sheep to slaughter are devour'd. (43–46)

Frontispiece to George Wither's *Britain's Remembrancer*, 1628. (Reproduced by permission of Henry E. Huntington Library and Art Gallery)

His lament, "Oh London, London, thou didst feel the Rod, / But never rightly lookt up to thy God" (123–24), along with the explicit allusion to Jerusalem among the "mighty Cit[ies] . . . which for their sins were wholly overthrown" (938–44)[18] effectively fulfills Christ's prophecy about Jewish willfulness and its consequence in Nashe's *Christs Teares*: "The dayes will come, when I shall be taken away from you, and then you shal wish (in vayne) that you had daunst after my pype, and borne a principall part in my Consort of mourning. Let all successions and Citties be warned by you, howe they neglect Gods calling: let euery priuate man be admonished by you, how he neglecteth Gods calling."[19] The ballad *Christs Teares* likewise exhorts "faire England" to

> repent while thou hast space,
> And doe not like Jerusalem
> despise Gods proffred grace.

"Faire Jerusalem," it recalls, "was cast unto the ground / For their great sinne and wickednesse." Pointing to England, the balladeer announces that God is similarly

> offended fore
> At thy great wickednesse,
> And that except thou dost repent,
> thy plagues shall he expresse.

Recalling that the victory over the Spanish Armada was providentially determined, the ballad bemoans that

> soone hast thou forgot
> his favour in the same,
> Which afterwards most grievously
> his wrath did so inflame,
> That then he plagued thee
> with pestilence and death,
> Whereby in Country and in Towne
> a number lost their breath.

Repentance is the only remedy for disease

> Lest he forsake thee quite,
> and turne away his face,

Because like to Jerusalem,
thou dost despise his grace.

The Plague's the Thing

The frequent identification of plagued London with Jerusalem on the eve of
its devastation drew heavily on the medieval *vindicta salvatoris* or "vengeance of
the lord" tradition that explicitly identified divine disfavor as the reason for the
holy city's destruction. Indeed, I posit that the ascription of common causality
produced the heavy reliance on the siege metaphor to describe plague. Even
William Bullein's 1564 medical manual *A Dialogue both pleasant and pietyful
against the Fever Pestilence* intimated that a wrathful deity inflicted plague. Bullein's text, which addressed the infected body politic just as much as it did the
afflicted body natural, reminded its readers that the devastation of both bodies
could be assigned to the "vengeance of God" that manifests "either by hunger,
sickness or the sword."[20] John Davies's *The Triumph of Death: Or; The Picture
of the Plague* (1609) identifies the "Two Plagues in one"—famine and infection—as "revenges fit for such a God, / Fit for his Justice, Power, and Majesty"
and "right jerks of divine Fury's Rod" (680–82).[21] In *A Description of the Great,
Fearful, and Prodigious Plague* (1626) Abraham Holland memorably characterizes plague in a catalog of mounting woe as

> dreary punishment, Heaven's curse
> That fatal Engine of Destruction, worse
> Than we can well imagine, which doth bring
> Terror on mortals, Death on everything,
> And Desolation unto Cities. (325–29)[22]

In *News from Graues End: Sent to Nobody* (1604), Dekker had lamented how
"God in anger fills his hand / With vengeance throwing it on the land." The
particular forms this vengeance assumes are later elaborated upon in a *A Rod
for Run-Awaies*, which reminds its readers that "*Iehouah*, when he is angry, holds
three Whips in his hand, and neuer drawes bloud with them, but when our
Faults are heauy, our Crimes hainous: and those three Whips are, the Sword,
Pestilence, and Famine . . . *Ierusalem* felt them all."[23]

What, specifically, did plague, a most dire form of divine vengeance, entail for
early modern England? In 1974, René Girard discussed plague as a metaphor for
social discord that is "endowed with an almost incredible vitality," because ours
is a world "where the plagues and epidemics in general have disappeared almost

altogether."[24] Girard could celebrate the incredible, and comforting, vitality of plague-as-metaphor precisely because it was a thing of the past for him; a horror that, by the mid-twentieth century, existed exclusively in language.[25] But for early modern English subjects beset with multiple outbreaks over the course of a single lifetime (assuming they were fortunate enough to survive even one), Girard's formulation would have been unthinkable. While the secondary use of the word "plague"—to bother or annoy—was first recorded in the 1590s and features, significantly, in Thomas Wilson's funeral sermon *Christs Farewell to Jerusalem, and last Prophecie,* which describes how the besieged "Iewes must be so plagued, in an allegorical sentence," plague was too tangible, too corporeal, too deadly, to be rendered in purely metaphorical terms.[26]

Michael Neill avers that "no other single phenomenon had a more decisive effect than the plague in shaping the early modern crisis of death."[27] Records suggest that the plague epidemic would assert itself about once every fifteen years or so. In the interim, a new generation would grow up and a critical mass of people would immigrate to London from the country until the population was dense enough for the disease to wreak havoc again. By the seventeenth century, a minimum of forty deaths had to be recorded in the Weekly Bill of Morality in order for the plague to be recognized as an epidemic. In 1603, of 31,861 burials, 25,045 were plague victims. The estimated population for that year was 141,000, which means that the plague claimed one in every five Londoners. While in 1625, there were 26,350 plague burials out of an urban population numbering 206,000, in 1665, the number swelled to a frightening 50,000, which "dwarfed the number of fatalities on both sides of the Anglo-Dutch war in the same year," to quote Gilman again.[28]

The onset of plague was savagely swift. Dekker's *A Rod for Run-Awaies* tells the story of a man who, about to send his wife to the market, changed his mind when he felt the "pricking in his arme, neere the place where once he had a sore, and vpon this, plucking vp his sleeue, he called to his Wife to stay; there was no neede to fetch any thing for him from Market: for, see (quoth he) I am marked: and so shewing Gods Tokens, dyed in a few minutes after."[29] The first sign of disease would be the dreaded bubo, which would usually appear within a day of infection and would "maketh the patient to feele as it were a coard or rope stretched in the place, or a hardened nerue with pricking payne." Buboes were swollen, often hot to the touch, and extremely painful. They were popularly termed "God's tokens," because they looked like coins or "coals" with their burning hot appearance and sensation. Ambroise Paré, royal surgeon to the French kings Henry II, Francis II, Charles IX, and Henry III drew attention to the "swift uiolence" with which buboes on the skin would grow to "iust bigness" that would "sodainly bring the patient to destruction." If "liuide or blacke" they were almost inevitably fatal. [30]

Bullein's *Dialogue against the Fever Pestilence* likewise describes the "sharpness of hot and burning humors" and the crust of the buboes "wrought by extreme heat and burning; therefore it may be called the burning coal or *Ignem persicum.*"[31]

The gruesome image of the bubo ravaging not just the body but also the diseased body politic was prominent in plague writing that attempted to rationalize the "vexed relationship between the individual sufferer and the suffering state as conceived under the aegis of a mysterious and angry providence."[32] It is prominent in Davies's *Triumph of Death*, where London's sinfulness provokes God's wrath to "Blister our City's public Body so" (831).[33] Davies struggles to hold out a tenuous hope for survival but cannot vanquish the dire prospect of future flare-ups that could destroy his sin-infested community:

> We see it will not out, but still it lies
> In our best City's Bowels like a Coal
> That threats to flame, and stil doth fall and rise,
> Wasting a part, thereby to warn the whole. (812–15)

There is no possibility of mistaking this blister as a badge of honor or of reconfiguring it as a tribulation chosen by God to try his faithful. It serves only to "warn," a winking ember of impending doom that "will not out" so long as England wallows in iniquity. In his *Gods Three Arrovves: Plague, Famine, Svvord, In three Treatises* (1631), William Gouge confirms this bleak interpretation: plague is not one of the "persecutions made by enemies of the Gospell" upon the truly religious for "triall or "to their honour that suffer" but ranks along with famine and war—the torments that beset Jerusalem—as "publike and generall" insignia of sin and fatal judgment.[34]

The link between individual suffering and national disaster inevitably begs the question of cause and culpability: do individuals suffer for national transgressions or is the nation afflicted because of the sins of its people? Thucydides's *History of the Peloponnesian War* toyed with this question when Pericles's famous funeral oration on the diseased political health of Athens was followed swiftly by the outbreak of plague in the city. For Dekker, one of our principal literary sources on the plague in early modern England, the link between the body politic and the body natural is unambiguous:

> The altring of a State
> Alters our Bodies, and our Fate … When Kingdomes breake,
> People dissolue, and (as with Thunder) Cities proud glories rent asunder.[35]

His *Wonderfull Yeare* opens ominously with the death of Elizabeth and resultant anxieties about the outbreak of civil strife, thereby transposing the internal
discord of the fevered plague-ridden body on a national scale. The image of the
dreaded inflamed buboes is implicitly evoked in the

> corruption, which did make [the realm] swell
> With hop'd sedition (the burnt seed of hell.)
> Who did expect but ruine, bloud, and death,
> To share our kingdome, and deuide our breath?[36]

Dekker's lamentation echoes Nashe's *Christs Teares*, which, as we saw in
the previous chapter, lingers on Jewish iniquity: "no remedy, or signe of any
breath of hope, was left in their Common-wealths sinne-surfetted body, but
the maladie of their incredulity ouer-maistred heauenly phisick. To desperate
diseases must desperate Medicines be applyde."[37] In Nashe's formulation, the
deadly siege of Jerusalem is one such "desperate Medicine," and the plague stalking London in 1593 is another. Unsurprisingly, Nashe's account of Jerusalem's
devastation is marked by the rhetoric of uncleanness and infection: no "Hogstie
is now so pollutionate as the earth of *Palestine* and *Ierusalem*"; Jerusalem is
an "vnmasked leprous face" and "vlcerous."[38] Furthermore, the city's deformed
aspect is only a partial index of the horrible disfigurement within, the consequence of vice: "Yet, were nothing but her face and out-side deformed, it were
some-what; her in-side is worst of all: her Hart, her Lunges, her Liuer & her
Gal, all are carioniz'd and contaminated with surfets of selfe-will. Her owne
hart she eateth and digesteth into the draught with riotte and excesse."[39] Lancelot Dawes's 1609 sermon *Gods Mercies and Iervsalems Miseries* likewise imagines Jerusalem as a festering body: "shee which at the first did onely pull little
sinnes with the small *cordes of vanity*, doth now draw greater transgressions
with the huge *cartropes of iniquity*, so that now *from the sole of her foot to the
crown of her head, there is nothing found in her but woundes and swellings, and
sores full of corruption.*"[40] Though the destruction Dawes alludes to is at the
hands of the Chaldeans rather than the Romans (his text is Jeremiah 5.1), the
image of the cankered and sore-infested body natural mapped onto the body
politic is common to other accounts of the Roman destruction. As is true of
Jerusalem's final devastation at Roman hands, her "Apostasie is so generall, her
disease (like a *Gangrena*) is spread through euery member of the body, her
malice is so incurable, that [God] cannot without impeachment of his iustice,
spare her any longer."[41]

Death the Invader

Employing somatic imagery to describe political spaces was popular in early modern England, thanks in part to Galenic medicine's establishment of a complex metonymic relationship between the macrocosm (body politic) and microcosm (individual healthy/diseased bodies) that Shakespeare, for instance, exploited to great effect in *Henry IV.II*, *Timon of Athens*, and *Coriolanus*.[42] John of Salisbury's famous twelfth-century comparison of the republic to a body where the head is a prince, the heart is the senate, and the eyes, ears, and mouth are judges and governors likewise survived well into Tudor and Stuart England—to wit, in Thomas Elyot's comparison of the "publicke weale" to a "body liuing compact" whose organization corresponds to the order that "God hath put generally in all his creatures beginning at the most inferiour or base, and ascending vpward."[43] The idea of the "body liuing compact" certainly animates Nicholas Barbon's (1640–98) *An Apology for the Builder: Or, a Discourse shewing the Cause and Effects of the Increase of Building*, which identifies the city as "the heart of a Nation, through which the Trade and Commodities of it circulate, like the blood through the heart, which by its motion giveth life and growth to the rest of the Body."[44]

Peter Heylyn (1599–1662), however, equates the city not with the heart but, more ominously, with the "Spleen or Melt in the body natural: the monstrous growth of which impoverisheth all its Members."[45] Heylyn's complaint that cities, like the aforementioned spleen, suck up "all the animal and vital spirits, which should give nourishment" to other parts of the body assumed a sinister cast during times of plague when the body count in urban spaces far exceeded that of the countryside. As Paul Slack famously notes, "it was plague that gave cities their reputation as consumers of men," thereby evoking for the metropolis a third related somatic image: that of the ravenous mouth.[46]

Jonathan Gil Harris contends that "early modern English versions of organic political analogy" are "fixated with illness" to a degree that has not been fully acknowledged in modern scholarship. Margaret Healy likewise argues that the early modern English people imagined their "conditions of disunity—problems relating to boundaries, internal structures and the relationship between parts—in much the same way as they imagine the physical body's conditions of disharmony."[47] The imagery of sixteenth-century health manuals, in particular, exploits the idea of the body as a bounded space akin to the city or fortress. Elyot's *Castel of Helthe* (1534) and Bullein's *Bulwarke of Defense* (1562) both imagine the body as an enclosed and barricaded space, "a little Fort . . .

against sickness."[48] When plague breached the walls of the individual body's "little Fort," it also wrecked the health of the commonwealth.

Siege and plague shared a common cause—a wrathful deity—but plague texts additionally borrowed the idiom of military devastation to describe suffering. Plague literature regularly translated Jerusalem's literal rout into gruesome metaphor, thereby attesting to the siege's cultural currency. Indeed, it is as a marauding general laying siege to a city that plague is most commonly figured in early modern narratives. Dekker's *Wonderfull Yeare* memorializes the onset of plague in London, "sister to great Ierusalem," as the "siege of the Citie," a "mortall siege." Underscoring the violence of the disease, Dekker hails it as "the tyrant not the conqueror, making hauock of all, when he had all lying at the foote of his mercy."[49] The image of "making havoc" with those who lie at the "foote of his mercy" carries echoes of Christopher Marlowe's hero Tamburlaine, who infamously abused the conquered Persian king Bajazeth by using the latter as his footstool. Dekker's text also implicitly invokes Nashe's famous allusion to Tamburlaine in *Christs Teares* (briefly discussed in chapter 1) where the Jews' obstinate refusal to heed Christ's warnings wreaks a terrible vengeance. In Nashe's reconstruction of events:

> When neither the White-flag or the Red which *Tamburlaine* aduanced
> at the siedge of any Citty, would be accepted of, the Blacke-flag was
> sette vp, which signified there was no mercy to be looked for; and that
> the miserie marching towardes them was so great, that their enemy
> himselfe (which was to execute it) mournd for it. Christ, hauing offered
> the Iewes the White-flagge of forgiuenesse and remission, and the
> Red-flag of shedding his Blood for them, when these two might not
> take effect, nor work any yeelding remorse in them, the Black-flagge
> of confusion and desolation was to succeede for the obiect of their
> obduration.[50]

In a sinister legerdemain, Nashe transforms weeping Christ into Tamburlaine. But in Dekker's pamphlet, it is plague that assumes the brutal conqueror's formidable aspect. Like "stalking *Tamburlaine*," plague manifests the wrath of a militant God. Having "pitched his tents, (being nothing but a heap of winding sheets tackt together) in the sinfully polluted Suburbes: the Plague is muster-maister and Marshall of the field" with "Burning Feauers, Boyles, Blaines, and Carbuncles, the Leaders, Lieutenants, Serieants, and Corporalls."[51] Here, the breached body functions at once as beleaguered

London, conquered Persia, and—when put in conversation with Nashe's plague pamphlet—besieged Jerusalem.

The white flag of peace, red flag of "correction," and "black flag of death and desolation" so favored by Tamburlaine feature, additionally, in Dawes's 1609 plague sermon on Jerusalem's miseries, which utters the portentous reminder: "he that was *Ierusalems* God, is *Britaines* God too, and therefore if shee parallel *Ierusalem* in her iniquities, let her take heed she tast not of her plagues."[52] Following precedent, Dawes characterizes the plague's ferocious progress through the city as the rampaging of a "man of warre," "a gyant refreshed with wine."[53] But for the sheer scale of military metaphor, we must return to Dekker. *A Rod for Run-Awaies* ominously announces:

> Wee are now in a set Battaile; the Field is *Great Britaine*, the Vantguard (which first stands the brunt of the Fight) is *London*: the Shires, Counties and Countries round about, are in danger to be prest, & to come vp in the Reare: the King of Heauen and Earth is the Generall of the Army; reuenging Angels, his Officers; his Indignation, the Trumpet summoning and sounding the Alarum; our innumerable sinnes, his enemies; and our Nation, the Legions which he threatens to smite with Correction.[54]

Dawes's comparatively modest "man of warre" is horribly multiplied in Dekker's text—the elaborate nature of the military metaphor attesting to the ubiquity of the danger. London may be the "Vantguard" but the plague invades the entirety of Great Britain, which, isolated from help (though not, alas, from disease), is as vulnerable as a walled city under siege. Resistance is futile when the attacking general is neither Tamburlaine nor Titus Vespasian but God Himself.

The image of death as a conqueror assailing the beleaguered body (politic) is scattered throughout plague literature, thereby suggesting the evocative power of siege stories such as that of Jerusalem. In John Taylor's *The Fearful Summer* (1625), "death his bloody fray doth fight / And kills eight hundred in a day and night."[55] John Davies exploits the image in *The Triumph of Death*, where the grim eponymous protagonist "like a Conqueror in Triumph rides, / And ere he came too near, each Creature falls" (533–34).[56] For Abraham Holland, London once was the "Delight of Nations," the "Center of the World" or *omphalos*, akin to Jerusalem at the height of its glory.[57] But the "innumerable powers" of the plague "lay siege unto this weak-wall'd Fort of ours" and in "desperate malice ready are to climb / The walls themselves" (305–9). London's heart offers bold rebuff and "much like / A strong Defendant, maketh good the

Dike," but ultimately fails, staining the "conquer'd Mass / With dying blood"
(309–13).[58] In Wither's formulation, the plague-infested metropolis is "like a
Town beleagur'd," and

> but that God had care
> By making others feel necessities
> which forced them to minister supplies,
> Thou hast been famisht. (414–18)[59]

Here, Wither hits on yet another feature of the Jerusalem siege: the deadly
famine that wrecked Jerusalem during the siege by Titus's forces. The kind-
ness of strangers may have kept London from the fate of besieged Jerusalem
in Wither's *Britain's Remembrancer* in 1628, but Davies, writing nineteen years
earlier, painted a grim picture of how "Fear of infection chokt Humanity" (537)
such that the poor, forbidden to venture abroad because of quarantine laws,
died of starvation when "no man sought them, that they might be fed" (541).[60]

Echo Jerusalem

Taking its cue, perhaps, from the siege histories by Morwen as well as Lodge
(1602), early modern plague writing was as much about the undoing of all
communal and civic bonds as it was about the "mortall siege" itself. Draconian
quarantine laws dealt a heavy blow to society as fear of infection eroded all
ties of fellowship. The plight of the diseased and at-risk indigents, many of
whom were forcibly removed to the pesthouse, was particularly dire. A Haver-
fordwest woman's complaint that the quarantine treated her "worse than a
whore" is corroborated by the bitter lamentations of a Salisbury mayor who
questioned whether "I came of a woman or a beast that I should do so bloody
an act [quarantine] upon poor people in their condition."[61] The discomfiting
likeness between quarantine and imprisonment and the forcible breaking up
of families by removal to the pesthouse fueled an "explosive" situation that was
exacerbated, as Alan D. Dyer notes, by "the injustice of the escape of the rich" as
well as the "collapse of the economic and administrative structure."[62]

Those who did remain reflected, in piteous terms, on the disintegration of
all communal obligations. William Cupper's *Certaine Sermons concerning God's
late visitation, London* (1592) laments how frequently during the time of plague
"a man's dearest friends and kinsfolks forsake him."[63] Dekker's *A Rod for Run-
Awaies* narrates the story of a man seeking refuge from plague with his brother
in the country, only to be threatened with having dogs set upon him because

his "Clothes smelt of infection."[64] A hapless Bury native recalled of the 1608 plague that he "could get nobody to help me and that all my household fled from me and left me comfortless (in respect that at the time my man died of the sickness) when myself and my wife were both lame."[65] Perhaps Samuel Pepys summed it up most succinctly when he noted that plague makes "us cruel as dogs to one another."[66]

The days of plague were unkind, marked not just by disease and painful death but also by the callousness and savagery reminiscent of the worst offenses described in besieged Jerusalem just before its capitulation. Dekker's *Wonderfull Yeare* paints how "in the dead houre of gloomy midnight," a man walking down the streets of London might hear the "loude grones of rauing sick men" and "Seruants crying out for maisters, wiues for husbands, parents for children, children for their mothers."[67] But rather than feel compassion, survivors were rendered indifferent to the plight of others in their grim determination to live. As Margaret Healy sums it up, "ideas about social decay, disorder and instability are thus encoded in the word 'plague.'" Plague "comes to represent the ultimate horror, that of both individual and social disintegration: only those two competing scourges, famine and war, match its effects."[68]

Plague in England certainly exposed a staggering capacity for venality on the part of the afflicted that is reminiscent of the barbarity that Josephus attributed to his people. Indeed, the language of depravation and depravity that characterizes the narratives of besieged Jerusalem is uncannily similar to the descriptions of social abuse during the plague outbreaks. In some cases, no more than a passing reference to the events and characters in Jerusalem was needed to conjure up images of keen suffering and exploitation that attested, yet again, to the trope's growing value as cultural capital. It is no accident that Dekker berates the abuses of the Church during the plague years by explicitly referencing three of the Jewish seditionists whose greed and reckless ambition were deemed responsible for so much of their compatriots' anguish: "Amongst which worme-eaten generation, the thrée bald Sextons of limping Saint *Gyles*, Saint *Sepulchres*, and Saint *Olaues*, rulde the roaste more hotly, than euer did the *Triumuiri* of *Rome*. *Iehochanan*, *Symeon*, and *Eleazar*, neuer kept such a plaguy coyle in *Ierusalem* among the hungerstarued Iewes, as these three Sharkers did in their Parishes among naked Christians."[69] Dekker's accusation against the three parishes articulated a popular suspicion that many clergymen, working hand in glove with sextons, had profited heavily from the plague by charging exorbitant rates for bells that were not tolled and funeral sermons that were not delivered. Dekker's cursorily glossed comparison of such "sharkers" to Jehochanan, Simeon, and

Eleazar presumes his readers' acquaintance with Morwen's *A compendious and most maruelous Historie*, which describes the "dwellyng place of the faythfull: nowe beare rule there suche men as prouoke and styrre Gods wrath agaynst it, and turne it away from their GOD, wastyng it as theeues."[70] Dekker's *Newes from Hell* likewise includes a throwaway but telling reference to the "three seditious Iewes in Ierusalem" who once again function as a byword for cupidity and reckless destruction.[71]

Even where those rebels are not mentioned by name, their actions cast a long shadow over the narrative. William Muggins's *London's Mourning Garment* (1603) assigns to death the same stalking rapaciousness associated with the three as it

> Rageth up and down
> And, secretly, his heavy visage shows,
> In every street and corner of the Town,
> Emptying whole houses, soon, whereas he goes,
> Taking away both old and young, God knows:
> The weeping Mother and the Infant clear. (169–74)[72]

Muggins's lines implicitly evoke parallels with Morwen's description of the "most sorrowful oppression[n] of them that liued, done by the sedicious" who, showing as little charity as death, "searched euery mans house and seller for foode. And because a certayne housholder withstoode them, they kylled him."[73] They likewise echo Lodge's depiction of the seditionists who indulged in "no end of robbing & spoiling rich mens houses, and of slaughtering both of men and women; [for] to iniure any person was a pastime."[74]

In *The Wonderfull Yeare*, it was Dekker's turn to linger over the way that plague overwhelmed the hapless Londoners: "Houses were rifled, streets ransacked, beautiful maidens thrown on their beds and ravished by sickness, rich men's coffers broken open and shared amongst prodigal heirs and unthrifty servants, poor men used poorly but not pitifully."[75] Dekker's language echoes yet another popular passage of Morwen's that received memorable treatment in both Nashe's *Christs Teares* as well John Stockwood's sermon on Jerusalem's destruction. Stockwood's prurient description of how the seditionists "laye in the market place with the graue matrons, and by forced rauished the chaste maidens in the open streats" is reinforced and exceeded by Nashe's obscene description of the verve with which they threw young children upon the "sacrificatory flame, and on the same Altar (after they were consumed) most sacriligiously rauisht theyr Mothers."[76]

The shadow of Jerusalem's misery hangs particularly heavy over *The Wonderfull Yeare* with its explicit allusion to the "hunger starued Iewes" at the mercy of the rebels within the city. Like the trapped denizens of Jerusalem, Dekker's plague-ridden London,

> like a prisoner must be kept,
> in thine own walles
> till thou hast wept
> Thine eyes out, to behold thy sweete
> Dead children heapt upon thy feete.

The obdurate sinfulness attributed as the root cause of both infection in England and siege in Jerusalem results yet again in a common rhetoric of betrayal and grievous loss. *News from Graues-ende*'s detail that "thousands weepe / And wring their hands for thousands dying, / No comfort neare the sick man lying," as fears swell of a "deadlyer siege ... Will your replenish walls ingirt" could refer just as easily to besieged Jerusalem as to plague-infested London.[77] No wonder then that "Purple plagues" and "Crimson Warre" are memorably equalized at the end of Dekker's pamphlet in a grim acknowledgment of their mutual powers of mass destruction.

Michael Neill's argument that "The death most to be feared ... is the mass death because of its extravagant multiplication of disfigured bodies" applies readily to the situation in both Dekker's London and Ancient Jerusalem.[78] Wither's grim assertion that he heard "naught but dying pangs and lamentations / If in the Streets I did my footing set" (170–71) confirms Dekker's account of the pitiable grief of "wofully distracted mothers that with disheueld haire are falne into swounds, whilst [they] lye kissing the insensible cold lips of [their] breathlesse infants."; the "ghastly vizages"; "loude grones of rauing sicke men: the struggling panges of soules departing: In euery house griefe striking vp an Allarum: Seruants crying out for maisters: wiues for husbands, parents for children, children for their mothers."[79]

The latter passage is clearly indebted to Lamentations 1:16, "For these things I weep: mine eye, *even* mine eye casteth out water, because the comforter that should refresh my soul, is far from me: my children are desolate, because the enemy prevailed," as well as to Lamentations 2:11, "Mine eyes do fail with tears: my bowels swell: my liver is poured upon the earth, for the destruction of the daughter of my people, because the children and sucklings swoon in the streets of the city." It also recalls the horrors predicted in Deuteronomy 28 should the Jews contravene God's commandments: "the man (that is tender and exceeding dainty among you,) shall be grieved at his brother, and at his wife *that lieth* in his bosom, and at the remnant of his children, which he hath yet left" (54). Then "the Lord shall make thy plagues wonderful, and the plagues of thy seed, *even* great plagues, and of long continuance, and sore diseases, and of long durance" (59).

Again it is Morwen's *A Compendious and most marueilous Historie* that powerfully realizes these prophesied horrors:

> And whersoeuer a man turned him, there was nothyng but desolation, pollusion (namely of the temple and al holy thinges), vproares, without all rest and refuge, no helpe, no succour, but euery corner of Hierusalem was full of howlyng and yelling, waylyng and weepyng, sobbing and sighing of women and chyldren. Here should ye heare the roaring and groning of wounded men, not yet though deade: there the mourning and lamentation for the elders that then were slayne by the seditious: yonder chyldren crying out for hunger.[80]

In siege, as in plague, the prostrations of grief unrelieved by another's ruth or succor become seared upon the memory, along with gruesome details of rotting corpses choking the streets. Davies's *Triumph of Death* bemoans how

> The *London* Lanes (themselves thereby to save)
> Did vomit out their undigested dead,
> Who by cartloads are carried to the Grave,
> For all those Lanes with folk were overfed. (344–47)[81]

Though Davies explicitly compares London to burning Troy ("Troynovaunt"), one could argue that his description owes as much to Josephus (or a variant thereof) as to Homer. Morwen's translation, for instance, dwells in unforgettable detail on Jerusalem "choked with carion doung, and most pestilent stynch of dead bodies, and blood of the wounded. Thy streates are strowed full of dead men, some runne through with glaues and iauelins, and other dead for hunger … corses lye cast out in the feelde, no better then the carkases of bruite beastes that be founde in desart places."[82] Lodge's translation of Josephus likewise records that "the houses were full of dead women and infants; and the streetes filled with the dead bodies of old men … the multitude of dead bodies was so great, that they that were aliue could not bury them, nor cared they for burying them, being now vncertaine what should betide themselues. And many endeuouring to bury others, fell downe themselues dead vpon them as they were burying them."[83]

For both Morwen and Lodge, then, the unburied dead are imbued with a particular horror that also animates many accounts of plague in England. Notable among these is T.D.'s *Canaan's Calamitie* (1618), which describes the mound of corpses in terms that apply as readily to either city:

> And by this wicked means it came to pass,
> The Streets and Temple full of dead-men lay,
> With wounds putrified, where burial was,
> Which rais'd a grievous pestilence that day:
> So hot, and fell, that thereof died a number,
> Whose foul infection all the Town did cumber.[84]

Thomas Clark's poignant *Meditations in my confinement, when my house was visited with the sickness: in April, May and June, 1666* specifically laments the lack of funeral rites for the dead:

> This Sickness also, after Death, doth seem
> To trample o're the dead with disesteem,
> And (Victor-like, o're Captives) with despite,
> Denies such Obsequies and fun'ral rite,
> Which in a solemn manner is most due,
> As we have seen in this late time, not few.[85]

Rebecca Totaro rightly notes that the denial of funeral rites for the dead recalls the "many famous classical episodes in which heroes and the sons of kings are refused burial by the enemy—the most egregious, final, and enduring form of military aggression, an act that makes clear there will be no mercy, forgetting, or forgiveness."[86] But the unmistakable parallel with besieged Jerusalem suggests another interpretation—the total collapse of civilized norms discussed in the previous chapter. As in the ballad *A Warning or lanthorn to London*,

> dead men covered all the ground
> of fair Jerusalem
> such Pestilence did there abound
> and so infected them,
> That many a thousand there did dye
> which still unburied there did lye

so is London strangled by the unburied dead, transforming from the "Kingdom's great Metropolis" into a vast charnel house, a "Golgotha of dead men's bones."[87]

Those lucky enough to survive in either city—if luck is the word—wander like apparitions. Morwen narrates that "they that remayne yet alyue in the citie, are as good as dead also, and maybe taken for no lesse. For they are weerie of theyr lyues, because of the pestilent dampe of the dead bodies, the outragious-nesse whereof, hath cast many into most daungerous diseases, and hath ben the death of numbers alredy."[88] Lodge likewise offers the sharply poetic detail of "yong men swollen like dead mens shadowes" who "walked in the market place, and fell down dead where it happened."[89] Both accounts may be discerned in Dekker's description of embodied sickness, "walke[ing] still in ghostly and for-midable shape vppe and downe my streets."[90] Once more, besieged Jerusalem supplies the requisite framework for comprehending tragedy.

Anthropormophiz'd Plague

Of course, it must be acknowledged that historians have long associated the plague with the disintegration of social order. Thucydides's account of plague in Athens (430 C.E.), which inspired, among other texts, Thomas Lodge's 1603 *Treatise of the Plague*, contains what we recognize as stock elements of plague writing: bodies strewn on the streets, disregard for the dead, holy places pol-luted by mounds of bodies, and the dissolution of the bonds of kinship under the weight of selfishness that is motivated by a frantic desire to live at all costs. While early modern English plague writing certainly follows this time-honored template, its reliance upon Jerusalem's tragic history of siege and destruction is nonetheless unmistakable (if largely overlooked). Two related tropes in par-ticular cement the indebtedness of popular plague accounts to Josephus/*Josip-pon*: the idea of plague as cannibalistic and the comparison of London to a grieving widow, specifically, to Miriam. Her piteous story of starvation became the perfect encapsulation of the greatest horrors inflicted by the plague. Her impossible hunger, manifesting in cannibalism, became the ultimate symbol for the relentless onslaught of the plague itself.

Again, it is Dekker, so attuned to the possibilities of the Jerusalem narra-tive, who explicitly compares the plague to a cannibal in *The Wonderfull Yeare*, when he expresses the intention to "arme my trembling hand, that it may boldly rip vp and Anatomize the vlcerous body of this *Anthropophagized* plague."[91] A few lines down, his depiction of London "forlorne like a widow, and disar-mde of all comfort" is beholden obviously to Lamentations but may also be read as a reference to Miriam. The allusion is spelled out decisively in *London Looke Backe at that Yeare of Yeares 1625*, in which Dekker fuses the narrative of Miriam's anthropophagy with its most famous biblical precedent—the story of the two Samarian women who made a tragic pact to eat their own children during the siege of King Benhadad (2 Kings 6: 28–29): "Thou [London] with *Ierusalem*, didst feele as grieuous a Desolation: eating vp, with *Mariam*, thine owne children, with *Samaria* thou wert besieged, though not (like *Samaria*) with *Benhadad*, King of the Aramites, and 32. Kings more with him: But with a farre more cruell enemy, (the Pestilence,) and an infinite Army of Sinnes, which to this very day, fight against thee."[92] In a variation on a theme, is it is not the plague but forlorn London, beggared and bereft, that consumes her own children. We are at once in first-century Jerusalem and in Ancient Samaria, both tragic instantiations of the horrors predicted in Deuteronomy 28. In that savaged world, hapless Jews "eat the fruit of thy body, *even* the flesh of thy sons and thy daughters, which the Lord thy God hath given thee, during the siege and straitness wherein thine enemies . . . enclose thee" (53). There, the "tender and dainty woman"—the embodiment of the glorious city—turns feral toward "her children, which she shall bear: for when all things lack, she shall eat them secretly, during the siege and straightness wherewith thine enemy shall besiege thee in thy cities" (Deut. 28:57). One recalls Paul Slack's formulation of the metropolis as the "consumer of men," a realization that also permeates *The Wonderfull Yeare*, which memorializes London's failing battle with "this hungry Plague, Cater to death, / Who eats vp all, yet famisheth."[93]

Dekker's "hungry plague" is anticipated by Bullein's *Dialogue against the Fever Pestilence* (1564), where the figure of Civis equates the plague to a "monstrous hungrie beast, devouring and eatyng not a fewe, but sometymes whole cities."[94] To be sure, Bullein's language conjures up not so much Miriam as the Whore of Babylon, a point also made by Healy in her excellent discussion of this passage. But in other plague literature, as Groves suggests, it is Miriam's tragic aspect that particularly haunts and chills. Drawing an analogy between the breached city, the plague infested metropolis, and the female body, Groves notes that, "in her embodiment of failed maternity, [Miriam] also incorporates the scriptural tropes for the fall of Jerusalem: a city that (in Lamentations) weeps sore into the night but cannot save her children."[95]

Thus it is that *A Looking-glasse for city and countrey* (1630) mourns London's decline by comparing the erstwhile "paragon of this kingdome for beauty & braue buildings" to a "widow . . . left disconsolate." Muggins's *London's Mourning Garment* implicitly draws on the same trope by personifying the city as an abandoned mother with "blubbered cheeks, bedewed with trickling tears / With mind opprest, lamenting griefs that flow." Muggins does not merely liken London to a grieving widow but lingers on the plight of the many mourning mothers in the poem who lament their insufficiency in the face of the inexorable demise of their progeny. One widow's lament that she could not save her "Chickens" directly harkens back to Luke 13:34—a passage that famously anticipates Jerusalem's destruction in Christ's sharp reproach:

> But now alas, a heavy Tale to tell,
> As with my Chickens I at pleasure slept
> Comes the great Puttock with his Talons fell
> And from me quite my youngest Chicken swept. (344–47)

Behind Muggins's lines lingers Luke's oft-quoted verse *O Jerusalem Jerusalem that killeth my prophets and stoneth them that I sent unto thee: how often would I have gathered thy children together, as a Henne gathereth her Chickens vnder her winges, but you would not* that also sounds in Nashe's *Christs Teares* with the clangorous regularity of a tolling bell.

The hen who fails to save her chickens is, of course, Jesus. But I suggest it is also Miriam, who in numerous texts on Jerusalem's siege elaborates painfully on her inability to save her child's life. The ease with which she could stand in for an English mother in distress is clear from *Canaan's Calamitie*, which describes her as a golden-haired mother weeping and wailing over the cold body of her little boy. Miriam's infamous vow to make her womb into a tomb for her son by returning him to her body reverberates in plague writing committed to amplifying the execrable horrors of the disease, the greatest of which was the mother's womb becoming a "fleshy grave" and "to the dead Child [a tomb]." Though Abraham Holland in this context speaks of stillbirth rather than cannibalism, his qualification of the English streets as "widow'd" functions in a metonymic relation to the tragic story of Josephus's notorious cannibal. London becomes Jerusalem, plagued and bereaved, just as Deuteronomy foretold. The prophecies come true.

Conclusion

The challenges of plague writing were manifold: to come to grips with tragedy, to advance a tenable cause for unendurable agony, and to grapple with the faint possibility of redemption and reprieve. Above all was the challenge to find an idiom that would adequately encapsulate the horror. Passages such as this from a plague sermon suggest the degree to which language strained to bear the weight of woe: ". . . what sighing of the sick, what groans of the grieved, what wailing of widows, what crying of children, what howling of orphans and what woeful lamentations are there all night in every street."[96] The preacher's reiterated "what . . . what . . . what" suggests the unspeakable—language's failure to accommodate pain. Narratives of Jerusalem's siege thus proved invaluable to early modern plague writing because of their analogous potential. London's suffering became terribly comprehensible when placed side-by-side with Jerusalem's adversity. Plagued London as besieged Jerusalem carried all the cold comfort of a formula. To be smitten by plague in London was to be like one of the Ancient Jews, degraded by violence, starvation, and pestilence. It was to identify in a real and unprecedented way, to partake in a shared acknowledgment of sinfulness. If, as Nashe maintained, no "image or likeness of Jerusalem on earth is there left, but London," then the burden of inheritance sat heavy indeed on English shoulders. But having such equivalence, as so much plague writing helps us realize, is also a boon: it is to be warned; to be exhorted; to be granted the charged gift of memory.

CHAPTER 3

Jerusalem in Jamestown

In 1609–10, settlers of the American colony of Jamestown beset by the Powhatan Nation endured what has come to be known as the "Starving Time." Hemmed in by the enemy, battered by the unrelenting winter, and frantic for food, the colonists consumed horses, dogs, cats, rats, mice, and snakes. When animal life proved hard to come by, they ate leather from their saddles and shoes. When all other options were exhausted, they fell upon the recent dead and drank their blood. Of some five hundred settlers at Jamestown in October, only about sixty survived that winter.

While an excavation at the site in 2013 uncovered the carcasses of the animals eaten by the hapless settlers, the discovery of the bones of a dismembered and cannibalized fourteen-year-old female soon attracted attention. Though this body, dubbed "Jane" by researchers, is the first tangible evidence that cannibalism did occur at Jamestown, it has long been speculated that the inclement conditions faced by the colonists had made them desperate enough to eat human flesh—perhaps even murder for it. In 1625, George Percy, president of the colony during the calamity and one of the fortunate survivors, penned a somber account of the colonists' gruesome diet during that terrible winter, when all endured "the sharpe pricke of hunger w[hi]ch noe man [can] trewly descrybe butt he w[hi]ch hathe Tasted the bitternesse thereof."[1] Intended as a rebuttal of the more popular version of events advanced by Captain John Smith, Percy's catalog of woe culminated with the confession that, "famin beginneinge to Looke gastely and pale in every face, thatt notheinge was Spared to mainteyne Lyfe and to doe those things w[hi]ch seame incredible, as to digge upp deade corpes outt of graves and to eate them. And some have Licked upp the Bloode w[hi]ch hathe fallen from their weake fellowes."[2] Percy's *Trewe Relacyon*, begun thirteen years after his return to England from Jamestown, circulated privately during the seventeenth century and was intended as a defense and explanation of his controversial leadership during the grim Starving Time.[3]

Grisly reports of cannibalism carried by runaways from Jamestown who escaped on a stolen boat christened the *Swallow* had already reached England as early as the summer of 1610. Despite the character of the storytellers, most of whom were deemed unsavory for deserting their beleaguered colony, the terrible tale gained credence in London. Unsurprisingly, the story was vigorously repudiated by the Virginia Company, the joint-stock enterprise responsible for the colony and its supply. Despite the company's best efforts, however, it was whispered that one of the colonists came to so relish the taste of human flesh that he could not refrain from cannibalism and had to be executed. Percy, anxious to justify the extreme actions of the settlers, cast about for other examples of similarly desperate recourse:

> If we Trewly Consider the diversety of miseries mutenies and famishments w[hi]ch have attended upon discoveries and plantacyons in theis our moderne Tymes, we shall nott fynde our plantacyon in Virginia to have Suffered aloane . . . The Spanyards plantacyon in the River of Plate and the streightes of Magelane Suffered also in so mutche thatt haveinge eaten upp all their horses to susteine themselves w[i]thal, Mutenies did aryse and growe amongste them, for the w[hi]ch the generall Diego Mendosa cawsed some of them to be executed, Extremety of hunger inforceinge others secretly in the night to Cutt downe Their deade fellowes from of the gallowes and to bury them in their hungry Bowelles.[4]

Percy drew his examples from recent colonial history, and they emphasize the fraught nature of colonial enterprise ("miseries mutenies and famishments") and the extreme vulnerability of settlers at the very outposts of civilization, where the rules that govern polite society no longer seem to apply.

Like most of his peers, Percy knew stories of cannibals in the Americas, and his *Observations Gathered Out of "A Discourse of the Plantation of the Southern Colony in Virginia by the English, 1606"* (1625) recalls the natives of Dominica in the West Indies who "eat their enemies when they kill them, or any stranger if they take them," and "lap up mans spittle, whilst one spits in their mouths in a barbarous fashion like dogs."[5] The bestiality Percy invokes here hearkens back to Columbus's misapplication of the word "cannibal" to describe the man-eating inhabitants of an island near Hispaniola that he connected to the dog-headed Scythians mentioned in Herodotus and Pliny.[6]

The uncomplicated equation of the cannibalistic with the bestial conveniently allowed Europeans like Percy to draw stark lines between culture and so-called barbarism.[7] Yet both the *Discourse* and *A Trewe Relacyon* betray a troubling inability to sustain the absolute differences between cannibals ("barbaric") and Europeans ("cultured"), and expose instead an anxious—if implicit—questioning of the reality of those differences. *A Trewe Relacyon* proceeds to recount a tale yet more horrific than the eating of "Jane." As president of the Jamestown colony, Percy was forced to mete out justice to a man found guilty of killing, salting, and eating his pregnant wife:

> And amongste the reste this was moste lamentable. Thatt one of our
> Colline murdered his wyfe Ripped the Childe outt of her woambe and
> threwe itt into the River and after Chopped the Mother in pieces and
> sallted her for his foode, The same not beinge discovered before he had
> eaten p[ar]te thereof. For the w[hi]ch Crewell and unhumane factt I
> adjudged him to be executed the acknowledgm[en]t of the dede beinge
> inforced from him by torture haveinge hunge by the Thumbes w[i]th
> weightes att his feete a quarter of an howere before he wolde Confesse
> the same.[8]

Whereas the London Council of the Virginia Company was anxious to dismiss the horror and quick to suggest that the man's murder and consumption of his wife was motivated by personal animus rather than by famine, Captain John Smith conjectured further on the macabre dish with grim humor in his *The Generall Historie of Virginia, New England and the Summer Isles* (1624), speculating whether the unfortunate woman's corpse would have tasted better "roasted, boyled or carbonado'd."[9] Indeed, the careful preparation of her body as described by Smith and Percy suggests a fastidious luxury associated more with ritual than with an act borne of desperation. As late as 1705, Robert Beverley bemoaned the event and the enduring infamy it brought upon the country. Certainly, the stigma of cannibalism proved hard to wash away. For centuries thereafter the Starving Time would be associated with Jamestown's nadir, the disintegration of its social contract.

Although Percy does not allude to Josephus's history of sporadic cannibalism catalyzed by extreme starvation, that history uncannily anticipates aspects of the Jamestown testimonies. Coincidentally, Josephus's account of the Roman siege had recently received fresh treatment in a translation by Thomas Lodge. Entitled *The Lamentable and Tragicall History of the VVars and Vtter Rvine of the Iewes* (1602), its second edition was printed in the same year that rumors of cannibalism in Jamestown first began to circulate. And even if Peter Morwen's 1558 translation of *Josippon* was the dominant version, it is significant that Lodge's translation, which strikingly collapses the civilization-barbarism binary through graphic descriptions of the degeneration of Jewish *civitas*, coincided with stories of similar unraveling in Jamestown. By relocating the irruption of disorder from the margins of the self and other to within the space of the self, Lodge's *Lamentable and Tragicall History*, I would argue, contributes an important voice to the circulating early modern discourse that interrogated and challenged the dichotomies of civilization/savagery and culture/non-culture.

This brings us back to Miriam, or Mary, as she is here known. In the buildup to describing Mary's gruesome act of cannibalism, Josephus's *Jewish War* paints Jerusalem as a cesspool of abjection. Consequently, it is quite sensitive to the widow's plight, presenting her motivation as a complex coalescence of desperation, compassion, and defiance. Her cannibalism, occurring as it does in the holiest of cities, is particularly disquieting for the way it exposes the permeable boundary between civilization and savagery. Unlike Abraham, who nearly sacrificed his child in dutiful obedience to his Maker, Mary was seen to actualize the ultimate expression of Jewish regression. Consequent upon Mary's ingestion of her own son, Jerusalem degenerates into a border space, wild and barbaric. Once the navel of the world (*omphalos*), God's city turns intestinal when it consumes its own flesh in an act that Claude Levi-Strauss memorably termed an "alimentary form of incest."[10]

In the Christian translations of Josephus that traditionally assigned to his history a providential and retributive dimension, Mary's cannibalism, unsurprisingly, came to symbolize the divine repudiation of the Jews.[11] As the story of Jerusalem's fall grew in popularity between the eleventh and sixteenth centuries, what Mary did increasingly came to be interpreted not as an act borne out of savage hunger and desperation but, rather, as a gross symptom of the spiritual malaise that many Christians believed infected the reprobate Jewish nation. There was even biblical justification for such a bias: exilic literature such as Jeremiah 19:9, Lamentations 2:20, and Ezekiel 5:9–10 all specify cannibalism as God's punishment for not keeping the Jewish Law and, particularly, for profaning the Temple.[12] But many early modern English Protestant accounts, especially the ones examined in this book, largely refrain from vilifying Mary in such simple terms. As I demonstrate, Morwen's Miriam, though a horrific simulacrum of the Virgin Mary, is also a figure of pity. The adaptations

Morwen inspired, such as Thomas Nashe's *Christs Teares over Iervsalem* (1593), emphasize the tragedy of her fate, even as they freight her action with perverse Eucharistic valences. She is both terrifying and tragic; at once dark Catholic, suffering Jew, and famished Protestant mother.

Lodge presents the cannibal mother as a tragic figure, but complicates the narrative tradition by eschewing the providentialist interpretation of Jerusalem's catastrophic decline that was favored by certain English Protestants.[13] Indeed, *The Lamentable and Tragicall History*, in the manner of George Percy's accounts, frustrates simple polarities to an even greater degree than the narratives peddled by Morwen and Nashe did. Rather than offer fallen Jerusalem as a warning to Protestant London, Lodge's translation steers clear of the Protestant appropriations of Jerusalem's history. While it is difficult to prove conclusively, there is strong reason to believe that Lodge was a Catholic convert. To be sure, his name appeared on recusant rolls until the end of his life. This religious bias may account—at least partially—for the absence in his work of Catholic resonances that imbued the work of his predecessors. Gone is the "handemayde," as well as the Eucharistic feast at which Miriam exhorts the rebels to "taste and see" the goodness of her son. Rather, Lodge's precise translation of Josephus advances a more secular reading of the tragic events in Jerusalem—a feature that would gain prominence in later seventeenth-century versions of the siege story such as William Heminge's play *The Jewes Tragedy* (c.1626).

This is significant because Lodge's repudiation of the providentialist interpretation of Jerusalem's devastation, coupled with the presentation of cannibalism as tragedy, produces a distinct effect. The forbearance shown to Mary in Lodge's "authentic" rendition of Josephus contrasts starkly with the censure he reserves for the seditionists whose tyrannical hounding of the Jewish people in the name of rebellion is figured as metaphorical cannibalism. In Lodge's work, the literal cannibalism of the desperate widow is transvalued as the lesser crime when compared to the extortion of the grasping zealots. Whereas Mary is accorded the stature of a heroine out of Greek tragedy, the Jewish seditionists are traduced for their savage infighting. Admittedly, several other accounts—Morwen's and Nashe's included—also contrast Mary/Miriam with the rebels who destroy her life. But Morwen also praises those very rebels for their ability to resist Rome and records such moments of triumph as when they "issued out with an horrible noyse & shoute, that they made the Romanes afrayde withal, in such wyse, that they fledde before the seditious."[14] Such episodes are markedly absent in Lodge's history, as he concentrates instead on the factionalism and internecine conflict that wrecked Jerusalem from within.

Lodge's bias becomes particularly meaningful when read in conjunction with early modern texts, such as Michel Montaigne's famous essays "Of the Cannibals" and "Of Crueltie" (trans. 1603), that erect a similarly unexpected scale of values whereby the New World consumers of human flesh are treated with greater charity than the Europeans who prey on their communities. The distinction that Lodge's translation makes between literal and figurative cannibalism and his justification of the former over the latter discursively overlaps with Montaigne's assessments of savagery and civilization, and—although they focus primarily on the plight of the European settlers—the narratives of Percy. To move therefore from *A compendious and most marueilous Historie* to *The Lamentable and Tragicall History* is to move from a distinctly Protestant interpretation of the cannibal episode to a reevaluation of seemingly stable secular categories such as culture and barbarism.

This is not to imply that Lodge's Josephus occupies the same political position as that of Montaigne or, indeed, that the aforementioned can be equated with Percy in simple terms. The cannibalism they describe is also differently motivated: by ritual practice in the case of Montaigne; by famine in Percy and Lodge. Montaigne's position, furthermore, is that of a skeptic freely entertaining doubt about the cultural and moral superiority of European colonists. Josephus's history, instead, is an elaborate and politically fraught *apologia* for his Roman overlords in which he consistently berates the Jewish seditionists for their ill-considered rebellion. It is not my intention to blur the notable political differences between these writers, nor to collapse the distinctions between ritual cannibalism on the one hand and survival-driven flesh-eating on the other.

But if we abstract the value system in Lodge's translation of Josephus, we find that it overlaps curiously with that of Montaigne. Like the latter, Lodge asks us to interrogate carnal cannibalism and to determine whether it is worse than spiritual or metaphorical cannibalism. The answer is a resounding no. Exploitation is consistently presented as the more pernicious form of anthropophagy—cannibalism of the spirit—in Montaigne and Lodge's works.

Although Percy's *A Trewe Relacyon* is penned exclusively from the perspective of the colonizer attempting to justify his leadership in dire circumstances, we may yet discern a similar underlying tension in the descriptions of the brutality meted out not just to the Native American enemy but also to dissenting settlers within Jamestown. His *Discourse*, for instance, is an unrelenting tale of abject misery, even dehumanization, suffered by a fledgling community cut off from the care and comprehension of the mother country. In this bleak account of settler life, colonization itself becomes cannibalistic as it indiscriminately consumes its own to slake its ambition. Thus, in each text, descriptions of the actual eating of people function discursively (deliberately or otherwise) to further denigrate and throw into sharp relief the exploitative cruelty of the people in control: the colonizers in Montaigne's texts, the English colonialists in Percy's accounts, and the seditionists in Lodge's translation. The horror of spiritual cannibalism is exposed not just by employing the rhetoric of savage and undisciplined consumption, but also, in every case, by setting it against descriptions of actual carnal anthropophagy.

The eating of human flesh by other humans, generally presumed to be the ultimate manifestation of intraspecies violence, has its more damning figurative extension in this literature, manifesting in internecine brutality, exploitation, and torture. Moreover, not only does cannibalism of the flesh function as a foil for an immaterial cannibalism that is deemed far worse, but also both literal and figurative forms of flesh-eating may be interpreted as occupying positions on the same continuum. The starving Jewish mother, the famished Jamestown settlers, New World anthropophagists, Jewish seditionists, French insurgents in the religious civil wars of the sixteenth century, Spanish conquistadores, and English colonizers all share a strange affinity as they stand at various points on this cannibal continuum.

The Tragic Cannibal

Lodge's *Lamentable and Tragicall History*, following its source text, insists on the unprecedented nature of Mary's cannibalism: "an act neuer heard of, neither among the Greeks, nor any other barbarous people, horrible to be rehearsed, and incredible: so that I would willingly omit this calamity."[15] And yet Josephus's audience would have known of other biblical accounts of cannibalism, such as the story mentioned earlier of the Samarian women in 2 Kings who made a pact to eat their sons during a terrible siege by Ben-Hadad of Syria. They would also have been familiar with the myth of Thyestes, who unwittingly consumed his sons—a story particularly well known to Hellenized Jews, according to Philo of Alexandria. Certainly, Josephus was not averse to drawing on *topoi* from myth and drama to embellish his history.[16] Indeed, he elevates the cannibal mother, "descended of noble and rich parentage" to a figure worthy of high tragedy. Like the besieged city to which she is confined, Mary is "inuaded" by famine.[17] Her choice is simple and terrible: either kill her starving child with her own hands or have others kill him. She can only hope that after death he will hound the rebels like the Furies in Aeschylus's *Orestia* do.

But it is to Euripides that Josephus appears to have been most indebted. Like Medea, his Mary is driven by "rage and necessity . . . to doe that which nature abhorred," and like Medea, she presents the murder of her progeny as "sacrifice."[18] As Honora Howell Chapman observes of the *Jewish War*, the combination of "anger, necessity, and an unnatural act committed by a mother" is striking, characteristics that Josephus and his first-century audience would have readily identified with Medea. Chapman even suggests that in killing, preparing, and serving up her son, Mary approximates a Medea-Agave hybrid—the tragic dismemberment of her son's corpse echoing a key moment from *The Bacchae*.[19] Even Pseudo-Hegesippus, who adapted the scene for his vehemently anti-Jewish retelling of the *Jewish War* in Latin, *De excidio urbis Hierosolymitanae* (c.370–75 C.E.), noted the parallels with Euripides's *Bacchae* and intensified them by having his Mary address the hand and foot of her baby in a manner reminiscent of Agave's address over the broken body of her son, Pentheus, whom she tore apart in ecstatic frenzy.[20] Mary's own speech to her suckling child—a rare instance of direct address by a woman in Josephus—is likewise charged with the theatricality reminiscent of Greek tragedy when she demands that her son become not just food for her belly but also, in Lodge's translation, a "tragical story to be spoken of by posterity."[21] The parallel with Medea is reinforced moments later with Mary's passionate challenge to the rebels to "be not more effeminate then a woman, nor more mercifull then a mother."[22] It is here that she most fully echoes that lamentable figure, at once monstrous in her impossible grief and awesome in her unrelenting fury.

Keen as Josephus was to assert the originality of his story, he relied implicitly both on his readers' awareness of the deeds and motivations of tragic heroines such as Medea and Agave and on the layered emotional responses their actions would generate. Lodge took care to preserve this complexity. Within the narrative, Mary's cannibalism provokes a range of reactions from horror and revulsion to profound pity. When the "vnnaturall fact" is recounted to the Romans, for instance, it is met with a multivalent response: "some of them would not beleeue it, others pitied them within the citie, and many hereat encreased their hatred towards that nation." As the report of the "hainous crime" is "bruted" all across the city, "euery man hauing before his eyes this execrable fact, trembled as though himself had done it."[23]

Lodge's translation functions within the tradition of presenting Mary as a tragic figure, a tradition upheld even by the very the Church Fathers who were quick to read her act as the climax of Jewish sinfulness. Origen, who used Josephus's history of maternal cannibalism to explicate the consumption of children by their mothers in Lamentations, emphasizes this pity when he notes, "So that the women may not seem on account of savagery to have eaten their children, it says they are compassionate; it attributes the suffering to the necessity of their lack [of food]."²⁴ Other Church Fathers such as Eusebius and Basil likewise regarded Josephus's account of Mary's cannibalism as a tragedy with all of the attendant emotional responses. This sympathy for Mary, sustained even in the versions of the story charged with Christian providentialist fervor, is particularly remarkable given the notorious libel against Jews as perpetrators of infanticide.²⁵ Indeed, St. John Chrysostom's claim that Jewish parents execute the ultimate abuse upon their children "without any necessity"²⁶ is precisely what the many accounts of Mary/Miriam's cannibalism derived from Josephus's contest.²⁷ And yet, even Chrysostom viewed Mary's act as one that "surpasses all tragedy."²⁸

Although the crime of cannibalism would have been instantly comprehensible as a punishment for sacrilege to any readers familiar with the Old Testament, the treatment of Mary's act consistently invites a more elevated and nuanced reception. This is certainly true of Morwen's representation of Jewish suffering in *A compendious and most marueilous Historie*, where Miriam's plight is presented as one worthy of pity. Significantly, Morwen's Titus is moved to tears by her plight: he "wept thereat, and was sory for the matter exceedyngly, holdynge vp his handes to heauen, and cryeing."²⁹

This presentation of Mary's cannibalism as tragic can be seen in the English accounts of the siege that preceded Lodge's translation of Josephus. John Stockwood, whose *A very fruitfall and necessarye Sermon of the most lamentable destruction of Ierusalem* (1584) celebrates Morwen's history as a must-read, depicts Mary as the tender-hearted mother who embraces her son, kisses him, weeps upon him, and, running backward because she cannot bear to witness her own horrific deed, stabs his heart.³⁰ For Nashe, it is "not hate, but hunger" that taught Miriam to "forgette mother-hood."³¹ *Christs Teares over Iervsalem*, following Morwen, underscores the charity of her act: "Ile bind thee to me againe, in my wombe Ile beare thee againe, and there bury thee ere Famine shall confounde thee." In a striking, unpredecented, and anachronistic move, Nashe's Mary draws an explicit parallel between her own motives and those of the New World anthropophagi: "Euen as amongst the *Indians* there is a certaine people, that when any of their Kins-folkes are sicke, saue charges of phisicke, and rather resolue (vnnaturally) to eate them vppe, then day-diuersifying Agues or blood-boyling surfets should fit-meale feede on them; so do I resolue, rather to eatte thee vp, my sonne, and feed on thy flesh royallie, then inward emperishing Famine shoulde too vntimely inage thee."³² The tension inherent in Miriam's justification of melancholic incorporation is parenthetically contained. It is "(vnnatural)" to consume one's kin but also necessary and excusable when the alternative is protracted suffering and degradation: witness the Indians.

In the previous chapter, I suggest that Nashe's text should be read as part of the plague literature that cited Jerusalem's destruction as an instance of divine wrath—a wrath that was felt deeply given the plague that ravaged London in the year of *Christs Teares*'s publication.[33] Miriam's story is explicitly directed to the "Mothers of LONDON" who are charged to "but imagine that you were *Miriam*. Wyth what hart (suppose you) could ye go about the cooquerie of your own chyldre?"[34] One imagines that those who had lost children would have naturally felt a deep sense of kinship with her. Others, as Catherine Cox suggests, might have received the story with mingled fear and hope, perhaps wondering if they could be brought to equal desperation.[35] That such alarmed self-reflection is Nashe's intention is clear from his admission that "whatsoeuer of *Ierusalem* I haue written, was but to lend her a Looking-glasse. Now enter I into my true Teares, my Teares for *London*."[36] The message of *Christs Teares* is unambiguous. Sin can bedevil the most holy. God's wrath will not spare a beloved nation. Savagery, at once the cause and manifestation of that punishment, can erupt at the heart of civil society.

In Lodge's punctilious rendering of the *Jewish War*, notably free from Catholic haunting, there is nothing to distract us from Mary's misfortune. Compared to the febrile prose of Morwen and Nashe, his account of the action may seem spare and restrained as it delineates the tragedy in a few precise strokes. But it is equally important to note that a seventeenth-century readership coming to Lodge from Morwen or even Nashe would have had little need of further dramatic embellishment. Mary's cannibalism was already recognized as an act borne of necessity, to be pitied as much as feared. Familiar as they would have been with the different versions of the story of the noble woman who *in extremis* ate her only son, Lodge's readers were already smitten with the horror of how easily civilized *topoi*—the holy city, the home, the genteel mother's arms—could turn brutish and hostile in dire circumstances.

Uncivil Strife

Even without the fresh example of Jamestown's horrors to unsettle them, the readers of the first reprint of *The Lamentable and Tragicall History* would have known something of the grey pinch of famine and its attendant vicissitudes. The poor harvest of 1608–9 and the "scarcity and dearthe of Corne" among all sorts of people, but "especially those of the poorer sort," had led to stringent measures, including harsh restrictions on the making of starch and ale so as to spare grain for consumption.[37] Thomas Dekker's 1609 pamphlet *VVork for Armourers* speaks powerfully of the hunger brought on by famine by staging an imagined war between wealth and poverty. Hunger is the great leveler as Dekker wryly notes, "one of the best commanders for warre . . . for no stone wall (of what height or strength whatsoeuer) is able to hold him out."[38]

But cannibalism is never merely a response to extreme hunger. As both Gina Hens-Piazza and Julie Faith Parker argue, cannibalism is about culture as much as it is about food, and the textual records of its occurrence say more about its relationship to the prevailing ethos of a society than its relationship to starvation.[39] As we know, cannibalism in the biblical tradition almost always represented the extreme state of devastation and decay consequent upon infidelity to God's covenant. Caryn A. Reeder also reminds us that cannibalism was a favorite *topos* of siege narratives (e.g., 2 Kings 6:28–29; Deuteronomy 28; Thucydides 2.70.1), "a powerful image . . . and indicative of the ancient fear of siege and its associated suffering."[40] Lamentations appropriately compares the war-torn Jerusalem of the Babylonian conquest to a bereaved mother, a widow driven to eat the fruit of her own womb (2:20, 4:10), and the very same ascription colors Josephus's history.[41] In her study of the cannibalism in 2 Kings, Hens-Piazza further speculates that "where accommodation and harmony are subordinate to or replaced by domination and control, cannibalism may constitute a response to famine." She notes that the hunger that motivates an act as desperate as cannibalism coincides, in these cases, with the rulers' voracious appetite for power: "The insatiable craving on the part of the powerful reigns over the hunger of the powerless, who eventually resort to cannibalizing in the face of threat."[42]

Modern theorizations of eating, and of cannibalism in particular, tend to explain the act in terms of the radical collapse of boundaries. Mikhail Bakhtin notes that "the body transgresses here its own limits; it swallows, devours, rends the world apart, is enriched and grows at the world's expense . . . Here man tastes the world, introduces it into his own body, makes it part of himself."[43] Although Bakhtin discerns a *jouissance* in the act of consumption, calling it "joyful, triumphant; [man] triumphs over the world, devours it without being devoured himself," Maggie Kilgour notes that the way Bakhtin describes eating sounds less like a dialogic ideal and more like a "monologic blood bath" that involves "the rending, the breaking of one term by another."[44] If man is fed at the world's expense then the relation is not one of reciprocity but, rather, one of self-enlargement. George Bataille would agree. For him "the eating of one species by another is the simplest form of luxury." For the "fragility and complexity of the animal body" to be destroyed in the service of another marks a "glorious" expenditure of energy.[45] If this is so, then, as David B. Goldstein observes, "The eating of one's own species, of one's own son, marks an even more spectacular expenditure, an expression of redundancy that forecloses all possibility of familial or generational growth. Performed by a mother, the act resides symbolically at nature's edge, at the point where human and inhuman meet, where carnivores gather at the fringes of the polis."[46] In a sobering and memorable summation, Kilgour asserts that "in the struggle between desire and aggression, between identification and the division that creates power over another, a struggle which is finally that between communion and cannibalism, cannibalism has usually won."[47]

The numerous symbolic valences that may accrue to the act of cannibalism—covenantal disobedience, radical generative foreclosure, the explosive expenditure of life, the violent collapse of boundaries, and the wrecking of community—are all writ large in Mary's act. But one may argue that the tragic dismemberment and consumption of the baby's body in Book VII of *The Lamentable and Tragicall History* is merely the final physical instantiation of the civic disorder and disintegration of Jewish society, one that aptly presages the eventual dispersion of the Jewish people.

Indeed, the language of dismemberment and cannibalism is everywhere in both Lodge's translation and his source, and long before we encounter the literal cannibalism of the child by his mother. Josephus identifies one principal group as responsible for the protracted catalogue of Jewish adversity: the mendacious zealots who forced the Jews into resistance against Rome. Lamenting the "miseries of my countrey," he identifies "the ciuill dissension that dismembred the same" as the "cause that brought it to confusion: and those tyrants that raigned amongst vs" that "forcibly drew the Romans with sword and fire to seeke the desolation of our holy temple."[48] Like Hens-Piazza's "sovereigns," they display the same moral turpitude, the same "voracious appetite" for power. As Josephus narrates it, the Jews had united under the attack from Rome, but in 68 C.E., with the cessation of hostilities precipitated by Nero's demise, they split into three factions. Jerusalem was divided between John of Gischala, Eleazar, son of Simon, and Simon, son of Gioras. The bulk of the *Jewish War* focuses on their infighting and the way their internecine strife weakened the city, leading to its inevitable fall to the Roman legions under the command of Titus Vespasian. It was "no forrainers," Josephus insists, but "our owne familiar friends, and countrimen haue been the actors of our tragedy."[49]

It is worth recalling at this juncture that as Josephus was a recent defector to the Roman side, his eyewitness account is particularly ambivalent. Having been captured at the battle of Jotapata, he was outside the walls with the Roman forces. From this vantage point, Josephus would later move to Rome and write the *Jewish War* as a pro-Roman *apologia* wherein the Romans, in a sense, save the Jews from themselves. It is a delicate and intricate political game of pleasing the Romans while sympathizing with the lot of his own people that he then plays. The seditionists who forced the Jews into an act of political defiance are thus the perfect targets for his fury. Merrall Llewellyn Price suggests that Josephus cannot be trusted when he writes about the brutality of the Jewish rebel factions. His descriptions are calculated to arouse such disgust in the reader that one can only assume that this is how he intended to shore up his credibility—through an utterly denigratory description of those that fought. Reeder agrees: "In *The Jewish War*, Josephus exploits 'non-combatants' as tools in his interpretation of the rebellion as misguided and even iniquitous from beginning to end."[50]

Regardless of the questionable nature of Josephus's bias, it manifests in striking fashion in *The Most Lamentable and Tragicall History*. Lodge's translation dutifully replicates the bitter hatred of the seditionists that marks his source material when he depicts Jerusalem rent to shreds by their unconscionable actions. It is worth noting something of Lodge's own political concerns here, for no translation, however accurate, is entirely free of the biases of its translator.[51] Josephus's history of the "vtter ruine" of the Jews through violent dissension would have resonated on a personal level with Lodge's own concerns about civil discord and the human propensity to wreck their own, concerns that characterize previous works of his such as the dire prognosticating play *A Looking Glasse, for London and Englande* (c.1586), the historical drama *The Wounds of Ciuill VVar* (1594), and *A Margarite of America* (1596), which emphasizes in graphic terms the human capacity for cruelty and mutilation.

The Wounds of Ciuill VVar is a particularly apt example of Lodge's dismay at the ruthless machinations and naked greed of those in power. As Andrew Hadfield suggests, it was probably intended to inspire an English audience to make connections between the protracted wars that eventually destroyed the Roman Republic and their own bloody past fraught with religious tensions and anxieties over Elizabeth I's succession. The waste and destruction of civil war and the unlimited capacity for human cruelty is starkly rendered in Lodge's play, notably in his comparison of men to beasts to the former's disadvantage:

Brute beasts nill breake the mutuall law of loue,
And birds affections will not violate,
The senceless trees haue concord mongst themselues,
And stones agree in linkes of amitie

so "what then are men that gainst themselues doo warre."[52] The unnaturalness of self-directed violence is heightened in later descriptions of the gracious

IOSEPHVS BEN-GORION

The Learned and Warlike Jew.

Frontispiece to Joseph ben Gorion's *The Wonderful and Most Deplorable History of the Latter Times of the Jews*, 1662. (Reproduced by permission of Henry E. Huntington Library and Art Gallery)

boulevards, where "earst the fathers of your state/ In robes of purple walked vp and downe" now "strewed with mangled members, streaming blood." Here, the patrician bodies of Ancient Romans are replaced by the hacked, mangled, and dispersed limbs of their progeny so that the color purple comes to be associated exclusively with gaping wounds, all because of "your seditious innouations, / Your fickle minds inclinde to foolish change."[53]

Arthur Kinney has argued for the unflinching spirit with which Lodge confronted the problem of human depravity in the grim turn of the sixteenth century into the seventeenth.[54] That depravity is on full display in his translation of Josephus. Above the carnage of the beleaguered city, the shadows of the unconscionable seditionists loom; they hover like birds of prey forcing fragments of food out of the mouths of the hapless Jews. But unlike vultures, they violate their own kind. Once again, it is the self-consuming nature of their violence that is searing. The ultimate horror of civil war equals and then exceeds the ultimate horror of cannibalism. The seditionists brutally beat old men clutching their victuals, and they drag women concealing crumbs in their hands by the hair and abuse them. Children with tiny particles of food they lift up and dash to the ground. Their cruelty is inexorable and, unlike Mary's cannibalism, it is spurred on by reckless cupidity and boundless ambition. It is they who precipitate the famine by capturing and destroying the granaries within the city, and when they find themselves in the terrible clutch of starvation, their response is vicious and abusive: "They also deuised most barbarous and cruell torments to extort foode from others: for they thrust sticks or such like into the cauitie of mens yards, and sharpe thornie rods into their fundaments: and it is abhominable to heare what the people endured to make them confesse one loafe of bread, or one handfull of corne which they had hidden."[55]

Lodge informs us that those who were "yet strong of body" were killed by the rebels on the assumption that they had food or would not otherwise be strong and fit. But the fate of those who "pined with famine" was no better, for they were also killed by the seditionists "who esteemed it no offence to kill them, who wold shortly after die though they were left aliue."[56] These violated Jewish bodies possessed no value or rights under siege, reduced to what Giorgio Agamben terms "bare life."[57]

Lodge provides an uncompromising and visceral account of the consequences of the zealots' rash ambition. When all food runs out, the very roofs of houses are covered with the moribund bodies of dying women and babies and the streets are clogged with the corpses of Jewish youth. It is here that we meet our "yong men swollen like dead mens shadowes," who stagger into the marketplace and "fell downe dead where it happened." A horrific index of the degree to which starvation and destitution contravenes all civilized decency is found in the description of the mounting heap of bodies, for "they that were aliue could not bury them, nor cared they for burying them, being now vncertaine what should betide themselues." Those who yet retained some small sense of the fitness of things fall prey to their own physical weakness and "fell downe themselues dead vpon them as they were burying them. And many being yet aliue, went vnto their graues & there died. Yet for all this calamity was there no weeping nor lamentation, for famine ouercame all affections."[58]

The famine that the rebels invite by firing the granaries is as cannibalistic as they are and, like them, it indiscriminately consumes the rich and the poor, the young and the old. In Lodge's account, families disintegrate as "wiues tooke the meate euen out of their husbands mouthes, and children from their parents, and mothers euen from their infants, which was the most lamentable thing of all."[59] In this belligerent climate, finer emotions such as benevolence and compunction are luxuries none can afford: "No body had now any comp[a]ssion, neither did they spare their deerest infants, but suffered them to perish euen in their armes, taking from them the very drops of life."[60] It is as if the grasping and intemperate behavior of the seditionists spreads like a cancer through the city, undoing all bonds of kinship and fellowship with tenacious fingers.

Thus, even though they recoil from Mary's "execrable meat," Lodge's rebels are the true anthropophagi. Their voracious appetite for power, which can be satisfied only by figuratively consuming their own community, is presented as far worse than Mary's pitiable act. It is they who strip her of all her possessions and leave her destitute; they who destroy food supplies indiscriminately in a bid to keep the people in their thrall; they who pollute the Temple; they who prosecute a senseless campaign against the far superior military might of Rome. It is fitting then that Lodge should employ the imagery of self-consumption and self-destruction to describe their petty infighting: "one may well call this a sedition raised out of a sedition; which, like a cruell and sauage beast in penury & want of others, turned his cruelty against his owne bowels."[61] Likewise, in setting fire to all of the granaries and provisions within the city, it is "as if vpon purpose, to the great aduantage of the Roman, they had consumed all that was prouided against the siege; so did they destroy their owne forces and strength." Thanks to their folly they are "taken by famine, which they could not haue felt, had they themselues not caused it. The citizens were in euery place a prey vnto those that were seditious on one side, and to them that besieged the citie on the other side, and like a great bodie torne in peeces between these two."[62] Again, those that "*Simon* robbed, he sent vnto *Iohn*; and those that *Iohn* spoiled, he sent vnto *Simon*: and so they did as it were one drink vnto another the bloud of the people, and diuide their dead carcases between them; insomuch that they disagreed onely for their desire of rule and domination: but both conspired to doe mischiefe and commit iniquitie."[63]

One may even discern traces of Gog and Magog in the depiction of these men who rent and feed on the body politic in such barbarous fashion.[64] The medieval Ebstorf *Mappa Mundi*, which depicts the known world inscribed on Christ's own body, relegates Gog and Magog to the northwest extreme where they crouch, biting the limbs of a naked human figure stretched between them. In a narrative memorable for the mother who reversed the normative vector of generation, there could be no better metaphor for the perverse behavior of the seditionists.

Indeed, by using cannibalism as a symbol for impiety and vendibility, Lodge draws on a familiar literary device that was popular in early modern texts such as Arthur Golding's translation of Ovid's *Metamorphoses*.[65] His use of cannibalism as a metaphor for perverse human behavior would have also been familiar from Shakespeare's plays. While *Titus Andronicus* is the most obvious and grotesque example, one cannot ignore the venal Shylock in *The Merchant of Venice* with his intent to feed on Antonio's flesh. *Coriolanus* famously uses eating—specifically cannibalism—to define its central issues, notably the pathological relationship between the titular hero and his mother Volumnia. In Janet Adelman's words, "the image of the mother who has not fed her children enough" is at the center of the play and "in this hungry world, everyone seems in danger of being eaten."[66]

In both *Macbeth* and *Timon of Athens* alike, cannibalism is linked to the corruption of the body politic.[67] Likewise, in the world of *Troilus and Cressida*, power again manifests as indiscriminating and insatiable appetite:

> And appetite, an universal wolf,
> . . . .
> Must make perforce a universal prey
> And at last eat up itself. (I. iii. 121–24)

In *Pericles*, it is "the great ones" who consume aggressively those less mighty than themselves. The "rich misers" are "whales: a' plays and tumbles, driving the poor fry before him, and at last devours them all at a mouthful. Such whales have I heard on a' th' land, who never leave gaping till they swallow'd the whole parish, church steeple, bells, and all" (II. i. 28–34).

Shakespeare here moralizes on what we might recognize as social Darwinism and exposes its obscenity and impropriety.[68] The great irony of sustaining oneself through self-consumption is writ large in *Pericles* in particular when Antiochus and the Princess pervert the socially acceptable means of propagating the family by nourishing themselves on human flesh. In that world of horrors, cannibalism shifts from metaphor to a real gross possibility: a daughter may eat her mother's flesh and parents devour "those little darlings whom they lov'd."[69]

Colonial Cannibals

It is this shift from cannibalism as metaphor to its carnal instantiation that marks the structure of Lodge's *Lamentable and Tragicall History*. Not only are these cannibalistic events juxtaposed on the continuum of intraspecies violence, but also the unequaled heinousness of the former is emphasized at every juncture. This lesson would have been familiar to anyone acquainted with Michel de Montaigne's essays "Of the Cannibals" and "Of Crueltie," which drew similar conclusions about metaphorical consumption. Translated by John Florio in 1603, these essays illustrated the porosity of the border between civilized and barbaric, and interrogated the system of values that govern so-called civil society. In clear and uncompromising terms, Montaigne berates the brutality of the Europeans in the face of whose venality the human flesh-eating American Indians appear more civilized and humane. It was worse:

> To mangle by tortures and torments a body full of lively sense, to roast him in peeces, to make dogges and swine to gnaw and teare him in mammockes (as wee have not only read, but seene very lately, yea and our owne memorie, not amongst ancient enemies, but our neighbours and fellow-citizens; and which is worse, under pretense of pietie and religion) than to roast and eat him after he is dead.[70]

In a startling reversal of expectations, it is the so-called civilized Old World that is truly bestial. Its torture of its own people, often conducted under a noble standard ("pietie and religion"), betrays an innate savagery. Here, one can trace the influence of Jean de Lery's *Historie d'un voyage fait en la terre du Bresil* (1578), which similarly associated cannibalism with the familiar brutality of warfare, economic inequality, and religious and political persecution, using it effectively as a trope for a wide variety of literal and metaphorical forms of violence that pervaded the so-called civilized world. Cannibalism, the supposed marker of absolute otherness, is seen to accrue more properly to the Old World so-called civilized societies. Praising the naturalness of the natives, Montaigne asserts, "the very words that signify lying, treachery, dissimulation, avarice, envy, belittling, pardon" are "unheard of." The New World savages are "close to their original naturalness," perhaps even free from the taint of Original Sin.[71]

As Stephen Greenblatt points out, Montaigne's witty discourse on cannibals deals more with the idea of cannibalism: he acknowledges the "barbarous horror" of New World cannibalism as a means to articulate the horror at home.[72] In the same context, Christopher Hill quotes a contemporary observer about the "Indians at home, Indians in Cornwall, Indians in Wales, Indians in Ireland." Commenting on this, Supriya Chaudhuri writes:

> It is in the representation of these "Indians at home" that the Renaissance writer is compelled to draw upon the most contradictory and self-reflexive elements of the contemporary discourse of cannibalism. Taken to constitute an extreme of wildness and incivility by which the norms of civil society may be measured, such figures are easily invested with allegorical resemblances to adversaries closer to home.[73]

For Montaigne and some of his contemporaries, then, the discourse of cannibalism was a means of self-appraisal, yielding a term that, in Chaudhuri's phrase, "can be turned back, not to its origin but to its originator." As she suggests, "the cannibal for Montaigne is ultimately not the other but the same . . . or at least, as this is how literature works, *possibly* the same."[74] Indeed, it is now a critical commonplace that early modern travel literature that discussed the nature and customs of others elsewhere invariably articulated them in relation to the inherited practices, conventions, and customs of those at home.[75] Wes William argues further that "in the context of sixteenth-century Europe to speak of cannibals is to engage in civil war talk."[76]

Appalled by the long years of civil conflict motivated by religious controversy, Montaigne is driven to wonder if other "savage" communities such as those in Brazil would credit the kind of barbaric cruelty the French inflict on one another. The unspeakable tortures in the name of religion are not confined to far-flung shores, he insists, but are daily inflicted upon friends, neighbors, kindred, the inhabitants of hearth and home. And this form of self-directed violence is no less cannibalistic than any violence encountered in the New World. Indeed, in an argument that should now seem familiar to us, it is so much worse. In a passage of crucial importance from "Of Crueltie," Montaigne asserts his bias in unequivocal terms: "The Canibales and savage peoples do not so much offend me with roasting and eating of dead bodies, as those which torment and persecute the living." He then elaborates:

I live in an age wherein we abound with incredible examples of this vice, through the licentiousnesse of our civill and intestine warres: And read all ancient stories, be they never so tragicall, you shall find none to equal those we daily see practised. But that hath nothing made me acquainted with it. I could hardly be perswaded, before I had seene it, that the world could have afforded so marble-hearted and savage-minded men, that for the onely pleasure of murther would commit-it; then cut, mangle, and hacke other members in pieces: to rouze and sharpen their wits, to invent unused tortures and unheard-of torments: to devise new and unknowne deaths, and that in cold blood, without any former enmitie or quarrel, or without any gaine or profit; and onely to this end, that they may enjoy the pleasing spectacle of the languishing gestures, pitifull motions, horror-moving yellings, deep fetcht groanes, and lamentable voyces of a dying and drooping man.[77]

Here Montaigne completely collapses the binary between New World savage and civilized European to reveal their affinity on the cannibal continuum. This is not to imply that Montaigne practices some nascent form of cultural relativism or exhorts the reader to judge an alien culture by its own standards. Flesh-eating is emphatically neither excused nor validated; it merely does not "so much offend" as figurative cannibalism does. Eating people is still wrong and the New World cannibals may well be called barbarous in regard of "reason's rules," but their barbarity pales in comparison to that of the monstrously infighting French.[78] The parallels with Lodge's Josephus are clear. Flesh-eating—whether ritual or survival-based in nature—is shudder-worthy, but internecine violence (of which Mary's cannibalism is both the final instance and consequence) is unforgivable.

The Consumed Colony

The affinities between Montaigne and Lodge as regards the value system they articulate are fairly clear. Less obvious at first glance, perhaps, is how Percy's narratives of settler life in Jamestown, written from the perspective of the colonizer, evince those same biases (despite his harrowing contemporaneous account of cannibalism motivated by extreme starvation).

George Percy, younger brother to the ninth Earl of Northumberland, was with the first party to land in Jamestown in 1607, remaining there until 1612 when the crises he describes so vividly were unfolding. Percy not only witnessed the Starving Time alluded to at the beginning of this chapter, but he also was central to its administration: first as president of the colony, then as chief commander under Lord De La Warr, and finally as deputy governor preceding the arrival of Sir Thomas Dale. As such, he wrote from the position of one deeply implicated; indeed, of one upon whose shoulders rested the responsibility for events at Jamestown. It is generally assumed that *A Trewe Relacyon* was Percy's attempt at self-justification. Noting the degree to which Percy tries in the account to shift blame on others in the colony, Mark Nicholls concludes that he "decided to concentrate specifically on protecting his own reputation, so producing a work that is more defensive than offensive, more concerned with exonerating George Percy than with advancing any sustained and painstaking critique of John Smith."[79] Forrest K. Lehman likewise concurs that Percy wrote to excuse his own failings, which he did by "laying blame on everyone else."[80] Percy does begin with the standard posture of *apologia*, acknowledging the versions of the story that had circulated and insisting that the time had now come to step forward and speak the truth, but as Kathleen Donegan persuasively argues, his aim to "manyfeste" himself also includes "representing that 'bitter experyense' and making himself and others manifest amid the colony's increasingly disastrous implosion."[81]

It is this act of making "manyfeste" the "bitter experyense" of the colony that makes Percy's *Observations Gathered out of a Discourse* and *A Trewe Relacyon* valuable texts that, when read alongside those of Montaigne and Lodge, deepen our appreciation of the complexity of early modern attitudes toward culture and barbarism, specifically in the context of colonial encounters. What makes Percy's writing so unusual is the grim catalogue of horrors that runs counter to the narrative expectations of the colonizing project in Virginia. While, on the one hand, the American colonies were viewed by the state as a dumping ground for the "swarmes of idle people" and "incorrigible and dangerous rogues . . . banished and conveyed" to spare the mother country from having to build more prisons, it was nonetheless hoped that some of these undesirable elements would be become productive and useful subjects of the Crown abroad.[82] The underlying conceit was that English cultural systems were not merely transferable but would also prove more bountiful and ameliorative in foreign climes, civilizing not only natives but also the unsavory elements within the settler community.

Even so, the authorities were not naïve about the impending dangers in the New World. The documents authorizing those in power to take stringent measures to maintain control within the colony also warn of inevitable problems with the American Indians as well as the need to stockpile food to avert the dangers of famine. Still, Percy dutifully strikes an optimistic note at the start of his *Observations*, recording with wonder and appreciation the fair country to which the colonists had been brought and at which, "I was almost ravished at the first sight thereof."[83] The account of the inland journey is replete with numerous mentions of "pleasant garden[s]" and "goodliest tall trees," "fresh fish and abundance of sea tortoises," "goodly grass, and abundance of fowls of all kinds," "excellent ground full of flowers of divers kinds and colors," "fine and beautiful strawberries, four times bigger and better than ours in England," "great store of vines in bigness of a man's thigh, running up to the tops of the trees, in great abundance."[84]

This rhetoric of plenitude is imbued with the associations of an earthly paradise to which the settlers have been providentially led, the presence of the "savages" notwithstanding. Yet Percy is unable to sustain this optimistic discourse and his report soon devolves into an unrelenting litany of death and disaster. As the violent skirmishes with the Native Americans become more frequent and food proves harder to come by, the leading colonists turn on one another and the authorized codes for organizing colonization and its official narrative collapse utterly. When Percy renders the dismemberment of the settler body in harrowing terms in *A Trewe Relacyon*—called by Philip Barbour "the most eloquent portrayal of the sufferings of the Jamestown colony ever written"—he presents, equally, the fragmentation of a single coherent authoritative version of the colonizing project. Although John Smith is largely credited with shaping the historical memory of the earliest years of American colonization, Percy's narratives reveal its underlying fissures. As Donegan notes, Smith "charts newly possible worlds but Percy proves that a discourse of catastrophe was sometimes the only way to write Virginia . . . While Smith creates new subject positions, Percy writes from the wreckage of old ones."[85]

Given the degree to which Percy's writing is mired in incertitude, it is easy to agree with Donegan's assessment that he closes down "the encyclopedic possibilities for inhabiting the New World and [renders] the alienation and violence of the settlement clear."[86] But Smith, too, relates the swift decline of the Jamestown settlers and, crucially, assigns primary responsibility for the disaster to the corruption and fractious behavior of members of the Virginia council, writing that it was "through the hard dealing of our President [Edward Maria Wingfield], the rest of the counsel beeing diverslie affected through his audacious command . . . through which disorder God (being angrie with us) plagued us with such famin and sickness, that the living were scarce able to bury the dead." In his own *True Relation* (1608), the first published account of Jamestown, Smith claimed that Wingfield had kept the stores (particularly "the Sack, Aquavitie, and other preservatives for our health") for himself and those close to him. He elaborated on these charges in his *Generall Historie of Virginia*, accusing Wingfield of "ingrossing to his private, Oatmeale, Sacke, Oyle, Aqua-vitae, Beefe, Egges, or what not" and leaving only the most meager of provisions in the common kettle.[87] In *A History of the Settlement of Virginia*, the council was full of "malice, grudging, and muttering" while the settlers were in "such despair, as they would rather starve and rot with idleness, than be persuaded to do anything for their own relief."[88]

Despite gesturing toward divine displeasure, Smith clearly assigns responsibility to the selfishness of those in authority. Percy likewise isolates and blames the actions of a few and, though history has (perhaps unfairly) impugned him for shifting responsibility—in Forrest Lehmann's words "No one, ally or enemy, is safe from the wide net of blame he casts"—we have only to look to Smith's histories for corroboration that infighting did weaken the community.[89] Percy's account lists instance upon instance of selfish policies implemented by the authorities. For instance, Captain Ratcliffe's fatal supply expedition to Werowocomoco "for want of circumspection" on the part of its leader resulted in the deaths of all but sixteen men, but more distressing was the venality of the others: Captain West's mission to Potoamack motivated him to desert his colony and turn his boat, now full of provisions, straight for England; and Captain Davis was found to be concealing a hoard of food at Fort Algernon during the Starving Time and, likewise, plotting to flee to England.

On a scale of horror, the petty selfishness of the colonists may seem less dire than the conduct ascribed to the Jewish malcontents by Lodge or that of the malevolent French denigrated by Montaigne. And yet the consequence of their infighting is no less catastrophic. It is important to note that Percy records a catalogue not only of death but also of brutality that includes the merciless executions of those who robbed the settlement's dwindling stores. Atrocity likewise characterizes the interactions with the American Indians. Building up to his account of the Starving Time, Percy describes the English messengers that are mutilated and killed by the Indians, their "Braynes cutt and skraped outt of their heades with Mussell shelles," as well as the English captain who is burned alive while his skin is scraped off and thrown into the fire before his face. English corpses are discovered with their mouths stuffed with bread—a telling commentary on colonial greed—as the product the colonizers demand is literally shoved down their throats.[90] With each instance that Percy recounts, he underscores the violence against English bodies that underpins the colonial enterprise such that the desecrated English corpses become a symbol of the native resistance to colonial cupidity.

The resultant retaliation by the English is equal if not greater in savagery to this violence, with the wholesale destruction of Native American villages through

arson and pillage. In the declension of Percy's optimistic narrative to a stark catalogue of death, we may locate an implicit (perhaps even unwilling) interrogation
of colonial values of greed, ambition, and the selfish pursuit of gain. Colonization,
Percy makes us realize, is cannibalistic in its violence: in the liminal space of the
settlement, English bodies are rent and consumed by English colonial ambition,
which manifests variously in the acquisitive tendencies of the settlement leaders,
the retaliatory violence of the Indians, starvation, and famine.

Interestingly, the Virginia Company's response to the catastrophe acknowledged the self-directed, involuted destruction at its core but declined all
responsibility for it. If the voyagers went out smiling and came back "rent and
disfigured," it was the fault of those "wicked Impes," the settlers themselves. As
one official tract intones, "Let the imputation of miserie be to their idleness and
the blood that was spilt upon their own heads that caused it."[91] Percy's reports
on the sick and starving articulates both the desperate need for acquiescence
and answerability on the part of the mother country—"if there were any conscience in men, it would make their hearts bleed to heare the pitiful murmurings
& outcries of our sick men"—as well as the embedded fear that such horrors
cannot and will not be witnessed.[92] Indeed, London's official response to Virginia's problems continued to abjure all culpability for its acquisitive imperialist
appetite. When the London Council for the Virginia Company admitted similar cases of hardship elsewhere, it was only to minimize the novelty and scale of
the disaster in the settlements. Thus, the council reminded its investors that the
Spanish had endured much the same order of hardship and indeed, of greater
degree in their colonial ventures: "aboundant" were their stories of "Fleets, Bat-
tailes, and Armies lost" and yet, with admirable "indefatigable industry and
prosperous fate," they overcame all adversity. If the Spanish could suffer and
triumph, then so could the English. The council's tellingly corporeal metaphor
of choice to describe Jamestown was that of a diseased body that could recover
if only fresh and hearty settlers were sent to replace their decaying counterparts. But, as Smith reports, the so-called fresh settlers were "all sicke, the rest
some lame, some bruised, all unable to doe anything but complaine."[93] Thus,
the all-consuming maw of colonial ambition ground down unchecked.

Percy's account of survival-driven cannibalism overlaps uncannily with Josephus's history of cannibalism in Jerusalem. Indeed, both are narratives of abjection, and the histories they relate are of decline, undoing, unsettlement, and
disarticulation. In her influential study of abjection, Julia Kristeva asserts that
while the "corpse seen without God, and outside of science is the utmost of abjection," its "most elementary and most archaic form" is "loathing an item of food."
Abjection is located in "The spasms and vomiting that protect me . . . The shame

of compromise, of being in the middle of treachery."[94] The "shame of compromise" is writ large in the histories of famished Jamestown and Jerusalem alike. In his 1610 report on the Starving Time, Spanish ambassador Don Alonso de Velasco asserted that some of the new arrivals had died "from having eaten dogs, cat skins and other vile stuff."[95] In his *Trewe Relacyon*, Percy lists with grisly precision a catalogue of abject comestibles that parallels almost exactly the items the Ancient Jews consumed in order to survive the siege on Jerusalem:

> Then haveinge fedd upour horses and other beastes as longe as they
> Lasted, we weare gladd to make shifte w[i]th vermin as doggs Catts
> Ratts and myce all was fishe thatt Came to Nett to satisfye Crewell
> hunger, as to eate Bootes shoes or any other leather some Colde come
> by and those beinge Spente and devoured some weare inforced to
> searche the woodes and to feed upon Serpentts and snakes and to digge
> the earthe for wylde and unknowne Rootes, where many of our men
> weare Cutt of and slayne by the Salvages.[96]

But abjection is something more than just a state of acute physical degradation; it is a state caused by "what disturbs identity, system, order, that does not respect borders, positions, rules."[97] In both Percy's text and Lodge's Josephus translation, abjection exceeds the physical state, signaling the total collapse of a seemingly stable identity.

Rather than celebrate the accomplishments of hearty, self-possessed Englishmen providentially led to a brave new world, Percy, feeling increasingly victimized, gives us a haunting portrayal of settler self-otherness (to borrow Donegan's phrase) in the description of skeletal figures, phantasmic counterparts of the attenuated Jews during the siege.[98] The "maugre and Leane" apparitions that "throwe extreme hunger have Runne outt of their naked bedds beinge so Leane thatt they Looked lyke anotannes (anatomies), Cryeing owtt we are starved. We are starved" recall once more Lodge's harrowing account of the young men reduced to "dead men's shadowes" that stagger into the marketplace to collapse and die.[99] In both narratives we see the slow dispossession of the body and with it the sloughing off of the markers of identity. In his *Observations*, Percy goes so far as to admit that, "There were never Englishmen left in a foreign country in such misery as we were in this new discovered Virginia."[100] But the label of "Englishmen" becomes increasingly impossible to sustain. They are soon just "men night and day groaning in every corner of the fort most pitiful to hear" or "sick men, without relief," dying "three or four in a night; in the morning their bodies trailed out of their cabins like dogs to be buried."[101]

The comparison of the settlers' cadavers to "dogs" is particularly piquant given Percy's previous blithe description of the Dominican cannibals who "lap up mans spittle, whilst one spits in their mouths in a barbarous fashion like dogs."[102] The ascription of bestiality to the indigenes "out there" can no longer be sustained. "Our sick men" are now bestial, descending the great chain of being from authorized imperial agents to moribund mongrels. A worse horror awaits them during the Starving Time, when a few of the perishing settlers "Runn away unto the Salvages" and are never heard of again. Whether they are killed or—most damning of all—assimilated, there is no way of knowing. At such moments, the markers of Englishness—being civilized, elect, superior—disintegrate utterly.

Conclusion

The notorious cannibal of Jamestown may be seen to parallel the cannibal mother of Jerusalem not only because both are driven to eat family members during extreme attrition but also because their acts of anthropophagy are the final incarnation of a more pernicious and rampant self-directed violence, catalyzed by rapacious greed, that threatens to consume their respective communities. But such figures of monstrosity can turn into scapegoats. As the obvious foci of horror, revulsion, and condemnation, they distract from a thorough engagement with the larger crisis of which their actions constitute only the climax. Donegan similarly notes that the episode of the cannibal husband served to divert attention from the real crisis in the colonies and allowed the London authorities to "resist a broader analysis of catastrophe in the settlement and focus instead on its most extravagant and punishable example."[103] Though Percy articulated no explicit condemnation of English colonial enterprise, he exposed the brutality and self-destructiveness that underpinned it more powerfully than his contemporaries did, and when read alongside Lodge, his writings reveal the incalculable horror of figurative cannibalism. Percy's *Observations* was published as part of cleric Samuel Purchas's popular compilation of travel writings *Hakluytus Posthumus, or Purchas His Pilgrimes* (1624), though the harrowing *Trewe Relacyon* would not appear in print until centuries after. At the same time, Lodge's *Lamentable and Tragicall History*, also advocated by Purchas, would go through twenty reprintings in the seventeenth century, suggesting its relevance to the ever-darkening political climate shadowed by clouds of civil war.

CHAPTER 4

From Providence to Politics

Not much is known about William Heminge other than that he was the son of First Folio co-editor John Heminge, and a rather opportunistic dramatist who capitalized heavily on his connection to Shakespeare by freely importing the latter's lines into his own work. Though not always a successful dramatist, Heminge clearly had an eye for the popular and the innovative. *The Fatal Contract* (c.1653) was the first revenge drama—a crowd-pleasing genre that reveled in unbridled violence, sexual perversion, and intrigue—to feature a female protagonist. Not only did Heminge fully exploit the novelty of a woman exacting bloody vengeance, but he went so far as to have her disguise herself as a Moorish eunuch answering to the name of Castrato. The outlandish ploy allowed him to "top his predecessors' grotesque art," and doubtless ensured the popularity of the play that Virginia Mason Vaughan has dubbed "the most graphic Caroline revenge tragedy."[1]

Equally fascinating, though less sensationalist, is a now largely forgotten play on the Roman destruction of Jerusalem that Heminge likely penned sometime in the 1620s. Printed in quarto by Matthew Inman in 1662, *The Jewes Tragedy, Or, Their Fatal and Final Overthrow by Vespatian and Titus his Son: Agreeable to the Authentick and Famous History of Josephus* (c.1628–30)[2] emphasizes Heminge's determination to bring this history to the theater. This is not to say that he was the first to dramatize Jerusalem's fall. We know of *The Destruccion of Jerusalem* (1584), which replaced the medieval *Corpus Christi* cycle in Coventry, as well as the now lost *Titus and Vespasian*, which saw ten performances by Lord Strange's Men at the Rose in 1592/93 before it was picked up by the Admiral's Men the following year. There is also evidence of a *Titus and Vespasian* being performed at court between 1610 and 1622, which Beatrice Groves suggests may well have been a new take on this topic.[3] Like its predecessors, *The Jewes Tragedy* set events familiar to anyone with even a glancing knowledge of the siege: the attack on Jerusalem by Vespasian and his son, Titus, in 70 C.E.; the consequent famine that devastated the beleaguered Jews; and the eventual destruction of the Second Temple through fire. All were common knowledge judging by the many reprints of Peter Morwen and Thomas Lodge, as well as the various references to the Jews' devastation in chronologies, sermons, ballads, and plague pamphlets. As we recall, in 1638, Thomas Jackson even suggested that the history of the siege had become more familiar than England's own history. When Heminge chose this topic, he could have presumed his audience's familiarity with the material in the same way that Shakespeare would have relied on his audience knowing about Richard III.

But *The Jewes Tragedy* merits close attention in part for what it reveals about shifts in the narrative tradition. Heminge's play eschews the conventional Christian moral and its accompanying providentialist rhetoric to produce a thoughtful secular analysis of the Jews' defeat. Rather than focus on providence and divine vengeance, it considers the political ramifications of Roman imperialism and Jewish resistance. By focusing heavily on politics, Heminge's work more closely resembles a Latin dramatization by Thomas Legge (1535–1607), whose *Richardus Tertius* (1579) has been lauded as the first chronicle play in England.[4] Legge's "famous tragedy" *Solymitana Clades*, which was performed at Cambridge around 1590, focused on the complexities of the Jewish rebellion and, like *The Jewes Tragedy*, invoked an explicit parallel between the Roman conquest of Briton and the subjugation of Judaea. However, there is no evidence that Heminge knew anything about Legge's drama, and in this instance, at least, his choices appear to have been his own.

Indeed, despite its dramatization of a trendy subject, *The Jewes Tragedy* fared rather poorly. Unlike *The Fatal Contract*, there is no indication that Heminge's play was ever performed in a public theater.[5] Prior to the publication of Carol Morley's 2006 critical edition, few had heard of this piece.[6] *The Biographia Dramatica; Or, A Companion to the Playhouse*, for instance, states merely the title of *The Jewes Tragedy* with the information that it was printed "some years after the author's death" and that "the plot is founded on the siege and destruction of Jerusalem, as related by Josephus, in the 6th and 7th books of his *Wars of the Jews*." Andrew Gurr, who served as chief academic advisor on the project to rebuild the Globe Theater, ignores the play entirely in his assessments of

Shakespeare's imitators, and *The Revels History of Drama* lists 1626 as the date of composition without further elaboration.[7]

When read in the context of the copious literature on the fall of Jerusalem, however, I would argue that both Heminge's choice of subject matter and the manner of its representation assume significance. Inman, his publisher, claimed that the play was "Agreeable" to Josephus's "Famous" history, thereby underscoring the continued interest in Jerusalem's fall in the 1660s. Both Morwen and Lodge enjoyed considerable popularity in the mid-1650s, especially during the controversy that then raged over readmitting the Jews into England— a controversy that generated a veritable cornucopia of polemical pamphlets, tracts, and sermons. Morwen's history was even reprinted by James Stafford as *The Wonderful and Most Deplorable History of the Latter Times of the Jews: With the Destruction of the City of Jerusalem* (1652). Suddenly the Jews—who had morphed into an abstraction in their three-hundred-year absence—were poised to become a very real political entity. When Inman unearthed and published *The Jewes Tragedy* in 1662, it was no doubt in a bid to capitalize on the fashionable interest in Josephus, suggested by the careful inclusion of his name in the title.

Inman himself may not have fully realized just how *The Jewes Tragedy's* politically enlightened retelling of the siege set it apart. In the drive to realize the secular and civic dimensions of his story, Heminge discarded much of the providential idiom that had dominated previous early modern versions of Jerusalem's devastation. His play has neither stock lamentation for divine abandonment nor extended prognostication of Jerusalem's fall. It also has a surprising dearth of apocalyptic omens. Heminge's Jews are not Christ-killing troglodytes, and conspicuously absent is any mention of heavenly punishment for contravening the Covenant—despite Titus's somber conclusion that "the gods are just" (5.8.196). In deviating from the traditional Christian retelling of the siege, then, *The Jewes Tragedy* is a remarkable, if neglected, contribution to early modern political and historiographical disquisition.[8] By turning to politics rather than to divine judgment to produce the Jews' tragedy, Heminge's play draws attention to second causes: the actions of human beings rather than God, the First Cause.

The result is a vividly realized examination of the consequences of political strife, influenced by contemporaneous controversies over divine providence, contingency, and the meaning of history. Heminge's inspiration may be traced to the political and religious climate of the period. The late 1620s had already witnessed a controversial interrogation of providentialism spearheaded by so-called Arminian forces. This remonstrance placed doctrinal emphasis upon free will and was interpreted as a challenge to the stock Calvinist convention of reading God's role in history as causative and deterministic, with secular events being mere indices of the divine disposition. I will show that, because of the way it disassociates political turmoil from heavenly judgment, *The Jewes Tragedy* may be usefully contextualized within the Arminian controversy, even as its ambivalence over the rule of chance and fate suggests that Heminge, while aware of tendentious debates on the role of providence, sought to stay away from them as much as possible.

In short, *The Jewes Tragedy* is a grim political allegory of contemporary internecine politics. It also anticipates the political and social culture of the Restoration court, which frequently derided apocalyptic and providentialist rhetoric. Heminge's play may thus be read as a compelling instance of the gradual shift in the seventeenth century away from a deterministic worldview, in which God assigns outcomes, to a more secularized conception of history that seeks explanations not in religious etiology but, rather, in human actions and interventions. Though not a trailblazer, or even a particularly well-written play, *The Jewes Tragedy* is a singular example of pre–Civil War disenchantment with providentialism.

The Providentialist Tradition

It is impossible to assess Heminge's secular slant, specifically as it pertains to Arminianism, without first recognizing the providentialism that imbued the narrative tradition. Heminge's knowledge of Jerusalem's destruction, like Legge's, was probably derived from Morwen's translation of *Josippon*.[9] As we saw in chapter 1, Morwen conformed to the tradition established by the sententious Christian apologists by emphasizing the providential destruction of the Jewish nation in order to encourage readers to apply the example of Jerusalem to present-day London. As Morwen had noted in his preface to the reader, "we should learne to know good from euyl" and by "the appliyng of their [the Jews'] deedes vnto our maners, with consydering the euent and successe they hadde of theyr actions, we may take eyther an example, or some admonition, or occasion to amende our lyues." He thereby emphasized a vital nexus between suffering and sin: the Jews are inflicted with "diuers kindes of miserie" as a consequence of their own iniquity ("they fell from GOD").[10]

Invariably, historical antecedents of *The Jewes Tragedy* predicated the Chosen People's fall upon their failure to correctly interpret Christ's strenuous warnings of impending calamity. Morwen's most memorable emulator, Thomas Nashe, citing Christ's prophecy about Jerusalem's destruction in Luke 19, readily

concluded: "In these words most euidently you see, he [Christ] cleereth himselfe, and leaueth them [the Jews] vnexcusable."[11] Unlike the "Temple-bosting
Iewes," who dismiss his warning, Nashe's Savior laments bitterly the impending alienation of his people: "O *Ierusalem, Ierusalem*, all this might'st thou have
auoyded . . . Saue thy selfe as well as thou mayst, for I haue forsaken thee; to
desolation haue I resigned thee."[12] But all to no avail.

A similar theme emerges in *Canaan's Calamitie* (1618) composed by T.D., variously identified as either Thomas Dekker or Thomas Delony. In a prefatory address
to the "Gentleman Reader's health," the 1677 version styles itself as a "Mourning
Song of Jerusalem's sorrows, whose destruction was prophesied by our Lord Jesus
Christ, while he lived among them: notwithstanding they neither regarded, nor
believed his words." T.D. emphasizes the heady recklessness of the "cursed Jews"
who, rather than quake at the enormity of their transgression, instead "cried with
one consent saying: His blood be on us and on our Children. Which wicked wish
of theirs the Lord brought to pass within a short time after . . . At what time
both City and Temple was brought to utter confusion: the misery whereof was so
extream, as the like was never before nor since."[13] In this sense, Nashe and T.D.'s
texts confirm the philosophy already at the core of Thomas Beard's influential
and oft-reprinted *The theatre of God's judgements* (1597), a vigorous denunciation
of human transgression that reinforced the view of history as "God's extra-biblical
revelation of himself," to quote Ronald J. VanderMolen.[14] In a by-now familiar
diatribe, Beard ascribes Jerusalem's fate to God's "fearfull indignation," motivated
by the "hainous" offences of the Jews, who "despise[ed] and reiect[ed] the Lord of
glory, whom God hath sent amongst them for their saluation."[15]

In addition to Christ's prophecy in Luke 19, it was traditionally reported
that signs and portents abounded in the weeks leading up to the siege. These
included a star shaped like a sword, a fiery comet, a strange light that spread
over the altar and Temple on the night of the Feast of Sweet Bread, a sacrificial
cow that gave birth to a lamb at that very feast, the massive Temple gate that
flew open of its own accord, a phantom army, a disembodied voice in the Temple that cried "Let vs goe hence" on the feast of Passover, and a rustic prophet
who pronounced the city's impending devastation.[16] Even Lodge's translation of Josephus, which focuses on factionalism in a manner that anticipates
Heminge's analysis of civil conflict, listed the omens in exhaustive detail before
concluding: "Thus the Iewes interpreted some of the signes as they pleased, and
at others they laughed, till by the ruine of their country, and their own woful
ouerthrowe, their iniquity appeared."[17]

Heminge's seventeenth-century predecessors and contemporaries alike were
all fixated upon the apocalyptic warnings presented to the Jews and their glib

dismissal of them. It has been argued that the providentialist interpretation of Jerusalem's fall, rife with "fearful signs" and wonders, was compelling precisely because it stoked the early modern fixation with providential ephemera. Alexandra Walsham observes that "no Protestant minister could pass up the opportunity afforded by a major conflagration, blizzard, drought, inundation, or epidemic to deliver a thundering diatribe on the doctrine of divine judgements." She even suggests that Morwen's version of the omens bears traces of the medieval prophetic legend of the Fifteen Signs before Doomsday—"a succession of portents it was believed would appear in the fortnight directly leading up to the Last Judgement." Groves likewise reminds us that Josephan portents "were a focus of early modern eschatological enthusiasm, as it was believed that the events which had foretold the destruction of the Temple would likewise precede the end of the world."[18] This was particularly true of the Civil War years as well as the lead up to the Restoration, when "reports of aerial armies and fiery swords hanging in the skies" saturated the popular press.

We saw something of this preoccupation in the plague literature discussed in chapter 2. Indeed, detailed descriptions of supernatural phenomena featured in almost every retelling of the Jerusalem story, regardless of the genre. Popular ballads, for instance, relished descriptions of the many signs and wonders that manifested on the eve of the siege. Notable among such ballads are *Of the horyble and woful destruccion of Jerusalem* by John Barker (1569), *A new ballad of the destruccion of Jerusalem* (1586), *A Warning or lanthorn to London* (1603), *A Warning to all England by the doleful destruccion of Jerusalem* (1604), and *A doleful destruction of Faire Jerusalem* (1624). Even a scientific tract on meteors such as Abraham Fleming's translation of Friedrich Nausea's *A Treatise of Blazing Starres in Generall* (1618) was interested in the "signs and tokens" that "Almighty God useth for more certainety of forewarning," recalling as an example "a sign in the ayre of *Titus and Vespasian*; his huge hoast against *Ierusalem*, to lay it waste; armed men with speares and lances, running to and fro in warlike wise."[19] Similarly, *The Levellers Almanack* (1651) recalled such "sounding of Trumpets, and beating of Drums in the Ayr," and prayed that "God avert those calamities from these Nations, and especially England."[20]

As may be imagined, then, the supernatural was emphasized in the many other narratives devoted to Jerusalem's fall. In *Christ's Teares*, Nashe observed that "It is not vnknown, by how many & sundry waies GOD spake by Visions, Dreames, Prophecies, and Wonders, to his chosen *Ierusalem*, onely to moue his chosen *Ierusalem* wholie to cleaue vnto him."[21] Nashe recorded that in the days leading up to the destruction, "the Element was ouer-hung with prodigies" as God "emblazond the ayre with the tokens of his terror." Astronomical

Apparitions in the sky during the siege of Jerusalem in R.D.'s *The strange and prodigious religions, customs, and manners, of sundry nations,* 1688. (Reproduced by permission of the Houghton Library, Harvard University)

anomalies abounded: "The Sunne did shyne all day as it is wont at his Euening going downe. The Moone had her pale-siluer face iron spotted with freckle-imitating blood-sprincklings; and for her dimme frostie circle, a blacke inckie hood embayling her bright head."[22] The Temple precincts are specially demar-cated as a site for supernatural occurrences. The raven—that favorite bird of ill-omen—"(with a fearefull croking cry) beate, fluttred, and clasht against the windowes. A hideous dismal Owle (exceeding all her kind in deformity and quantity) in the Temple-porche built her nest. From vnder the Altar there issued penetrating plangorous-howlings and gastlie dead-mens grones."[23] Jeru-salem's sinfulness, as befitting her status as navel, disrupts also the natural rhythms of the earth "which left to be so fruitfull as it wont."[24]

John Taylor's *The Severall Sieges, Assaults, Sackings, and Final destruction of the Famous, Ancient, and Memorable Citty of Jerusalem* (1616), which presents "Our Savior, weeping on the Mount" and prophesying the wrack of the city, likewise catalogued the myriad supernatural phenomena—comet, phantom army, mysterious voice, monstrous sacrifice—that presaged destruction.[25] *Canaan's Calamitie* also expends considerable effort detailing the harbingers of Jerusalem's doom, the "Signs and Tokens shewed before the Destruction, Alluring the Jewes to repentance," and "their little regard thereof, interpreting all things to be for the best, flattering themselves in their sins."[26] T.D. insists that God heaped wonder upon wonder

> All to reclaim them [the Jews] from iniquity:
> That so he might remoue his plagues away,
> Which threatened their destruction every day,

only to have the Jews dismiss His warnings with unparalleled insolence.[27] Though the omens "many men amazed, / When they beheld the uncouth sight so strange," they "did interpret to the best, / Thinking themselves above all oth-ers blest."[28] They are "cock-sure" even as they "stand upon the brink of desola-tion." In conclusion, T.D. begs "All faithful Christians [to] warning take by this, / Interpret not Gods fearful signs amiss."[29] In 1677, John Crowne's spectacular heroic drama *The Destruction of Jerusalem by Titus Vespasian* (1677) returned to the familiar lament for the Jews' failure to interpret the prognostications of their doom.[30] Crowne's Jerusalem is a magical space where "the stormy air is fill'd with prodigy / A numerous Army in the skye appears, *every troop a bloody banner bears*," and the ghost of Herod shrieks calamity from the battlements (1.2.3).[31]

Given this pervasive construction of Jerusalem's prodigy-plagued destruc-tion as divine punishment, *The Jewes Tragedy* may be expected to adhere strictly to the providentialist tradition. Even if "authentick" is hardly the apt epithet for Morwen's mangled account of Josephus's history, with its Christian interpolations and anachronistic justifications, it bore the weight of authority for early modern English readers eager to consume stories of Jerusalem's devastation. Indeed, Heminge's eschewal of the charged Protestant rhetoric of Jerusalem's destruction is more akin to Lodge's repudiation of the same in *The Lamentable and Tragicall Historie*—though there is no evidence that Heminge used Lodge as his source. True, the emphasis on political hostility over Christian moralizing fractures the providentialist paradigm of divine retribution for deicide in a manner akin to Lodge, but in curtailing the supernatural dimension, I would hold that *The Jewes Tragedy* goes one step further.

Politics over Providence

In Heminge's play, Vespasian and Titus are no longer the instruments of divine vengeance, and the Jews are not destroyed for killing Christ. The impetus behind the tragic events of the siege is entirely secular and terrestrial. A brief summary of the plot shows that *The Jewes Tragedy* offers the lesson of the deleterious consequences of relentless imperial ambition when provoked by territorial unrest. The play opens in Nero's Rome, to which the Jewish King Agrippa, a Roman puppet, flees in fear from insurgents. The Roman commander Vespatian (Heminge's spelling), recently victorious over the Britons, is deployed to Judaea to quell the uprising led by the nefarious trifecta of Jehochannan, Skimeon (the historical Simeon), and Eleazar, the son of the High Priest.[32] At this point, the action moves to Jerusalem. Tensions mount between the old order symbolized by the High Priest Ananias and his cohort—who are naturally wary of Rome's military might—and the hot-headed rebels. The historical Josephus or Joseph (as he is named in the dramatis personae) then makes his appearance as a captain in the Jewish Guard and son of the priest Gorion.[33] Joseph becomes increasingly aware that his suffering countrymen are powerless to withstand the Roman juggernaut, and casts his lot with Rome. Scenes of terrible suffering follow as the obdurate zealots prove determined to pursue personal vendettas at the cost of the Jewish nation. Notable among these is Eleazar's conspiracy to topple his father, the High Priest, and his descent into madness following the patricide. Act 4 contains scenes of the piteous suffering of the besieged Jews, and, of course, the notorious Miriam who consumes her son in due course. The play climaxes with a desperate Jehochannan setting fire to the Temple to precipitate the final destruction of Jewish life as it was. A victorious but somber Titus confers the herculean task of restoration upon

Joseph. In the same breath as the commander promises that "*Romes* General / Will find a way to raise your ruin'd State," he acknowledges that "The gods are just; we must submit to fate" (5.8.195–96).

It is already evident that *The Jewes Tragedy*, while distilling the essential narrative of Jerusalem's destruction, makes key alterations by way of original characters and scenes, all of which reinforce the play's commitment to eschewing supernatural explanations. The patricide subplot is Heminge's invention, as is the character of a mercenary, Zareck, whom he has inciting infighting among the insurgents.[34] Heminge also takes the liberty of promoting Joseph, who escapes the fate of his historical prototype. There is no suggestion that the Joseph of *The Jewes Tragedy* will live out his remaining years in Rome writing pro-Roman histories of his people's devastation.

That said, it is Heminge's neglect of the Josephan portents that constitutes the truly radical divergence from traditional accounts of Jerusalem's destruction. Indeed, for a play that is longer than *King Lear*, it is remarkable that *The Jewes Tragedy* should devote less than ten lines overall to describing the standard signs of divine displeasure. Contrary to Fredson Bowers's assessment that the "supernatural is freely employed for portents,"[35] Heminge makes only the briefest allusions to the traditional omens associated with the siege story. All we get is the mysterious voice in the Temple, and a blink-and-you-miss-it mention of a flaming sword in the sky:

> [Chorus] A bloody Sword hangs blazing in the Sky?
> A Strange and uncouth voice was heard to cry,
> *Come let's away from hence?* The Iron gate
> Ope's of it self to let in Jewries fate:
> To tell ye more my aking heart would break. (4.11.9–13)

Unlike the denizens of Nashe's "gorgious strumpt, *Ierusalem*," who merely scoff at the omens, the Chorus in *The Jewes Tragedy* seems baffled by the impending apocalypse. Its tone suggests wonderment, confusion, a hint of disbelief—the struggle of a people in shock whose "aking heart[s]" and minds are too bruised to make any sense of what they have heard and witnessed. But rather than exploit the moment, Heminge, who otherwise revels in emotional excess, disregards the phantasmagoria and their effect. The ghostly voice is mentioned only once more, by an "amazed" Skimeon just as the Temple is set on fire (5.7.25–26). All other portents of Jerusalem's fall are expunged. When providential rhetoric is employed, it is rid of the supernatural: Ananias's terrified proclamation of a "prodigious sight" in Act 4 refers not to a comet or ghostly army, but rather to

the sight of his treacherous son poised over him with blade drawn (3.5.5). The
rest is silence.

Indeed, *The Jewes Tragedy* consistently betrays a reluctance to infuse the
political with the providential. Consider, for instance, Act 1, Scene 1, which
takes place in the fractious court of Nero, and offers a striking attempt to shift
away from omens and auguries. The opening speech is loaded with Nero's enu-
meration of "signes prodigious," which he interprets as harbingers of Rome's
impending military ruin:

> Our Bulls for Offerings to the God of War
> Fall dead untoucht by hand of Holy Priest;
> And such as wounded dye by sacred Knife,
> Their Intrails spotted tells us all's not well,
> The Gods are sure displeas'd. (1.1.9–13)

To be sure, Nero's court is mired in prestidigitation with none more super-
stitious and charm-ridden than the emperor himself. But though Nero's
frantic mind demands the assurances of "some luckie signs" (1.1.38) when he
commands the priests to offer sacrifice upon sacrifice, his courtiers exhibit
discomfiture at their emperor's dependence on auguries, and attempt to shift
the conversation to the terrestrial—specifically to the vicissitudes of empire-
building. In response to Nero's fretting, a nobleman tersely reminds his
emperor that

> Our War . . . can import no less,
> The *Persians'*, *Grecians'*, and the *Galls'* revolts,
> With ill success in *Jewry*, these can tell
> Most mighty *Cesar*, that all is not well. (1.1.14–17)

The implications are unmistakable: Nero does not need omens; the truly
meaningful signs are earthier and bloodier than the spotted entrails of a bull.
The real problem in Jerusalem is the "fury of a frantick mind, / The factious
Commons in their heat of blood" (1.1.60–61). If that were not enough, Heminge
has Nero misread the signs. When Vespatian arrives in triumph to announce
a glorious victory over the Britons, Nero, apparently forgetting his previous
gloomy interpretation of the auguries, determines that the "Gods are pleas'd
indeed" (1.1.105). Even before we get to Heminge's portent-light Jerusalem,
then, the Roman emperor's whimsical flip-flopping suggests that divinations
and apocalyptic prophecies will count for very little in this world.

From the outset, the play drives a wedge between political crises and "providential ephemera" (to borrow Walsham's phrase), and discards the latter.
When, on rare occasions, phantasmagoria do feature in *The Jewes Tragedy*,
they signify individual rather than collective guilt. Persiphone and the Three
Furies, classical figures for whom there is no historical narrative precedent,
emanate from the fevered dreams of Eleazar, who swiftly sinks into madness
upon murdering his father. But his "ghastly apparitions" signify on a purely
private level. They have no world historical connotation. Nor do they utter any
of the contingent prophecies ("repent, or else") seen in other accounts of the
siege. Persiphone and the Furies give Eleazar a taste of the inexorable fate that
awaits him personally: the horrors of hell. Rather than warn, they function in
a punitive capacity.

The bias against the supernatural only intensifies in subsequent scenes, as
the reader is plunged into the gritty details of the rebellion precipitated by
Jehochannan and Skimeon, who chafe bitterly under Roman yoke. When characters repeat themselves or echo one another, their talk is never of omens but,
rather, of the gravity of the political situation. The plight of the "factious Commons," first mentioned in the opening scene in the Roman court, is invoked in
the very next scene by the zealots in Jerusalem, who rage openly at the myopic
obduracy of their compatriots obsessed only with quotidian survival. Skimeon
and Jehochannan berate the "ragged multitude" (1.2.20) who resist their incite-
ment to rebellion because their

> stupid brains are stuft with nothing else
> But their mechanick skill, whose highest strain
> Of Cunning is to get some musty meat
> To feed the hungry maw, or ragged clothes
> To cover nakednesse. (1.2.36–40)

It is telling that our first perspective on Jerusalem comes from the seditionists—whose voices, though biased, are memorable—alerting the audience
immediately to the social and political conflicts that will be the Jews' true undoing. The leitmotif of the "factious Commons" returns in Act 2, Scene 3, with
Joseph's captain fearing that they have finally been "seduc't / And gather head
against the sacred priests" (5–6).

In addition to abjuring the Christian reading of the fall of Jerusalem, *The
Jewes Tragedy* balks at interpreting the horrors of besiegement—war, famine,
death, exile—as divine punishment. The High Priest, Ananias, takes recourse
to a non-religious explanation for Jerusalem's swift decline:

O *Jerusalem*! Is thy decrepid Age already come!
Or art thou hastned by untimely means
To end thy dayes of honor? (1.4.112–15)

If the reference to the "decrepid Age already come" suggests the fulfillment of
a dire divine prophecy, then that prophecy is not one we ever hear. Instead,
The Jewes Tragedy is all about the "untimely means": its investment is in the
"heavy weight / Of sad oppression" under which "wretched Jewry" labors
(1.4.67–68).

Where writers like Nashe and T.D. pepper their narratives with lurid
descriptions of the providential signs heralding divine castigation ("the many
and sundry waies GOD spake"), Heminge emphasizes repeatedly the prevailing socioeconomic and political predicament. Jehochannan and Skimeon
express outrage at having to submit to Rome's puppet-prince in Judaea. Agrippa
is a "mungril Prince," a "sacriligious thief," "Bastard-Issue, sprung from *Herod's*
Race, / Of low discent in bloud, obscure and base" (1.4.71–75). Meanwhile,
the people are a "raving multitude [who] will not endure / To pay the *Roman-
tribute*" (1.4.181–82). As Ananias bemoans to Gorion:

Are not our Towers defac't! our Walls unbuilt?
Our Forces weakened, and our treasure spent?
Our countrey ruinate, our people too
Imbroile in native blood? O *Gorion* see,
Judaea wars with *Rome*, *Rome* with the world,
The world is conquer'd, and yet *Jewry* stands
In opposition. (1.4.168–74)

Ananias's lament echoes Gorion's own threnody for the "weakness of our State"
and the "furious tempest" that drives Jerusalem "on the Rocks / Of Forreign and
Domestick Enemies" (1.4.177–80).

In Act 2, Scene 3, it is Joseph who takes up the dirge when he describes the
"maze of misery" in which "the State of Jewry stands," and the impossible choice
it faces. Should the Jews

prise our Honours, or our Countreys good,
We must with resolution bid defiance to *Vespatian*.
If we embrace a peace, we raise a war
Amongst our selves; and so we make a breach
For *Rome* to enter. (2.3.36–40)

Though Joseph's acknowledgment in Act 4 of the inevitability of Jewish defeat may suggest a providentialist bias ("the heavens have fore-decreed your over-throw"), it is folded into a larger commentary on Rome's martial prowess: Vespatian's cavalry numbers ten thousand and his infantry is forty thousand strong. Rather than dwell on their past transgressions (the killing of Christ, for example), the Jews in Heminge's play look to their political counterparts, figured as the colossus of Nebuchadnezzar's dream, to realize their doom is sealed:

> The great *Caldeans Golden Head* is laid,
> The mighty *Persians silver Arms* are lopt;
> The *Grecian thighs of brass* are broken down:
> What's then remaining but those *Iron Legs*
> On which the sturdy Roman Empire stands,
> And stamps the World to Powder: Ah my Lords
> Will ye contend with Fate? (4.4.25–31)

Joseph underscores the Jews' defeat as one that grows organically out of preva-lent political conditions. The "sturdy" Roman war machine is the natural inher-itor of the imperial mantle of the once-great Chaldeans, Persians, and Greeks whose might now lies shattered like a broken colossus. There is little sense that Rome's victory over the Jews is providentially predetermined or supernaturally reinforced by a justly wrathful Judeo-Christian entity seeking vengeance for the death of His Son.

Heminge's Fractured World

The Jewes Tragedy's refusal to stage divine punishment allows it, instead, to lay extensive political groundwork to explain the tragic events of the siege. The question is why the play makes this choice when providential rhetoric featured prominently in the discourse of Heminge's contemporaries, not to mention in the source material. Heminge did not need to privilege the political over the providential, and yet he obviously did. I posit that his departure from the pulpit and the press may be best understood in the context of the vitiated political and religious atmosphere of the mid-late 1620s.

Recall that *The Jewes Tragedy* was composed at a time when England was still laboring under Charles I's ill-advised military campaigns against the Euro-pean powers. It is also worth noting that, unlike his pacifist father, Charles spent nearly half of his reign at war—with Spain and France as much as with his own subjects. His foreign policy in the early years was marked by European conflicts: the breakdown of his marriage negotiations with the Spanish Infanta, for one, escalated the tensions that had resurfaced during the last years of James I's reign and manifested in an ill-considered war in 1625, encouraged by the Duke of Buckingham, that involved combat both on land and sea. The English forces were dogged by defeat, most notably at Cadiz where their lack of military discipline and their inferior technology were embarrassingly evident. Charles, however, turned a blind eye to the debacle and busied himself instead with the French Huguenots at La Rochelle. But instead of suppressing that Protestant group as he had agreed to do—one of the secret conditions of his marriage to the Catholic Henrietta Maria—he reneged and mounted an ill-conceived defense of the fortress, thereby driving a wedge between the French and the English crowns. With one disgraceful defeat following another, Parliament refused to finance the king's wars, thereby driving Charles to extraordinarily punitive lengths that further alienated him and his cause.

It is in this context therefore that we may comprehend Heminge's preoccupation with the Jewish rebels' foolhardy determination to prosecute war against a powerful enemy. Given the stalemate caused by Parliament's refusal to finance the king's wars, it is only fitting that Heminge presents the Jews' tragedy as the natural outcome of a poorly conceived military offensive against an imperial superpower, aggravated by turbulent partisan politics. Judaea's campaign against the Romans is dogged by dissension in the ranks, with the hotheaded younger generation chafing at the cautious strategy of the old guard who would rather placate the Romans than make war on them. The villainous Eleazar assigns responsibility for the "strange distraction of the times" to the misgovernment of those "whose poor decrepid brains are fitter far / For drowsing pillows, than for bloody war" (3.2.47–48), an accusation echoed by his co-conspirator Jehochannan when he curses "the black tempest of a shipwrackt State" (3.5.85). In a memorable encounter with his father in Act 3, Eleazar fuses his personal hatred of Ananias with the larger woes of the government:

> Look, look but upon thy self, and see
> Of what decrepped age and misery
> Thou art compos'd: behold the reeling State
> Distracted, feeble, sick, and ruinate,
> Turn'd topsie-turvie by thy doating brain. (3.5.27–31)

Like his fellow rebels, Eleazar assigns much of the responsibility for Jerusalem's decline to the enfeebled sensibilities of the Sanhedrin, whose "doating" suggests both overindulgence and senility. Skimeon concurs: in a time when Jewry lives in a "hodgepodge of confusion," he resents that his initiative should be counter-manded by "babling Priests" such that the "rough sword of War / [Is] guided by the rusty hand of Peace" (1.2.49–51). The strident cacophony of voices demand-ing war in debilitated Jerusalem would have been unnervingly familiar to the witnesses of Charles's mulish military ambitions.

As factionalism threatened to become the real devil of the Civil War years, the infighting associated with the siege came to be lamented by preachers and historians alike. William Hampton, whose *Proclamation of Warre from the Lord of Hosts* (1627) was published in the same decade that Heminge is believed to have composed *The Jewes Tragedy*, declared that "*Ierusalem* had not so soone beene wonne by *Vespatians* sonne, had it not beene for ciuill discord within the Citie; and nothing [is] more to bee feared for the ruine of our Nation, then ciuill dissention, domesticall foes."[36] In a moment of supreme irony, the always divisive Archbishop Laud (1573–1645), preaching on Psalm 122.3 ("Jerusalem is built as a City that is at unity in itself"), blamed factionalism for the city's vul-nerability to "forraine malice" for "faction within the walls was a helpe to *Titus*, and his siege without."[37] In 1658, John Spencer, notable Hebraist and Master of Corpus Christi College, likewise determined that "a Kingdome diuided within it self cannot long stand."[38] While not necessarily superseding the providential-ist narrative, it would seem that Jerusalem's fractured political world was start-ing to make a big impression.

Debates over Providence

Topical in its staging of military turmoil exacerbated by civil discord, *The Jewes Tragedy* was equally influenced by the urgent debates on the role of providence, as we shall see below. Indeed, this background is crucial to comprehending the significance of Heminge's decision to construct the play as he did. Carol Morley maintains that Heminge may have been less interested in perpetuating the providentialist narrative because "it is unlikely that [his] religious sympa-thies were sufficiently Low Church, or 'godly,' to engage with Morwyng's own doctrine."[39] But I maintain that the contemporary political scene—fractured, polemical, at once fascinated and repelled by providentialism—equally influ-enced Heminge's artistic choices.

It is here that we must grapple with the raging Arminian controversy. Charles's Continental wars coincided with an internal rift in the Church of England that took the shape of fierce disputes over questions of predestina-tion, contingency, and human agency.[40] For scholars like Nicholas Tyacke, the "basic issue" plaguing the late 1620s was the conflict between alleged Calvinist and Arminian tenets—translated as the question of "divine determinism versus human free will."[41] Arminianism, named for the Dutch theologian Jacobus Arminius (1560–1609), placed doctrinal emphasis upon free will in marked contrast to the perceived Calvinist credo. In his view, divine providence was neither causative nor deterministic. Rather, God maintained providential control over the world primarily by setting moral precepts that ought to be obeyed. To quote Arminius in "On the Providence of God," providence "preserves, regulates, governs, and directs all things" and "nothing in the world happens fortuitously or by chance." Furthermore, "nothing can be done without the will of God, not even any of those things which are done in opposition to it; only we must preserve a distinction between good actions and evil ones, by saying, that God both wills and performs good acts but that He only freely permits those which are evil."[42] Though Arminius believed that God preserved, regulated, and directed all things, he nevertheless imagined a scope for the mediation of the human will. Consequently, as Tyacke notes, Arminius's contemporaries felt that he had seriously curtailed and circumscribed divine providence by shifting control of human history from the First Cause to second causes, from a sovereign and determinist deity to autonomous human beings.

Of course, Augustine had formulated the idea that secular history could have no meaning without reference to divine providence and this notion had been avidly enforced by Protestant reformers such as John Calvin and Philip Melanchthon. Although Calvin insisted that "nothing happens except what is knowingly and willingly decreed" by God, he decried the capacity of human beings to discern divine will based on historical observation, and repeatedly warned his readers to refrain from presuming to pass precipitate judgment on things unknown.[43] Yet if Calvin maintained that the universe was deterministic and that nothing was a matter of chance or contingency, he was also reluctant to employ secular history as a simple index of divine disposition. Even as "nothing happens but what [God] has knowingly and willingly decreed . . . as the order, method, end, and necessity of events, are, for the most part, hidden in the counsel of God, they have the appearance of being fortuitous."[44] In *Tvvo Godly and Notable Sermons*, Calvin again cautions "when we speak of the counsel of God, we may not always dispute, who hath so induced him we may not imagine reasons, as to say, for this cause hath God so determined, or wherefore would he do so."[45]

By Heminge's day, prominent religious figures such as George Hakewill (1578–1649), author of *An Answere to a Treatise Written by D. Carrier* (1616) and *An Apologie of the Power and Providence of God in the Government of the*

World (1627), likewise criticized those who would "turn every accident into an argument for their own purposes."[46] Hakewill stressed final judgment— "judgment after this life, rewarding every man according to what he hath done in the flesh"—rather than judgment in history.[47] Though he believed in "particular providence," he deemed it mysterious and beyond human discernment and therefore was at pains to avoid citing examples in which God judges humans using providentially ordained suffering.[48] But English divines such as William Prynne, Henry Burton, John Bastwick, and John Rous railed against Arminian sympathizers for diminishing God's power by "depriving him, not onely of his all-disposing prouidence . . . but likewise of his absolute soueraigne power ouer all his creatures."[49] Like Thomas Beard, who famously cited the Roman destruction of Jerusalem as a prime example of divine wrath in *The theatre of God's iudgements*, they too regarded the ordinary course of history as the special revelation of God's judgments.

Although Tyacke's critics have questioned his claim that the rapid rise of Arminianism in the 1620s destroyed Calvinist consensus,[50] they generally agree that Arminianism played a role in the religious and political climate of Heminge's day. The debate over predestination was highly topical and the merits of Calvinism versus Arminianism were hotly debated at the York House conference of 1626. Charles himself was accused of harboring pro-Arminian sympathies that many of his detractors condemned as pro-Spanish. The last Parliament before Charles I's Personal Rule (1628–29) again spent a considerable time debating what they saw as the encroachment of Arminianism. Charges of heterodoxy were leveled, among others, at Charles's favorite, the then-prelate William Laud who had been made Privy Councilor in 1627, and it was widely claimed that Arminians were receiving preferment in ecclesiastical appointments.

Additionally, it is possible to discern a connection (as Tyacke did) between Arminian thought in the late 1620s and the "anti-determinist" views of Epicurean atomists. In *English Epicures and Stoics*, Reid Barbour agrees that Epicurean philosophy featured largely in Stuart England, manifesting in debates on the scope and reach of God's providence in relationship to human intention and endeavor, which in turn inevitably led to questions about the "idleness or activity of God."[51] Barbour cites numerous examples of the Epicurean insistence on free will, including George Sandys's popular commentary on Ovid, which acknowledges the same. But it was Thomas Jackson's *The Treatise of the Divine Essence and Attributes* (1628) that made a concerted attempt to reconcile providence with an element of fortuity.

Jackson also fell under suspicion for advocating views similar to Arminianism, though the extent of his perceived anti-Calvinism has been debated by Tyacke as well as by Peter White.[52] For Jackson, "all real effects, all events possible, whether necessary, causal, or contingent, are eminently contained, the perfect knowledge of his [God's] own essence necessarily includes the perfect knowledge, not only of all things that have been, are or shall be, but of all things that might have been or possibly may be."[53] In other words, contingency as well as necessity could be decreed; freedom of choice need not be incompatible with the immutability of the divine will. Jackson was concerned that his argument for some measure of free will would be misinterpreted as a "heathen epicurean" attack against providence. Nevertheless, as Barbour observes, he continued to strive for a middle ground between "the perfections of providence" and "the Epicurean allowance of contingency, in a definition of divine decrees that tends to 'hold the mean between chance or fortune and absolute necessity.'"[54]

It is not surprising, therefore, that the contentious Arminian question of the degree of free will and human agency should have been reckoned alongside calculations of the operation of chance in the universe.[55] When Thomas Gataker undertook to assess the role of chance in everyday life in *Of the Nature and Use of Lots: A Treatise Historicall and Theologicall* (1618, enlarged and reprinted 1627), he did so partially in opposition to the clerics who advocated an unrelentingly deterministic providence. Gataker sought to carefully distinguish between "natural" lots that depended on chance and biblical lots, which were divinely determined.[56] It strikes me that Heminge's awareness of this discourse is suggested by his inclusion of two scenes in *The Jewes Tragedy* that deal with the casting of lots in which the characters choose to interpret the outcome as proof of heavenly direction.[57] The employment of the lottery system as a decision-making device in *The Jewes Tragedy* occurs first in Act 1, Scene 4, and is promoted by the High Priest himself, who casts lots to apportion the respective commands of those sworn to protect Judaea from the Romans: Eleazar gets charge over the Edomites, Joseph is given Galilee, and the Sanhedrin takes Jerusalem. The more memorable equation of providential intervention with the lottery system occurs in Act 2, Scene 7, when Joseph, gravely wounded and in danger of being set upon by his own starving cohort, entrusts his fate to the heavens by casting lots to determine who shall be killed and consumed first.

Joseph's recourse to the lottery system is ostensibly motivated by the desire to "free each person from the bloody guilt / Of wilfull slaughter" (104–5). As Joseph explains to his soldiers, they will

unite our selves by two and two,
Then cast by lots which couple shall dye first:

The couple first to dye shall likewise cast
Which of them two shall kill his fellow . . . (2.7.109–12)

But Joseph has no intention of dying "Without his Makers leave," and he clearly
believes that his preservation through the lottery system is miraculous. The
diverse application of the lottery system in *The Jewes Tragedy* gives credence
to Keith Thomas's assertion in *Religion and the Decline of Magic* that the casting of lots in the seventeenth century was still regarded as a "readily available
instrument for settling daily problems with God's aid," despite the fact that
its use incurred the disapprobation of Church leaders.[58] Certainly, Ananias
and Joseph's desperation to believe that their respective lotteries are divinely
directed is comprehensible given that they exist in a world apparently devoid
of God's presence. But one imagines that in the context of the spirited coeval
debates on contingency, agency, and providence, Heminge's potential audience
may have been more ambivalent in their response to the lottery scenes.

The point of this discussion on shifting providential perspectives in the late
1620s is not to postulate that Heminge was Arminian or Epicurean. Rather,
it is to observe that Heminge's preoccupation with the civic dimension of his
story, and generally careful abjuration of providentialist rhetoric, may be attributed, at least partially, to the fact that he wrote in a world that relentlessly, even
tendentiously, deliberated the scope of divine providence and its role in secular
political affairs. For all its messy plotting and ill-conceived characterization,
The Jewes Tragedy's commitment to politics over prodigies reveals it to have
been a perspicacious work. Its author was attuned not only to fashionable histories but also equally to the fluctuations in contemporary political and theological discourse, and was deeply sensitive to the fissures in his world.

Post-Restoration: Secular Drives

Despite its political and theological nuance, *The Jewes Tragedy* held little appeal
prior to the closing of the theaters, when recycled plays were all the rage. By the
time it was published, however, the theatrical and political scenes had under-
gone remarkable change. Recent scholarship posits that the seventeenth century became increasingly aware of providentialism as a dangerously politicized
discourse. Walsham has persuasively argued that, in the years leading up to
the English Civil War, every phenomena became the sign of divine displeasure
against the Laudian and Caroline regime, and Laura Lunger Knoppers likewise
notes that, in the early Restoration, spectacular natural disasters became "contested sites, open to varied and contradictory interpretations."[59] For Michael

Witmore, "what changed during the sixteenth and seventeenth centuries was not the kinds of causes (natural or supernatural) that could be assigned to strange phenomena, but rather the kind of divine purpose or intention these phenomena were understood to express." He suggests that the potential for "divergent" and "disruptive interpretations" of the meaning of wonders led natural philosophers to "eschew open speculation on the value of wonders as signs as the seventeenth century progressed."[60]

As prophecies and prodigies increasingly became pawns and weapons of sectarian conflict, they became less valuable as reliable signs of divine intention. Walsham's study surmises that the continued manipulation of ephemera by unscrupulous propagandists probably contributed to undermining the credibility of both the discourse and the genre, especially in the second half of the seventeenth century, as familiarity with the "strange but true" gradually bred contempt. Certainly, in the aftermath of bloody civil strife readers grew increasingly suspicious about the authenticity of individual prodigies, especially those that were commandeered to buttress an enemy cause.[61] Paul Boyer calls attention to the way Charles II's accession "cooled [the] orgy of apocalypticism" that had so beset the years of the Civil War.[62] Apocalyptic or providentialist language was seen as the provenance of the Puritan revolutionaries against which Charles II's court, the "new Rome," embodied rational Augustan values. Jonathan Rogers correspondingly argues that the Civil War radicals, "always on the lookout for portents of doom, were themselves portrayed as a kind of portent—a gross aberration of the natural order" in the immediate aftermath of the Restoration.[63]

Rogers's reading is borne out by Abraham Cowley's exuberant *Ode on the Majesties Restauration and Return* (1660), which denounces explicitly the providentialist fervor of the radicals who discerned congruency between besieged Jerusalem and England.[64] Cowley recalls the terrible predictions that "God's Triumvirate of Desolation," the "three dreadfull *Angels* . . . / Of Famine, Sword and Plague" (103–4), would fall upon England in the same way that they had beset Jerusalem, and notes that frightened Englishmen read

th' *Instructive Histories* which tell
Of all those endless mischiefs that befell,
The *Sacred Town* which *God* had lov'd so well. (114–16)

In the glow cast by Charles's return, Cowley could dismiss those purveyors of apocalyptic nightmares as nothing more than "Vain men" who "thought the Divine Power to find / In the fierce *Thunder* and the violent *Wind* (137–38), and dismantle their prodigies with ease:[65]

Wher's now that *Ignis Fatuus* which e're-while
Mis-lead our *wandring Isle?*
Wher's the *Imposter Cromwel* gon?
Where's now that *Falling-star* his *Son?*
Where's now that *large Comet* now whose raging flame
So fatal to our *Monarchy* became?
Which o're our heads in such proud horror stood,
Insatiate with our *Ruine* and our *Blood?*
The *fiery Tayl* did to vast length extend;
And twice for want of *Fuel* did expire. (207–16)

The anonymous *Vox Populi* of 1660 corroborates Cowley's anti-apocalyptic, anti-prodigious stance: "But now those Meteors which we feared and felt / Are by a Northern Star to vapours melt."[66] The doomsday portents of the 1650s and 1660s dwindle in the radiance of the pure shining star of Charles II's majesty. As Steven Zwicker observes, the early Restoration was distinguished by the way the royalists shied away from absolute claims of biblical prophecy to embrace a more stable Augustan rhetoric.[67]

Because Heminge steers clear of presenting Jerusalem's destruction as providential, his play ends up interrogating the very narration and transmission of history. Of course, the Restoration ethos did not entirely or uniformly discard the providential idiom.[68] In John Dryden's *Astraea Redux: A Poem on the Happy Restoration & Return of His Sacred Majesty Charles the Second* (1660), Charles, "toss'd by Fate" (51), waits for "Heav'n's prefixed hour" (147).[69] The Royal Proclamation of June 5, 1660, was likewise characterized by providential rhetoric praising "Almighty God" for manifesting "his own Immediate Goodness Wisdom and Power, in his Late Providence towards us and our Kingdoms" and who "by the Interposition of his own Power and Wisdom, after a long and tedious Exile returned us Home to our People."[70] A few years later in 1666, portentous events such as the plague and Great Fire would generate a further storm of belligerent providentialist discourse with writers such as the author of *A Short Narrative of the late Dreadful Fire in London* feeling compelled to illustrate "the dreadful effects of providence."[71] Like so much popular literature on Jerusalem's destruction, these narratives articulate an assured link between crime and punishment that, if hardly comforting, offers some coherent meaning to events.[72] But increasingly, the post-Hobbesian world tended to place more emphasis on the human ability to control and shape history, and the earliest years of Charles II's reign were characterized by an effort to prevent further fracture in the social order by consciously renouncing an excessive providentialist discourse.

Thus, when writers such as Dryden and Edward Hyde, the Earl of Clarendon, resorted to providential explanations for political events they also strove to understand the link between cause and effect in the human secular realm.[73] The result was a somewhat strained literature that often sought to wed the miraculous with the political. Such tension may be discerned, for instance, in the opening to Clarendon's *The History of the Rebellion and the Civil Wars in England* (1702–4), which announces:

> If God had not reserved the deliverance and restoration of the King to himself, and resolved to accomplish it when there appeared least hope of it and least worldly means to bring it to pass, there happened at this time another very great alteration in England, that, together with the continuance of the war with Holland, and affronts everyday offered to France, might very reasonably have administered great hopes of a speedy change of government to the King.[74]

Even as Clarendon acknowledges the operation of divine grace in the restoration of the monarchy, he emphasizes that it was tensions with France and Holland, not to mention Oliver Cromwell's weakening hold over both the army and Parliament, that enabled Charles's successful return. As Jessica Munns argues, it is "worldly events, and most memorably very human personalities that predominate in Clarendon's account."[75] Politics is no less a player than providence is.

Indeed, Clarendon's sensitivity to the changing nature of historical discourse underwrites his painstaking efforts to balance the providential with specific, secondary, civil, and economic causes that emphasize the culpability of individual players. The same scrupulousness characterizes John Evelyn's account of the Restoration in his diary,[76] which, like Clarendon's history, emphasizes the political maneuvering that went into Charles's return even as it celebrates the hand of providence in restoring the king. Such texts illustrate Daniel Woolf's premise that the "clearer the immediate motives and drivers behind history the less likely were historians simply to shrug their shoulders and attribute outcomes directly to fate, chance, or providence."[77]

Conclusion

It is in this world where providentialism warred with realpolitik, and apocalypse with Augustan rationalism, that *The Jewes Tragedy* was recovered. While I do not mean to suggest that Heminge's play was finally deemed publication-worthy during the Restoration solely because of its secular approach, it is clear that his depiction of the siege of Jerusalem constitutes a rare—perhaps even refreshing—non-providentialist take on a by-now fashionable story that generated renewed interest in the recent political storm over the readmission of the Jews to England, about which I shall say more in the next chapter. Cromwell had been inspired to consider the restoration of the Jews based on millenarian ideas about the approach of the messianic time, which demanded the return of the Jews both to Palestine to herald the Second Coming, as well as to England in order for it to secure a place among the blessed nations.[78] Charles II's own relationship with the Jews was more prosaic: rumors circulated of a deal brokered with the Amsterdam Jews granting royal protection in exchange for arms, ammunition, and/or money. Yet even if nothing can be proved, as David Katz notes, it is clear that the restored monarchy's attitude toward the Jews amended significantly, and when angry petitions for their re-expulsion were brought to Charles, they were generally ignored.[79] John Locke's first draft of his famous "Letter Concerning Toleration" (1667) even cited the treatment of the recently readmitted Jews as the yardstick for measuring amity and accord.[80]

Heminge's rather remarkable portrayal of a doughty nation humbled by the forces of imperialism may well have attracted the moderates in the pro- versus anti-Jewish controversies of the early 1660s. At the same time, Heminge's unabashed valorization of Romans like Titus would have appealed to the Restoration court's Augustan self-fashioning and, perhaps, even stoked its own imperial design. Given that Charles's burgeoning imperial ambition was largely inspired by the Roman model, Heminge's generous depiction of the military prowess of Titus and Vespatian, coupled with their innate nobility and generosity of spirit, should have appealed to Restoration readership. That said, the devastation that ensues in *The Jewes Tragedy* as the result of empire-building must have resonated in the wake of the First Anglo-Dutch War (1652–54), especially with the renewal of tensions between the English and the Dutch in their bid to establish naval supremacy in the early 1660s. By pitting the Roman claim to empire against the Jewish claim to liberty, the play would have tapped into yet another serious contemporary concern. While one might not go so far as to say that Heminge adjudicates between the competing claims of empire and freedom, *The Jewes Tragedy* does function as a perceptive political allegory that at once lauds imperial enterprise and highlights its dangers and losses.

In the new dispensation where tolerance and unity were watchwords and internecine violence anathema, it is fitting that *The Jewes Tragedy* should have finally seen the light of day. This is not to imply, however, that a genial spirit of philosemitism reigned in Restoration England, or that *The Jewes Tragedy* became an instant success. But Heminge's demonstration of the corrosion of political stability through selfish ambition, communal hatred, and ill-conceived rebellion holds up the Jews' tragedy to the English nation as a poignant reflection on human culpability. Above all, it signals an evolving historical consciousness that would reshape not just the siege narrative but also other 'politic' histories in the late seventeenth century.

CHAPTER 5

Exile and Restoration

In her powerful meditation on belonging, Simone Weil suggests that to be rooted is perhaps the most important and least recognized need of the human soul.[1] The Ancient Jews would have affirmed the significance of Weil's claim but most likely contested its designation of rootedness as the "least recognized" need. For them, the knowledge of being rooted in the land as a special mark of covenantal favor with God constituted their very sense of selfhood. As Walter Brueggemann has argued persuasively, the two dominant histories of Genesis are of land. Genesis 1–11 chronicles the history of a people fully rooted in the land who thereby presumed they were inviolable, only to be extirpated for their colossal impudence. Chapters 12–50 then tell the counter-narrative of Abraham migrating in powerful expectation of land and belonging. As Brueggemann notes, both accounts set the parameters of what he calls "land theology" in the Bible and define the Jews' lives in terms of loss and anticipation, of uprooting and re-rooting, "of being dislocated because of impertinence and being relocated in trust."[2]

This relocation in trust is precisely that which is foreclosed in the story of Jerusalem's destruction by the Romans. Though recent scholarship posits that emigration from Israel was a gradual process rather than a large-scale eviction during the first centuries of the first millennium, early Christian moralists habitually identified banishment as the worst of the calamities that befell the Jews after the destruction of the Second Temple.[3] The dominant myth was that Titus Vespasian destroyed the Holy City and expelled its denizens in the manner of Nebuchadnezzar, who had destroyed the First Temple and exiled the

Judaeans to Babylon in 586 B.C.E. In point of fact, different biblical and Tal-mudic texts, as well as *midrashim* (biblical exegesis) on the destruction of the Temple and exile, almost always refer to the First Temple's destruction. Indeed, the oft-cited description of the Jews as "a certain people scattered abroad and dispersed among the people in all the provinces of thy [the Persian emperor's] kingdom" comes from the Book of Esther (3:8) and pertains specifically to the Babylonian exile.

Israel J. Yuval has argued convincingly that early Tannaitic and Amoraic sources about the first-century siege accuse the Romans only of destroying the Temple but not of exiling the people. Nevertheless, a myth of exile took shape that explicitly connected the final fall of the Temple with the radical expul-sion of the community.[4] *Galuth* or exile became the incontestable reminder that the Jews had failed in the end to fulfill the promise of Abraham. The Church Fathers, unsurprisingly, interpreted the crushing of the Bar-Kokhba Rebel-lion (132–36 C.E.) and consequent dispersal as the final unraveling of their covenanted relationship with the divine.[5] Voiced memorably in Eusebius's *His-tory* and *Praeparatio Evangelica*, Origen's *Contra Celsum*, Tertullian's *Adversos Judaeos*, Jerome's *Commentary*, and Augustine's *City of God*, the Roman "exile" was presented as a fulfillment of the prophecy in Isaiah 1:7: "Your country is desolate, your cities are burned with fire: your land, strangers devour it in your presence, and it is desolate, as overthrown by strangers."

Both crises of exile—Babylonian and Roman—held special interest for the early modern Protestant nation. Though Robert J. Wilken is right to note that the return from Babylon was not one of unqualified rejoicing but, rather, one marked by disappointment, disillusionment, and a humiliating sense of obliga-tion to the Persian overlords, it nevertheless functioned as a sanguine analog for the English Protestants in self-imposed exile on the Continent during the reign of Mary Tudor. There, they drew on the Babylonian captivity not just to explain their plight, but also to insist on the hope of a restored Protestant church at home. Their interpretation of the Jews in Lamentations (with whom they identified) was of a people bemoaning their losses but holding steadfast to the promise of redemption and return. For instance, the Bishop of Durham James Pilkington's (1520–1576) polemical exegesis, *Aggeus and Abdias Proph-etes, the one corrected, the other newly added, and both at large declared* (1562), published upon his homecoming from Germany, drew an unmistakable anal-ogy between the restored Jews and other Marian exiles emboldened to return.[6]

Indeed, the expectation of restoration after dislocation proved a popular trope well into the seventeenth century, especially with Puritans who had been exiled by the Star Chamber in the 1630s, but who had started to return to

England from the Netherlands between 1640 and 1642. John Greene's 1644 sermon *Nehemiah's teares for the affliction of Jerusalem* draws on Jeremiah's account of Babylonian exile to comfort the reformed churches that had been brought "very low" in England, Ireland, and Germany. According to Greene, recalling the "low, afflicted and despised condition of the Jewes then in Judea" would "hereof helpe to support the spirits of Gods people in their most sad dejecting times: you have heard there is a new heaven and a new earth promised, a Jerusalem to come downe from heaven, a glorious building going up."[7]

Unsurprisingly, then, that same comfort is markedly absent in the early modern accounts of the Roman devastation. Unlike the Babylonian exile, the post-siege dispersal of 70 C.E. carried with it no hope of return. Early modern texts identified the Jews' exile as irrevocable, the just consequence of "unthankefulleness" and impiety. To parallel these exiled Jews was to invite a prospect of loss unrelieved by the glimmer of recovery. Thus, *The Lame[n]tacion of England* (1558), attributed to Thomas Cranmer, who had been executed by Mary Tudor the previous year, identifies the Catholic queen as a "scourge" and "rood" to "plage England, for their vnthankfullness." In this aspect, it anticipated a 1558 sermon by Edwin Sandys, Archbishop of York (1519–1588), alerting the Protestant Church to its wanton disregard of divine grace. Sandys railed against the "great vnthankfulnesse" of Jerusalem as a consequence of which the Jews were sent into "exile and miserable bondage." God "burnt vp their holie citie, he destroied their glorious temple, he left them to be deuoured with pestilence, with hunger and with the sworde the accustomed instruments of his wrath," Sandys warns. There is little hope of redemption, just heavy punishment for sin and ingratitude: "Insomuch as euen to this day the remnant of that elect and chosen people is scattered farre and wide, and doth liue in all contempt hatred and slauerie."[8]

The representation of the Jews' final and irreversible expulsion is the focus of this chapter. However, the correspondence that interests me is not the familiar one between the exiled Jews and the faltering Protestant Church of mid-sixteenth-century sermons. Rather, I focus on the curious similitude between the besieged Jews of 70 C.E. and the exiled/recently restored court of Charles II—a court that, incidentally, prided itself on its tolerant attitude toward the Jewish community that had been readmitted into England in the mid 1650s. My case study, as we shall see below, is John Crowne's spectacular heroic drama in two parts, *The Destruction of Jerusalem by Titus Vespasian*, which premiered at the Theatre Royal in January 1677. Performed by His Majesty's Servants and later dedicated to Charles II's Catholic mistress, the Duchess of Portsmouth, the play is set against the backdrop of the Roman siege of insurgent Jerusalem and focuses on the star-crossed lovers Titus, the newly appointed Roman commander and soon to be emperor, and Berenice, a Jewish princess. The play's preoccupation with the trope of banishment, though frequently passed over by scholars of Restoration drama, speaks powerfully to the nightmare of dislocation endured not only by Jews officially readmitted to England between the mid-1650s and the 1660s, but also by the court, whose members may have comprised Crowne's audience at the Theatre Royal. Like Heminge's politically nuanced *Jewes Tragedy*, which was finally published during the early years of the Restoration, Crowne's drama resists the uncomplicated vilification of the Jewish nation that permeates some of the earlier texts on the siege. Rather, his conscious employment of exile rhetoric makes for a fascinating study in the context of both returns—Jewish and royalist—that marked the second half of the seventeenth century.

The result is a layered discourse on exile and restoration. On the one hand, the traditional equation of exile with condign punishment becomes almost impossible in a text presented before a court that had worked energetically to reinscribe its own banishment as something other than divine retribution for sin. Furthermore, the juxtaposition of the hapless subjects of the play with its restored audience implicitly challenged the popular fear that expulsion was irrevocable. Indeed, the notion of reversible exile had already seeped into the cultural and political fabric and had been voiced by mid-century millenarianists who supported the restoration of the Jews to England, and, ultimately, to Israel. Certainly, a major impetus for readmitting the Jews to England was the Puritan eschatology advanced by Judeo-centric exegetes such as Thomas Brightman (1562–1607), who maintained that scriptural prophecies called for the Jews to be, quite literally, resettled in the Holy Land.

On the other hand, Crowne—an able political satirist—proffers a meticulous study of rootlessness and the trauma of dislocation that contradicts both the court's attempts to reconstitute its own checkered history of banishment, as well as the jubilant clamoring for the Jews' restitution to Israel. For all its bells, whistles, and burning temples, *The Destruction of Jerusalem* is a somber take on exile and the factionalism that can result in such totalizing loss.

Crowne's *Destruction of Jerusalem*

Like William Heminge, Crowne recognized the merit of transposing a fashionable history into dramatic spectacle. Unlike Heminge, however, his efforts were wildly successful. Both parts of *The Destruction of Jerusalem* met with such "extravagant applause" that it is believed the play aroused the envy of Crowne's patron, the dissolute Earl of Rochester, who promptly "commenced an enemy to the bard he before had so much befriended."[9] Stuart Gillespie and David Hopkins describe it aptly as a "heroic extravaganza," replete with sieges, battles, and feats of martial valor.[10] It boasted a stellar cast with Edward Kynaston and Charles Hart playing the principal male leads Titus and Phraartes, and leading ladies Mrs. Marshall and Mrs. Boutell as Berenice and Clarona. According to John Downes, the play incurred "vast expence in scenes and cloathes" with a series of magnificent sets: the lavish Temple Gates, the chaotic streets of "starving Jerusalem," and "the blazing Temple sinking to destruction in a sea of fire."[11] This Jewish history was, after all, a hot topic, and Crowne knew exactly how to keep fanning the flames.

Unlike Heminge, Crowne was also helped by the theatrical fashion. Heroic dramas of love and valor set in exotic locales were all the rage during the Restoration. *The Destruction of Jerusalem*, following Elkanah Settle's *Empress of Morocco* (1673) and John Dryden's critically acclaimed *Conquest of Granada* (1670–71), drew heavily on the stock elements of heroic tragedy by presenting a tale of exotic cultures in conflict, with a hero divided between the contradictory claims of empire and desire. The ill-fated affair between Titus and Berenice was certainly a popular tale. By the late seventeenth century it had become something of a theatrical fashion, with Pierre Corneille and Jean Racine in France producing plays on the subject in the same year (1670). Indeed, Crowne's model was Racine's *Bérénice*, which had been adapted by Thomas Otway for the Duke's Company the previous year.[12]

Despite its theatrical success, *The Destruction of Jerusalem* has been dismissed as a cheap derivation lacking both Racine's complex psychology and Dryden's mastery of verse and dramatic structure. Consequently, scholars of Restoration drama overlook Crowne's singular artistic decision: his choice of setting. It may come as a surprise, given the pervasive interest in the Roman siege that we have thus far seen, that *The Destruction of Jerusalem* is the only play to set the doomed love story between Titus and Berenice in that wartorn city. This was an anachronism, to be sure, for the affair unfolded a few years after, in Rome. But unlike Corneille, Racine, and Otway,[13] who meticulously followed the historical accounts, Crowne saw merit in superimposing the fractured love story upon the saga of the assailed city rife with conspiracy and rebellion. Thus, *The Destruction of Jerusalem* joins *The Jewes Tragedy* as the only other seventeenth-century English play to juxtapose Roman and Jewish society in Judaea.

As with *The Jewes Tragedy*, critical response to Crowne's play has plodded along a spectrum ranging from utter disregard to outright bafflement.

A. T. Bartholomew in *The Cambridge History of English Literature* comments on how "incredible" it is "that such a piece ... could ever have gained the marked success it undoubtedly enjoyed."[14] Arthur Franklin White likewise deemed the play's success "very remarkable" given how "uninteresting" it is: "the couplets are mediocre, the characterization is artificial, and the emotion is forced."[15] Bartholomew and White are in august company. As early as 1731, Charles St. Évremond in a letter to the Duchess of Mazarin, marveled that it should have met with as "wild and unaccountable success as Mr. Dryden's *Conquest of Granada*."[16]

All of these commentators failed to take note of the play's setting. As I have demonstrated, besieged Jerusalem had consistently captured the early modern English imagination. Certainly, this was lost on J. Maidment and W. H. Logan, who, editing Crowne's works in the nineteenth century, attributed his choice to stage the events in Jerusalem to a pervading fascination with Orientalism following the success of Dryden's *Conquest of Granada*. As they surmise, Crowne had hoped to be "as successful with the Jews and the Romans as the Laureate ... had been with the Moors and the Spaniards."[17] For the most part, since then, the setting has been dismissed as a mere excuse for a flashy denouement. White identified the spectacular burning of the Second Temple orchestrated with the help of William Davenant as the reason for the play's early popularity, but exhibited little interest in what it may have signified for Crowne's audience.[18] Robert Hume, while stressing the visual impact of the play—which he describes as "a *lush* work"—is doubtful that it had any "significant intellectual or political design."[19] Recently, Don-John Dugas notes that the play was so "resplendent with elaborate scenes and effects that we should not be surprised that contemporaries enjoyed it," but he, too, is uninterested in the import of the "foreign setting."[20] Richard Capwell's extensive investigation of Crowne's sources similarly dismisses the "historical material" as "merely background for the love stories."[21] Only John B. Rollins, in his study of Crowne's apocalyptic rhetoric, acknowledges that "the center of the play is, as the title suggests, the destruction of the city of Jerusalem."[22]

As a popular entertainment, then, *The Destruction of Jerusalem* builds on conversations about the ruin of the Temple and the expulsion of the Jews that had surfaced in the histories, sermons, ballads, and apocalyptic pamphlets, and in the political memoranda on the decision to readmit Jews into England in the 1650s. Yet again, Peter Morwen's translation of *Josippon* appears to have been the favored source, but this time in a new guise, for it is likely that Crowne was most familiar with the version reprinted by James Stafford in 1652. Freshly edited by James Howell, it bore the new title of *The Wonderful and Most deplorable History of the Latter Times of the Jews*.[23]

Unlike Morwen, both Stafford and Howell were ardent royalists. In his epistle to the 1662 edition, Stafford leveled praise for the way that Howell mapped the "ugly and enormous *Crimes*"—the worst manifestation of the "true Jewish spirit"—onto the excesses of the English Civil War. Indeed, he insisted that this edition's true value lay in its perceptive equation of "*Crimes* and *Crying sins*, which raigned in Jerusalem before her last and utter destruction" and the "spirit of *Sedition*, instable and stubborn *Rebellious hearts* ... *murmurings* at *Government*, and an itch after *Innovations*"[24] with Puritan high crimes and misdemeanors. Stafford agreed that the regicide of Charles I bore "a kind of analogy" to the Crucifixion, and indeed, was even more deplorable in one respect: "Nay the *Jews* (whereof there are swarms now in this City) will not stick to say, that was a Murther beyond theirs; for what they did, they did it out of *blindness* and *ignorance*: for they neither knew nor acknowledged *Him* to be *King* of the *Jew*: But the *English* did accuse, and arraign, they did condemn and murther King CHARLES by the *name of their own king*, the *King of England*."[25] By comparing regicide to crucifixion, Stafford is unabashedly polemical in his equation of the English Republic with fallen Jerusalem, even more so than Morwen who, for all his insistence on the siege as requisite Protestant history, readily acknowledged its purely intellectual value to antiquarians.

Stafford's anti-Jewish rhetoric closely echoed that of Howell, the first Historiographer Royal, who virulently opposed readmission for the "swarms" of Jews into England—a matter that was memorably (if inconclusively) debated in Cromwell's Whitehall Conference in 1655. Howell's own "Epistle Dedicatory," written from the Prison of the Fleet in February 1650, was an exhortation to fellow royalists that likewise relied on a parallel between republican England and sinful Jerusalem. Indeed, Howell framed Morwen's history as evidence of the treachery and fractiousness of the Jews and, thereby, of their innate undesirability. Citing the fall of the Temple as an example of how the flower of grace can wither, he noted that the loss of the Covenant occurred during Passover— one of the holiest events of the Jewish calendar—so that what should have been a time of sanctity became, instead, an hour of mourning and deprivation. The "Epistle" lingers on the horror of alienation with its mordant descriptions of the remaining Jews, scattered around the globe, "no better then slaves wheresover they take footing," and occupying the lowest professions: "Tollmen" in "some inferiour places in the Custom-houses," or else "Spies and panders for intelligence."[26] They are presented as both deformed in body and mean and twisted in soul and spirit. A stench emanates from them so foul and noxious that Howell sends up a hearty supplication that "England may not be troubled with that sent again."[27]

By contrast, Crowne's *Destruction of Jerusalem* recovers the more discerning spirit of Morwen and even Lodge. Not only does it subvert Howell's identification of Jew as bestial and dastardly, but it also flies in the face of its source by allowing for the construction of a new parallel between exiled Jews and royalists. Whereas both Howell and Stafford's dedicatory epistles dismiss the Jewish nation as a whole—a move reminiscent of the more virulent sixteenth-century sermons—Crowne's play, like the histories of Morwen and Lodge before him, distinguishes carefully between the Temple priests and the zealots, reserving its ire for the latter. *The Destruction of Jerusalem* largely resists glib identifications, with the notable exception of equating the Pharisees with the Puritans, a comparison of which Stafford and Howell would doubtless have approved, though they would much rather have tarred all Jews with the same brush. Crowne leaves his audience in little doubt that Jerusalem is responsible for its own downfall but even as his drama celebrates Titus Vespasian's *virtu*, it resists the ready and uncomplicated vilification of the Jewish people. Even as he exploits a fashionable trope, Crowne achieves a rather refined and layered presentation of the Jews' plight that, if not quite philosemitic, resists anti-Semitic homogenizing. Instead, it is the desolation of exile—the Jews' imminent fate—that is most apparent from the perusal of this drama that enacts the very agonies of dispossession that its audience had once endured.

Royalists in Exile

The affliction of exile, so much a part of the Jewish experience, is something that also emerges quite powerfully in the writings of several displaced royalists who left England in the aftermath of the Civil War. Historians of royalist exile such as Eva Scott describe evocatively the "weary, sad-hearted men who maintained the cause of Charles I" only to "[follow] his son across the seas, into the wilderness of a foreign kingdom."[28] Paul Hardacre likewise conjures up images of "suffering, material and intellectual poverty, frustration and paralysing unhappiness."[29] Though it is important to remember the varied nature of royalists' experience in exile—in Geoffrey Smith's words, they exhibited a "diversity of behavior . . . in response to the unfamiliar and difficult situations with which they were confronted"—several remained mired in wretchedness, and almost all suffered acute material deprivation at some point.[30] Even John Stoye, whose controversial *English Travellers Abroad* reconfigured royalist exile as closer to the Grand Tour than wandering in the wilderness, acknowledged that the "poverty, of this second residence abroad [would have been] strange to some of them."[31] Though one must acknowledge Timothy Raylor's thesis that when men like John

Evelyn, Roger Pratt, Robert Lord Montagu, or Francis Mortoft went abroad in the 1640s and 1650s, "they were not going into exile, [but] were, to varying degrees, strategically absenting themselves from troubles at home," the writings of other exiles betray the tremendous strain of alienation, with its "mental and material wounds," to borrow Philip Major's phrase.[32]

For these royalists, privation, in particular, left deep scars. James, Duke of York, admits ruefully on the first page of his memoirs that "Nothing was so rare as money,"[33] and in 1653, Edward Hyde, Earl of Clarendon, expressed bitter amazement that he "did not know that any man is yet dead for want of bread."[34] The Cavalier Captain Thomas Carnaby likewise bemoaned his impecunious circumstances in 1657, confessing that he was "in danger to perish for want of bread and clothing."[35] For those sundered from loved ones and the lifestyle to which they were accustomed, anxious and afraid, this was an overwhelming ordeal. Memorable among these unfortunates is Sir Francis Windebank, secretary of state to King Charles I, who, denounced in 1640 to the House of Commons as a Catholic sympathizer and protector of recusants, made a "passage ... full of hazard" in an open boat across the Channel to France. His was a bleak voyage and a bleaker sojourn. After drifting from France to Italy and back again, he died, bitter and heartsick, in 1646. His nephew, in a letter to Windebank's son, Thomas, describes Sir Francis as "very much dejected" and languishing in the conviction that he and his family were "utterly ruined."[36] Margaret Cavendish's *The Cavalier in Exile*, which eloquently recounts the ordeal of her husband William Cavendish, Marquess of Newcastle, likewise stresses the "often hazarding of his life ... the losse of his Estate, and the banishment of his Person by his necessitated Condition, and his constant and patient suffering."[37]

Upon Charles II's return, panegyrists such as Edmund Waller and Richard Flecknoe sought to reconfigure the trauma of his dispossession as an "opportunity for a solid education" in foreign courts that molded him into an effective ruler. Dryden's *Astraea Redux* (1660) is likewise a carefully manipulated account of Charles's displacement that compares it to the biblical David's salutary absence from Israel when

> Forc'd into exile from his rightful Throne
> He made all Countries where he came his own.
> And viewing Monarchs secret Arts of sway
> A Royal Factor for their Kingdomes lay. (75–78)[38]

It is understood that like "banish'd *David*" (79), Charles II upon his restoration would make "his proud Neighbours rue" (81) their unfortunate alliances with his enemies. Exile, in this eulogist narrative, is but a short-lived phase: a time for opening the mind and training the spirit, a rigorous finishing school. To be sure, some Cavaliers undoubtedly thrived—or at the very least survived—in some style. In his study of Cavalier exile, Smith notes that even William Cavendish developed during his sixteen-year stint "the art of living on credit to a level of refinement never approached by his fellow emigres."[39] We have reports of Thomas Dalyell and William Drummond, who flourished in the court of the Tsar in Russia. Others like Thomas Killigrew traveled extensively on the Continent, while the Anglican clergyman Dr. Isaac Basire, though beginning in peril ("sequestered, plundered, and forced to fly"[40]), wandered through France, Italy, and the Levant before ending up in Transylvania where he was persuaded to accept the chair of Theology at the University of Weissemburg.[41] Indeed, most royalists did survive to return to England with the restoration of the monarchy. But the haunting murmurs of the less fortunate and less hardy (even if they endured long enough to return) grow ever louder when juxtaposed with plays such as *The Destruction of Jerusalem*. Even Charles II was occasionally shown to be a pathetic figure, a penniless monarch, a "stateless king in exile."[42] If anything, the strenuousness of the effort to recuperate royalist Continental exile as a kind of neo-biblical fortunate fall, a time to both "regret and bless," suggests only the depth of the wounds that exile inflicts.[43] It is to that horror that we now turn.

Exile in Crowne's *Destruction*

In his "Reflections on Exile," Edward Said described the experience as the "unhealable rift forced between a human being and a native place, between the self and its true home." Insisting that the "essential sadness can never be surmounted," Said, after the fashion of Shakespeare's Romeo, identifies exile as "like death, but without death's ultimate mercy."[44] Moses Finley agrees: banishment, especially in the ancient world, was deemed "the bitterest of fates. The exile was stripped of all ties that meant life itself; it made no difference in this regard whether one had been compelled to flee or gone from home in the search for land by free choice."[45] Exiles, to quote Said again, are "cut off from their roots, their land, their past." Theirs is "fundamentally a discontinuous state of being." To counteract their debilitating loss, they seek new armies or states with which to identify. Sometimes they attempt to reconstitute their lives by choosing to see themselves as part of a "triumphant ideology or a restored people." But "the crippling sorrow of estrangement" besets the exile even as she or he tries to accommodate to a new world with its new values. History, in Said's words, may contain "heroic, romantic, glorious, even triumphant episodes in an exile's life," but these achievements are "permanently undermined by the loss of something left behind forever."[46]

The Destruction of Jerusalem anticipates such twentieth-century philosophical and psychological assessments of exile in its presentation of the two original characters at the start of the play. Phraartes is a Parthian prince who loses his kingdom because of a conspiracy between the Romans and the Parthian rebels, while Monobazus is the brother of the neighboring Adiabenan king who unjustly accuses him of treason and turns on him in battle. Phraartes is distantly descended from Jewish kings but neither he nor Monobazus is a Jew. Both men enter the play as rootless aliens, ejected from their familiar worlds. When the city comes under siege, they pledge to defend it against Rome—a common enemy. The princes' generosity toward the Jews is partly motivated by their hatred for the Romans but is more directly the product of their desire for Jewish women: Phraartes for the High Priest's daughter, Clarona, and Monobazus for Berenice herself. Clarona eventually yields to Phraartes's passion, but their joy is short-lived, and she is killed in the attack upon the Temple spurred by the Pharisees in Part 2 of the play. Monobazus, for his part, saves Berenice's life, but she does not repay him with her love. Instead, upon discovering that it was he who killed her brother, Agrippa II, she evicts him from her retinue. Both princes eventually die heroic deaths as they strive to defend the burning city.

Although non-Jewish, Phraartes and Monobazus provide a powerful commentary on exile and dislocation that is pertinent to the worlds within and outside of the play. One could argue that *The Destruction of Jerusalem* foregrounds the themes of exile and dispossession by opening the play with liminal characters that Said would identify as occupants of the "perilous territory of non-belonging."[47] Phraartes is strikingly disconnected from the world of the Temple, its ritual and covenant. His reaction upon beholding it in Act 1, Scene 1 of Part 1 is one of utter bemusement:

> Ha! At Devotion still! Can the tir'd Air
> Obtain no truce from Sacrifice and Prayer?
> They are importunate, with their great power
> They let him scarce enjoy one quiet hour;
> But ply him still with Sacrifice so fast
> He's Cloy'd with new, er'e he digests the last. (1.1.1)

In this, the opening speech of the play, Phraartes presents Temple ritual as a travesty that reduces God to a glutton. The image of Yahweh as the hapless recipient of "gay Splendid follies" (1.1.1) who, in the onslaught of oblation, craves a single moment of tranquility attenuates the image of the omnipotent God of Abraham, Isaac, and Jacob. Phraartes thus stands for the outsider, an ironic bystander, though he "springs / Of *Jewish* blood by a long Race of Kings" (1.2.1). When questioned about the gods of his people, Phraartes replies that there are none, "or if any, the Slaves worship me, / Though now a Villain does prophane my Throne" (1.1.1). Indeed, his atheism, which was strongly criticized after the play's premiere, connotes his alienness.

Derek Hughes implicitly recognizes this when he acknowledges that Crowne's "enduring literary image of mankind" is that of a "gathering of strangers," which expresses "the incoherence of a world where creeds are determined by culture."[48] When Phraartes confesses aesthetic appreciation for the splendor of the Temple—"Heaven does in no place appear, / Treated with such Magnificence as here . . . / Were I a God I would expect no less" (1.1.1)—his perspective is akin to that of a tourist before curiosities. "This is some charm'd and visionary Land," he mutters at the close of Act 2 of the first part of the play as he gazes out from the Temple precincts,

I scarce can trust the ground on which I stand . . .
Wonders, not Fishes, spawn within their Seas
And all the winds that blow breathe Prophecies. (1.2.3)

Again, Phraartes's words betray his status: Jerusalem, a place of augury and of portents, is undeniably alien to him. His language of marvel and wonder signifies a fundamentally discontinuous relationship with the people among whom he now resides.

Monobazus's dislocation is even more pronounced. More than any other character, he embodies Melvin Seeman's categories of alienation: powerlessness, normlessness, isolation, cultural estrangement, social isolation, self-estrangement, and the overpowering feeling of personal worthlessness.[49] Monobazus is introduced in Part 1 as "the brave unknown Prince" (1.2.1) and as a slave to "wandring Fortunes" (1.2.2). His presence in Jerusalem is accidental; when betrayed by his brother, he goes by his "own doom to willing Banishment" until "Roving the world," he "hither chanc't to stray" (1.2.2). Berenice, with whom he falls instantly in love, offers a tenuous means to anchor him in a new space, but the hopelessness of his desire only intensifies the illusive nature of his new life.

Monobazus's desire for Berenice, like Phraartes's love for Clarona, may also be read in the context of Said's theory of compensation for disorienting loss. The determination with which both men speedily fall in love with Jewish women and ally themselves with their cause assumes a new meaning in light of their dislocation: the prospect of reintegration. Monobazus's passion, however, is doomed to remain unrequited. Not only is Berenice beloved of mighty Titus himself, but in a cruel twist of fate, it is Monobazus who kills her brother. In Part 2, he unthinkingly saves Titus's life and thereby seals the fate of the people he had sworn to fight for. It is not that he is a turncoat; merely that he is discombobulated. Without his rightful place, he vacillates in everything but his love. Berenice orients him such that he is prepared to do anything that might benefit her personally, even if it betrays her people and his new cause. As a consequence, Monobazus remains marginalized, alien and unnatural both to his lady's heart and to her land:

> My cruel Fate pursues me every where.
> My name can like a Charm, uncalm the Sea
> Where e're I wander, there no peace can be. (2.4.1)

The exile/belonging binary, foregrounded by the introduction of the foreign princes, is the first and arguably most significant of several binaries that Crowne erects in this play, including love/conquest, duty/desire, public/private, and imperial/domestic. Though both princes are celebrated as saviors "drop't from Heaven," they remain baffled by their adopted country and are ever "Strangers to [its] Faith and Bloud" (2.2.1). When, at the close of Part 2, Phraartes and Monobazus opt to surrender their lives in Jerusalem's service, it is largely because "to live and reign, we know not how nor where" (2.5.1). And even though each receives news of the recovery of his kingdom, the breach proves too wide to span. Restoration comes too late for them, and is made yet more unattainable by the loss of the women—Clarona is killed in the siege, and Berenice spurns Monobazus over her brother's murder. In the face of totalizing loss, then, it is entirely, if tragically, appropriate that the two princes make their final exit preparing to "Plunge into deeps and never be perplext / Be Kings this moment, and be nothing next" (2.5.1).

The declension from being to nothingness—the trajectory of the exile— is presented as the tragic lot of Jerusalem itself. Once the terrestrial mirror of heaven, the city becomes the creature that perishes when cut off from the familiar and nurturing. God's city is a "distrest place, which Earth and Heaven forsake" (1.1.1). As the High Priest Matthias bemoans in Part 2,

> Heav'n his presence has withdrawn from hence:
> He none of all his wonted ways replies,

By Angels, Visions, Dreams, or Prophecies;
From his own Temple he has ta'ne his flight,
And given it to Owls, and Birds of night. (2.2.1)

The Jews' impending eviction also colors a curious conversation about death
and the afterlife between Clarona, Matthias's daughter, and Phraartes, as they
seek refuge in the Temple precincts. Distressed by her lover's unbelief, Clarona
conjures a sobering image of herself separated eternally from Phraartes,

wandring on wild Natures Heath,
When we from these poor Cottages are thrown,
Having no dwellings, and desiring none. (2.3.1)

Clarona speaks of the spirit world that awaits those who shuffle off their mortal coil ("these poor Cottages") but the metaphysical wilds of her limbo assume
dire political significance in the context of the siege. Inevitably, the majestic
Temple and its splendid altar will also give way to the rude dwellings of the
exiled ("these poor Cottages") and her destitute people will, quite literally, wander on "wild Natures Heath" in search of new homes. In Clarona's speech, future
and present, eschatological and political, collapse to create a cycle of eviction.

In a poignant turn, it is the already displaced Phraartes who attempts to
comfort his beloved by focusing on what they have rather than what they stand
to lose:

But let us this fantastick talk give o're,
These Fairy thoughts shall pinch thy soul no more;
Let us not think of Lands remote, unknown,
But eat the Fruits and Spices of our own. (2.3.1)

But it is Phraartes, not Clarona, who is guilty of "fantastick talk." For Phraartes,
ever more "the Pagan King" and "Heathen," has no right to the possessive plural
pronoun. His talk of the treasures of "our" land is as outrageous as the pretense
that Clarona's fears are mere "Fairy thoughts." The "Lands remote, unknown"
are not phantasmagoria but, rather, the adumbration of alien shores, and the
only reality Clarona's people will know for centuries.

As if in recognition of this, the play produces paean upon paean to Jerusalem's fleeting splendor in the manner of the exile, comparing present desolation
with past glory. Even Titus is captivated by the city's charm. He is introduced
in Part 2 in the unenviable position of a man divided, one who recognizes true

grace but must be the architect of its destruction. "Yet I would fain this splendid City save," he confesses: "Me thinks it does a Noble Town appear; / Gods
Might forsake their Heaven t'inhabit here" (2.1.1). But the play knows better.
God does not forsake heaven for Jerusalem; rather, it is Jerusalem that is abandoned and cast out. As the dying Matthias reminds his fatally wounded daughter, "Our Temple, Nation, Glory, Faith are gone; / And what wou'dst thou do
in the world alone?" (2.5.1).

The *topos* of exile dominates Part 2 of *The Destruction of Jerusalem* in
descriptions of the beleaguered city and its desperate people, but it is notably
also used to characterize the doomed love of Titus and Berenice. Here, Crowne
intensifies his employment of a motif that Racine and Otway had used quite
sparingly. In Racine's *Bérénice*, exile is almost exclusively figurative: banishment
is the sundering of lovers. This amatory exile is the lot of King Antiochus of
Commagene, a prototype of Monobazus, who languishes "wandering in Cae-
saria" after Berenice elects to follow Titus to Rome (1.4.233–34).[50] Otway's
Titus and Berenice sustains a similar equation in Antiochus's hopeless desire
for Berenice—"Perhaps I'le ever banish her my heart. / She left me cruelly, and
let her go" (2.1.254–55)—as well as Titus's projection of his lovelorn future self:

> Mourning at court, and more exil'd than she
> My Reign but a long Banishment shall be,
> From all those Joys that wait on Pomp and Power. (2.1.120–22)

Both Racine and Otway's presentations of the heart's exile are in the
Petrarchan tradition, of which Sir Thomas Wyatt's English translation of
Petrarch's Sonnet 35 "How oft have I, my dear and cruel foe" is a prime example:[51]

> If I then it chase, nor it in you can find,
> In this exile no manner of comfort,
> Nor live alone, nor where he is called resort,
> He may wander from his natural kind.
> So shall it be great hurt unto us twain,
> And yours the loss, and mine the deadly pain. (9–14)

Both Petrarch and Wyatt figure absence from the beloved as exile, thereby
heightening "the tension between possession and loss, characteristic of desire."[52]
The conceit of the "banished" lover derived from Petrarch was instantly rec-
ognizable to early modern Europeans and it cast a familiar shadow on both
Racine and Otway's dramas. Crowne, by contrast, presents a more layered exile

Image of Titus Vespasian from Joseph ben Gorion's *The Wonderful and Most Deplorable History of the Latter Times of the Jews,* 1662. (Reproduced by permission of Henry E. Huntington Library and Art Gallery)

that interweaves political and amatory banishment. While it may be argued that Racine and Otway's banishment becomes a political reality when the doomed lovers part because of the state's decree, the exilic rhetoric employed by their Titus and Antiochus is consistently metaphorical. Only Corneille's Tite comes close to collapsing the metaphor when he offers to step down as emperor to wander in foreign lands with Bérénice. But in the end, he, like his literary counterparts, prefers the Petrarchan exile of the heart.

Crowne emphasizes the political reality of exile by merging the destruction of Jerusalem with the parting of Titus and Berenice. In the context of the very real banishment endured by Phraartes and Monobazus and the imminent dispersal of the Jewish people, the exile that Berenice, in particular, is fated to experience far exceeds the lovelorn pining of the stock Petrarchan lover. Though Berenice's gloomy promise to live out her exile in a cave gestures to the stylized lamentation of Elizabethan lyrics like Edward Dyer's "A Fancy," in which the lover anticipates the transformation of the landscape in the absence of his paramour,[53] Crowne presents a steady ironizing of the amatory exilic trope by juxtaposing it with the actuality of destruction, dispersal, abandonment, and ejection on a national scale. In this way, the play's trajectory is a movement from figurative to literal exile. Consider Berenice's casual equation of eviction with a lover's neglect at the beginning of Part 2 of *The Destruction of Jerusalem*:

> A foolish dream tormented me tonight;
> What, matters not, now I have you in sight.
> But ha! I in your looks a sadness spy;
> You only to my words with sighs reply.
> Must all your thoughts to Fame devoted be?
> Can you afford no room in 'em for me?
> If present thus you banish me your mind,
> My Image sure does cold reception find
> In your retiring heart, when I am gone. (2.1.1)

Banishment is here leached of its political essence: "thus you banish me your mind." In Act 3, Berenice again metaphorizes exile when she insists that Titus's "neglect" is a fate "worse than death" (2.3.1), whereas Titus himself consistently projects the Petrarchan lover even as he decrees that his mistress be banished from his retinue and lands. Too afraid to face Berenice directly, he presents himself via a messenger in Act 4 as "an Imperial exile in my Throne" whose life without his beloved "will be in sorrow spent. / And all my reign a glorious banishment." The irony inherent in the oxymoron "glorious banishment"—a stark

contrast to the inglorious and violent dispersal of the people he subjugates—
is reinforced in a direct address to Berenice later in the same scene where he
imagines his future politically victorious self "Great as a God, as solitary too; /
Ador'd, but banis'd from the sight of you" (2.4.1).

The exilic rhetoric of Titus and Berenice becomes more resonant and sub-
stantive as the threats of real expulsion—Berenice from Rome and the Jews
from Jerusalem—loom over the text. By the end of Act 4, Titus, like Corneille's
Tite, is overcome with grief at the prospect of impending loneliness and briefly
contemplates defying the will of Rome by going into banishment with Berenice:

> Without Renown or Empire I can live,
> But not without the Queen; she, only she,
> Fame, Empire, Glory, all things is to me. (2.4.1)

Eventually, however, the quiddity of political exile proves overwhelming for
Titus, and in a fascinating exchange with Berenice in the play's final act, he
brings together the political and the amatory forms, only to choose the sweet
torments of the latter:

> For Madam, say, wou'd not your Spirit loath
> An abject Prince. Who should such meanness shew,
> He poorly should for Love to Exile go?
> Yet this inglorious Exile I must chuse,
> Or Throne, Life, Glory, You and all must lose. (2.5.1)

Painful as the exile of the heart (now amended to "inglorious Exile") may be,
true abjection remains the lot of the political exile. An absence, a void, synony-
mous with loss, the political exile stands to lose "Throne, Life, Glory, You, and
all." It is as if Titus understands this distinction for the first time, and once real-
izing it, can do little more than retreat into metaphor.

Berenice, for her part, reinforces the tribulations of true exile in a scornful
challenge to Titus's extravagant rhetoric:

> You of your own distractions can complain;
> But mine, though greater, I lament in vain.
> Say all your grief is more than a pretence,
> You have Renown your loss to recompence,
> And by your own free choice your self undo;
> But I am into Exile sent by you.

Despis'd, forlorn, disgrac'd, inglorious made,
Nothing in my obscure and mournfull shade
To comfort me, for all the wrongs I bear,
But death,—whose aid I will not long deferr. (2.5.1)

Berenice's powerful speech effectively undoes the antithetical "glorious ban-ishment" that Titus initially envisioned for himself. Contrary to his assertion, there are no "splendid steps to ruine" (2.4.1) but paths "obscure and mournfull." Amatory exile allows Titus to remain "great as a God," but the banishment that consigns Berenice to an undistinguished, secluded place, alien and mean, "some Cave [where] this troubler of the world shall hide" (2.5.1), at once exposes and undermines her Roman lover's histrionics.

"Despis'd, forlorn, disgrac'd, inglorious made," Berenice is finally reduced to the state of her fellow Jews. Although she had displayed little affinity for them earlier, preferring Titus to Yahweh ("Titus is Heaven, and all the gods to me"), one may argue that she is most fully realized as a Jew in expulsion. To be sure, the sympathetic touch with which Crowne presents both her sorry plight and that of her people is noteworthy given the consistent antagonism displayed by royalists like Stafford and Howell in the previous decade. Again, this is not to say that the Jews are exonerated of all wrongdoing. Repeatedly, the play empha-sizes their responsibility for their own fate: their misinterpretation of signs and prophecies, their failure to amend their ways, and their arrogant insistence that Jerusalem is "the world" and therefore impregnable.[54] At the same time, it empathizes with their loss and commends the heroism of Matthias and his Temple cohort as well as that of the "noble *Jews*" who "in Battel chose to fall,/ And bravely with their Country perish'd" (2.5.1).

The Advent of Philosemitism

Crowne's *Destruction* suggests that the Jews' experiences of dislocation, humili-ation, and crushing loss, while on a different scale, had become comprehensible to the restored monarchy. Certainly, his nuanced presentation of the siege of 70 C.E. was performed in an altered political climate ostensibly marked by amity toward the Chosen People readmitted into England. In fact, the perception of early modern Jews had been shifting in certain religious circles throughout the seventeenth century, prompting the convening of the Whitehall Conference to discuss their possible return. Stafford and Howell's distaste for the Jews had been consistent with the politics of Charles I, whose attitude had been anything but conciliatory. This anti-Jewish sentiment had similarly prevailed through the

Interregnum with the likes of William Prynne objecting in inflammatory terms to the prospect of readmission. But the Jews had already found unexpected allies among several radical Protestant groups who celebrated them as heirs to the Covenant between God and Abraham and the subject of biblical prophecies about a restored Davidic kingdom in the Land of Israel.

In his book on early modern hermeneutics and the impetus to read eschatological prophecy literally, Andrew Crome suggests that the key element in the emergence of "Judeo-centrism" in the seventeenth century was an "appropriation and logical development of Reformation hermeneutical norms to reread Old Testament promises to the Jews."[55] Using Thomas Brightman as a case study, Crome analyzes the exegetical drive in the early seventeenth century to recover the meaning that scriptures would have had for their original readership—a task, he notes, that required the biblical commentators committed to historicist/literalist interpretation to ask uncomfortable questions about such issues as the restoration of the Jews to the Holy Land.[56] A resultant tension thereby emerged between the "mystical" application of biblical prophecies of restoration and renewal to the Reformed English Church and the very literal interpretation of Jewish restoration favored by Puritan exegetes such as Brightman, whose "consistent literalism" (to borrow Crome's phrase) in writings such as *A Revelation of the Apocalypse* (1611) and *Shall They Return to Jerusalem Again* (1615) produced vocal support of the Jews' return to Palestine, and predicted a millennial future founded on a Jewish empire. Correlating post-biblical history with the Book of Revelation, Brightman interpreted moments in the latter such as the apocalyptic pouring of the sixth vial into the Euphrates as preparing the way "for the Jews of the East, that, after they have embraced the faith of the Gospel, they should return to their own country: when there shall be a great preparation of war; partly by the Turk against these new Christians in the East, partly by the Pope in the West."[57]

Brightman's vision of the Jews' return to Israel involved their triumph over the Turks and the papacy, as well as their eventual conversion to Christianity. Other millenarian ideas about the approach of the messianic time insisted on both the return of the Jews to Palestine to herald the Second Coming, as well as their readmission to England in order to secure its place among the blessed nations in accordance with the prophecy in Deuteronomy: "among all people, from one end of the earth even unto the other" (Deut. 28:64).[58] That a number of Jews shared this millenarianist belief is suggested by the medieval Hebrew name for England: Kezeh ha-Aretz, "the end of the earth." For these believers, however, returning to England was only a step toward ensuring the advent of the Jewish messiah. Some millenarianists even identified the apocalyptic year as 1666—eleven years before Crowne produced *The Destruction of Jerusalem*. So dominant was this belief that Rabbi Menasseh Ben Israel in the Netherlands made it a prominent element of his plea to Oliver Cromwell and the Rump Parliament to readmit the Jews, stating that "the opinion of many Christians and mine do concur herein, that we both believe that the restoring time of our nation into their native country is very near at hand."[59] In a canny move, he praised the English nation for its reformed zeal: as a result of eschewing the "Papistical religion," it was "no longer our ancient enemy" but rather "excellently affected to our nation, as an opposed people whereof it has good hope."[60] The noted Hebraist and Dissenter Henry Jessey (1603–1663), who energetically advocated the return of the Jews, went so far as to identify the English as the people that prayed for Jewish restoration more than "any other Nation that we have heard of," and lauded the English for believing "the promises touching the calling of the Jews, and the great riches and glory that shall follow to Jews, and us, Gentiles."[61] Cromwell, for his part, emphasized the Christian obligation to convert the Jews, reasoning that they could not possibly receive the true Gospel if they were not allowed among people who professed it.

Crowne himself had had little to do with the radical Puritan position and, as I shall show, made a scathing comparison between the Puritans of his day and the Jewish zealots partially responsible for Jerusalem's ruin. But by the time *The Destruction of Jerusalem* premiered, royalist attitudes toward the Jews had also shifted significantly. As mentioned in the previous chapter, the exiled Charles and his fellow royalists had sought favor with the community of Jews in Amsterdam who, for their part, claimed to have disassociated themselves from the politics of Menasseh Ben Israel and his support for Cromwell. Instead, they wished Charles a speedy restoration and some, it is rumored, proffered him arms as well as money. In return, Charles is believed to have made it clear that, unlike Cromwell, he did not expect the Jews to convert to Christianity upon their return, and that they would be free to live and worship under his restored regime. There is no evidence that the Amsterdam Jews extended to the exiled monarch anything more concrete than their felicitations, although one cannot entirely discount the possibility of the conclusion of some clandestine agreement.[62] All that is known for certain is that when angry petitions for the Jews' removal were brought before Charles II almost immediately upon his accession, the Merry Monarch let them die a bureaucratic—and therefore entirely effective—death. Not only were the newly returned Jews and those who had lived incognito in England before openly allowed to remain after centuries of exile, but they also enjoyed the protection of the restored monarch after 1664. Restored crown and returned religious minority, once united in a common (if unacknowledged) experience, were now avowedly linked in symbiotic concord.

England's Seditionists

The clemency exhibited toward the Jews was consistent with Charles II's first imperative: to prevent further fracture in the social order. Under his rule, non-Christian sects such as the Jews and the few Muslims in England appeared to enjoy greater leniency than even several Protestant factions did, prompting the dissident theologian Edward Bagshaw to furiously query why the radical Protestant sects were treated with less toleration.[63] It is not surprising, then, that when John Locke prepared the first draft of his "Letter Concerning Toleration" in 1667, he should cite the treatment of the recently readmitted Jews as the yardstick for measuring accord.[64] Indeed, the toleration of the Jews had become an established and incontrovertible fact to be cited: "'tis strange to conceive upon what grounds of uniformity any different profession of Christians can be prohibited in a Christian country where the Jewish religion . . . is tolerated."[65] Locke's own position regarding toleration of dissident sects slackened eventually but he maintained absolute and confident conviction in the toleration of the Jews, their practices and rituals. Locke's letter is imbued with the consciousness of a new dispensation in which "tolerance" and "unity" are watchwords. It is quite appropriate, therefore, that *The Destruction of Jerusalem* should exhibit a degree of graciousness, or at least of political understanding, toward the Jews and their history. It is also equally fitting that the play's ire should be reserved for the characters whose turbulent envy of authority corrodes communal stability and, ultimately, precipitates exile. If the changing position of the Jews in seventeenth-century England was one possible reason for the play's radical sympathies, then Crowne's need to critique those who threatened political stability and invited chaos in his own historical moment was likely another.

As demonstrated in previous chapters, civil conflict dominated early modern iterations of the siege narrative. Even Morwen's *A compendious and most marueillous Historie* lamented the "doggidnesse and intestine hatred" of the Jews as they turned on each other, "subiectes agaynst theyr princes, and subiects agaynst subiects."[66] Where the Jews did succeed in coming together, they were lauded as objects worthy of emulation. Even the author of one of the anti-"Martin Marprelate" tracts (1589)—which defended the Anglican hierarchy from certain Puritan writers who used the pseudonym Martin Marprelate to attack stringent censorship laws effected by the Archbishop of Canterbury—alludes to such Jewish unity, albeit in a tongue-in-cheek manner. "Cauliero Pasquill" urges Puritan readers in a mock exhortation to unite in resisting the Episcopalian Church by remembering that: "Though the Iewes at the siege of Ierusalem were pressed by theyr enemies without the walles, and punished wyth such a mortalitie within, that the carkases of the dead did dunge the grounde, yet they neuer went to the wall, till they grew to be factious, & fell to taking one another by the throate."[67] Nevertheless, the dominant image was of the zealots' rapaciousness and self-destruction, which precipitated the desolation of their city and the final exile of their people. This ascription had been particularly popular with supporters of the Crown who denounced the religious radicals for undermining national unity. *The Subjects Sorrow: Or, Lamentations Upon the Death of Britains Josiah, KING CHARLES* (1649) excoriated the Puritans, who in the beginning "pretended *God, Religion, the Church, [their Cause]*," but who instead "have dealt with us as that Faction among the Jewes, who called themselves *The Zealous in the Warre with* Titus *did under pretence of defending Religion, and the Law, they possessed themselves of the Temple, yet were themselves the first who put fire with their owne hands into the holy places*."[68] The author of the infamous King's Book *Eikon Basilike* likewise denounced Charles I's enemies who "pretend[ed] to build *Jerusalem*" by comparing their divisiveness to "the fury of those Zealots whose intestine bitterness and divisions were the greatest occasion of the last fatal destruction of that City."[69]

Crowne sustains this royalist bias by identifying the Pharisees under John and Eleazar with Puritan radicals; indeed, they are explicitly designated "zealots" and "Proud Separatists."[70] A "usurping sect" whose power Matthias justly sought to curb, the Pharisees are motivated by "their own revengeful humour." Sworn iconoclasts driven by petty hatred, they advocate the vandalizing of the Temple and its "brazen images" as an act of "Pure Reformation" mandated by heaven.[71] John, in particular, is presented as a hypocrite who "creep[s] in power by unperceiv'd degrees," a fawning rogue who employs "every Art and subtlety." Like the serpent in Milton's *Paradise Lost*, his is a

> lurking Treachery that's hid
> In humble fawnings, and in fierce pretence
> To each punctilio of obedience. (1.1.1)

The theme is continued in the epilogue to Part 1, where Crowne identifies the "Fanaticks" of his own country as "Jews uncircumcis'd," descendants of the Pharisees "Shewing their sires, the Pharisees, from whom / They and their cheats by long succession come."

In his study of *The Destruction of Jerusalem* and Judeo-Christian apocalyptic literature, Rollins suggests that the equation of the Puritans and the Pharisees offers "a commentary on contemporary events and, in particular, the coalition of interests that had, by the mid-1670s, allied itself against the Crown."[72] The

1670s, running counter to the hopes and promises of the 1660s, had been beset by rumors of plots of every kind, and natural phenomena such as eclipses of the sun and moon were once again, in the fashion of the pre-Civil War and Civil War years, translated as dire prognostications of the kind that purport-edly beset Jerusalem before its fall. While a great many of these fears proved imaginary, the real danger, as Rollins persuasively argues, was "the threat of political chaos arising within the country itself."[73] It is thus unsurprising that Crowne should perceive an affinity between the machinations of the Phari-sees and those of the Puritans who had allied themselves against Charles I, and who continued to thwart his son in the "rekindled political firestorm" of the 1670s. In opposition to the Pharisee-Puritans, the High Priest Matthias is presented as a Laud-like figure and is even addressed as a "Romish priest" (2.3.1) in a deliberate anachronism. The implication of the "Hero ruined by the sneaking Saint" in the epilogue to Part 1 would have been impossible to miss for Crowne's Restoration audience. By raising the specter of past sectarian con-flict—the very conflict that culminated in the beheading of Charles I and the exile of the royalists—*The Destruction of Jerusalem* employs historical events to produce a powerful commentary on contemporary political unrest and its long roots in the previous decades.

Conclusion

Crowne's grandiose spectacle about Jerusalem carries serious meaning in its presentation of the endemic Restoration nightmare of a nation divided, a nation exiled. In this, it follows in the footsteps of William Heminge's *The Jewes Tragedy* with another pertinent commentary on internecine conflict. Through its equation of the Pharisees with the Puritans, *The Destruction of Jerusalem* warns about the perils of factionalism and bigotry in a way that would have res-onated powerfully with the Restoration court that had endured civil war and banishment. In so doing, it deviates from archetypal Restoration heroic plays that strove to reconstruct English society and politics along traditional lines in the aftermath of the crises of the 1640s and 1650s.[74] David Evans notes that "royalist writers such as John Dryden and William Davenant idealize attributes of a romanticized earlier time [in heroic plays], when longstanding, hierarchi-cal social bonds and a carefully wrought mythology of political order ensured a stable nation."[75] Gerald MacLean agrees that Restoration culture of the 1660s mobilized "many different psychic, political, and poetical registers seeking to reinscribe monarchic ideology in ways that would make the king's return seem acceptable and unquestionable."[76]

Less than twenty years later, however, Crowne's play, which reconfigures exile as fracture and irrevocable loss, showed itself to be fundamentally at odds with this design. Rollins is right to note that *The Destruction of Jerusalem* departs even from other late seventeenth-century apocalyptic texts that afforded the reader comfort should they take heed of warning. Crowne's narrative of all-encompassing loss, devastation, personal betrayal, expulsion, dislocation, and alienation offers next to nothing by way of hope or positive exhortation. Rather, by reinforcing the congruity between the Pharisees and the Puritans on the one hand, and displaced Jews and royalists on the other, it exposes the deep-seated anxiety over sectarian conflict and exile at the heart of Restoration politics.

Epilogue

"Worthy to Be Known and Read of All Men"

In mid-July 1634, the city of Oxford was treated to a performance of the destruction of Jerusalem that starred very special actors: puppets. Titled *Jerusalem in its Glory, Destruction*, and divided into "5 or 6 parts," the show depicted Vespasian's army entering Judaea, Titus laying siege to the city, the resultant famine that forced the inhabitants to eat everything from horsemeat to babies, the final breach of the city walls, and Titus's slaughter of the remaining Jews. For its content, *Jerusalem in its Glory, Destruction* appears to have relied heavily on John Barker's popular ballad *Of the horyble and woful destruccion of Jerusalem* (1569) and, indeed, would have been directed to a similar audience.[1]

That said, these puppets attracted more than the rank and file. Our information about this performance comes from the records of Thomas Crosfield (1602–1663), who was a tutor at Queen's College. Crosfield's diary has interested scholars primarily for its vivid portrait of university politics during the tenure of William Laud as chancellor (1629–33). But the entries also reveal an energetic man of wide-ranging interests who sought out lectures on music, history, moral philosophy, anatomy, natural philosophy, geometry, and even private lectures on Arabic. Somehow he managed to find time to attend the puppet show, which he must have enjoyed, because he was back in the audience the following year when it was staged again at Moot Hall.[2]

Crosfield ascribed the show to one William Gosling, a former pupil of the great antiquarian William Camden (1551–1623), who had been reduced to puppetry when a thieving maidservant made off with the money he had inherited from his wife. Although Crosfield may have been mistaken about the show's owner—other sources suggest it belonged to a Captain Pod—there is no doubt that he saw puppets play out Jerusalem's destruction twice within the space of twelve months.[3] In each case, the show appears to have included a bit about the city's transfiguration at the end of days. But the chief focus was the tragedy that had proven so popular in other media—namely, the siege and its attendant horrors.

Oxford would become invested in Jerusalem's destruction yet again in the 1680s. The principals of this story, however, would move in vastly different circles from the good folk who may have cheered on that midsummer afternoon fifty years before. The protagonist on this occasion was Edward Bernard (1630–1697), professor of Astronomy and noted Orientalist, who was commissioned by Oxford University Press to edit a massive scholarly edition of Josephus's works. That this endeavor was eagerly anticipated is clear from the enthusiasm expressed by many of Bernard's peers, including the philologist Pierre Daniel Huet (1630–1671) of the Academy Francaise, who assured him in 1684 that "expectation is great among all the learned of your Josephus, and no one's is greater than mine."[4] The chief catalyst for the project was John Fell, Bishop of Oxford (1625–1686), whose ambitious plan had included printing annotated editions of Josephus's Greek and Latin writings alongside a new edition of the Septuagint, the Coptic gospels, the Aramaic Targums, Greek and Latin Fathers such as Clement, Ignatius, and Polycarp, the Syriac writings of the Eastern Church Fathers, and even Maimonides's *Mishneh Torah*. As Thomas Roebuck notes, Fell believed that this was "Josephus's context . . . a product of the Judaic culture of the first century AD." His intention was to produce an erudite and comprehensive source "that might help illuminate that culture and, in turn, the origins and development of the early Christian church."[5] But the enterprise may also be read as a repatriation of Josephus—removing him from the sweaty crowds into the hushed halls of academe.

The undertaking failed. But the story of its failure is fascinating, as Roebuck demonstrates. Bernard had sought out the most prominent Josephan scholars all over Europe and made concerted attempts to access manuscripts in libraries across the Continent. While the famed Dutch manuscript collector Isaac Vossius (1618–1689) obligingly supplied collections of the Latin translation of Josephus, the most prominent Josephan scholar of the day, Johann Andreas Bosius (1626–1674), who had devoted a decade to collecting variant manuscripts from all over Europe, dismissed the project, claiming that Bernard could not possibly have access to the many "helpful manuscripts" he himself had studied.[6] That

the emphasis was all on how many variant readings could be cited and annotated is suggested also from a letter written by the Irish scholar of chronology,
John Baynard, in which he cautioned Bernard that "no man can p[re]sume he
has the Author if he has no more but one copy."[7] Baynard need not have wor-
ried. As Roebuck points out, "Bernard was not attempting to produce a new
manuscript recension of Josephus." Rather, his aim was "to amass as many textual variants as possible to insert into the edition's footnotes."[8]

Despite non-cooperation from key Parisian libraries, Bernard compiled a
prodigious collection of variant readings, to which he added so many annotations that the main text was completely overwhelmed. Even Vossius urged Bernard to pare down his ambition, but to no avail. Finally, a frustrated Bishop Fell
turned to Henry Aldrich (1647–1710), Dean of Christ Church. The result, in
1687, was an edition of the first two books of the *Jewish War* that, while drawing on the variant readings of the Greek manuscripts Bernard had assiduously
collected, eschewed his copious annotations and arcane knowledge. Bernard's
own exacting labors yielded four books of *The Antiquities* (his real passion) that
were only published by the press in 1700, three years after his death.

At a time when, to quote Daniel Woolf, history was passing from a "minor
pastime of a small number of monastic chroniclers and civic officials into a
major area of study and leisurely pursuit of university students, lawyers, aspir-
ing courtiers, and ordinary readers" and thereby becoming a "broadly appealing
genre that straddled the worlds of scholarship and literary culture," the failed
Oxford University Press edition of Josephus poignantly attests to the pitfalls
of academic exclusivity and scholarly obsession.[9] Intended for an audience of
highly accomplished intellectuals, it broke under the weight of its own esoteric
ambition as Bernard became mired in his own erudition.

Elsewhere, though, Josephus's siege continued to function both as an
effective barometer for crisis and as a subject worthy of intellectual curiosity.
Laurence Price's *Englands Golden Legacy: or, A brief description of the manifold
Mercies and Blessings which the Lord hath bestowed upon our sinful nation* (1657)
returned its readers to the familiar scene of Christ weeping over Jerusalem's
iniquities to encourage them to stay virtuous during economic hardship.
Its epistle dedicated to "all Christians" emphasized the scale of the author's
ambition: to expound on the "bitter calamities and extremities of that glorious & unparaleled City of Jerusalem" that he might "give warning to the
world, that every man may take heed of that fearful sin of Ingratitude."[10] The
language of Price's epistle—"all Christians ... the world ... every man...."—
bespeaks a broad and democratic outreach, counterbalanced within the piece
by explicit comparisons between ancient Jewish calamity and contemporary

English despair: "some hanged themselves, some drowned themselves, some cut their owne throats, all which was done for want of serving God; as many have lately done in the City of London, and in other parts of England, the more is the pity."[11]

Price's account of the siege is laconic and omits details that are "too tedious here to be told." Instead, he offers a highlights reel, all the while pointing his readers to the larger and familiar "testemony for the same, both from the Scriptures, & other sufficient Authors."[12] That Josephus need no longer be named is, in and of itself, quite suggestive. His siege story was, by this point, almost proverbial. Thanks to his emulators, the "sufficient Authors" who had said so much, Price had the luxury of saying so little.

Compression likewise marks R.D.'s *The Strange and Prodigious Religions, Customs and Manners of Sundry Nations*, first published in 1683 and reprinted in 1688. His history, "Faithfully collected from ancient and modern Authors; and adorned with divers Pictures of several remarkable Passages therein," is explicitly designed to entertain the inquiring mind. "If the Variety and Greatness of Subjects are capable of affording satisfaction to a Reader," R.D.'s history pledges "abundantly to satisfie thy Curiosity." The result is a handy compendium of topics on which "the greatest Pens . . . have filled many large Volumes, and [which] would require a great deal of time to read over."[13] Among these is the Roman siege, a brief account which, R.D. coyly admits, "will not perhaps be an ungrateful Undertaking."[14] The result is a highly compacted, often word-for-word abridgment of the *Josippon*, numbering a mere fifty-two pages, that hits familiar high notes such as the civil discord instigated by the zealots, the famine, and Miriam's cannibalism.

R.D.'s successful conspectus confidently presupposed knowledge of historical events such as the siege, and with good reason. The late seventeenth century had witnessed many a reprint of such material, with accounts of Jerusalem's tragic decline proving to be enduringly fashionable. Ballads about the city's final fall first produced in the sixteenth century were reprinted as late as 1690. John Crowne's spectacular *Destruction of Jerusalem by Titus Vespasian*, printed the same year T.D.'s *Canaan's Calamitie* was reissued (1677), was itself reprinted in 1693. Hardly surprising, then, that writers and preachers continued to allude to the siege in divergent contexts with little or no preface, so convinced were they that these inferences would be understood and appreciated.

In 1682, John Flavel recalled in his *Two Treatises* how "plainly Christ did fortel" the Roman devastation of Jerusalem and its Temple, thereby reiterating a familiar refrain: that "the Israelites are made examples to us, plainly intimating that if we tread the same path, we must expect the same punishment."[15] *Great*

Britain's Warning-piece; or Christ's Tears over Jerusalem (1689), a self-styled "ferocious Exhortation to a timely Repentance," castigates its readers for their affinity with the sinful Jews with the assurance of one treading familiar ground. In 1689/90 Gilbert Burnet, preaching before the Court of Aldermen, urged his audience to be vigilant against Catholic ascendancy. Recalling how the Jews became complacent after beating back the forces lead by Cestius Gallus only to be routed by Titus, he reminded them that just as "the next return of the Romans was more formidable and proved in Conclusion fatal to [the Jews] . . . If we . . . grow to have milder Thoughts of our Enemies the modern Romans . . . we may soon [be] undeceived."[16] In 1697, John Cockburn's Good Friday sermon preached in Edinburgh used Luke 23—Christ's address to the weeping women of Jerusalem—to recall the "sore and heavy Calamities" that befell that holy city, namely "what afterwards fell out at the Destruction of *Jerusalem*, viz. That during the strictness of the Siege, some were reduced to that strait, that to pre-serve their own Lives they Eat the flesh of their own Children."[17] Citing Christ's prophecy of Jerusalem's destruction, he assured his congregation that "*whoever is pleased to read Josephus his History will find, That all was actually accom-plished upon Flavius Vespasian and Titus his Son invading Judaea; Besieging and Sacking of Jerusalem.*"[18]

As if to encourage such inclusive perusal, yet another edition of *The Won-derful and Most Deplorable History*—that ever-popular mid-century reprint of Peter Morwen's translation of the *Josippon*—was reissued in 1699. But perhaps the universal appeal of the siege in the late seventeenth century is best summed up in the title of an anonymous tract published in 1675: *The world surveyed: or, A brief account of many remarkable passages wherein the omnipotent works of God are brought to our knowledge* includes *A relation of that dreadful famine that befel the memorable city of Jerusalem, while grass, hay, leaves, and barks of trees, dogs, cats, with the dung of fowls and beasts was their desirable food.* As its author insists in the very title, such a subject was "*Worthy to be known and read of all men.*"

Notes

Introduction

1. Beatrice Groves, *The Destruction of Jerusalem in Early Modern England* (Cambridge: Cambridge University Press, 2015).

2. See James Carroll, *Constantine's Sword: The Church and the Jews, A History* (Boston: Houghton Mifflin, 2001), 108.

3. Unless otherwise indicated, all biblical references are taken from the Geneva Bible.

4. Robert Wilken, *The Land Called Holy: Palestine in Christian History and Thought* (New Haven, CT: Yale University Press, 1992), 43.

5. Francis White, *Londons VVarning, by Jervsalem* (London, 1619), 49.

6. John Lawrence, *A Golden Trvmpet, to Rowse Vp a Drowsie Magistrate . . . drawne from Christs comming to, beholding of, and weeping ouer Hierusalem* (London, 1624), 14.

7. Richard Maden, *Christs Love and Affection towards Jerusalem* (London, 1637), Cr.

8. Thomas Cooper, *Certaine Sermons vvherein is contained the Defense of the Gospell* (London, 1580), 188.

9. John Brinsley, *Tears for Iervsalem, or, The compassionate Lamentation of a tender hearted Saviour over a rebellious and obdurate people* (London, 1656), Aaa3r.

10. *Great Britain's Warning-piece; or, Christ's Tears over Jerusalem* (London, 1689), 8.

11. Thomas Wilson, *Christs Farewell to Jerusalem, and last Prophesie* (London, 1614), C8r–Dv.

12. M. E. Hardwick, *Josephus as an Historical Source in Patristic Literature Through Eusebius* (Atlanta: Scholars Press, 1989), 17–18.

13. See Wataru Mizugaki, "Origen and Josephus," in *Josephus, Judaism, and Christianity*, eds. L. Feldman and G. Hata (Detroit: Wayne State, 1987) 325–37; pages 331–33 deal specifically with the *Fragmenta*.

14. Cited in Heinz Schreckenberg and Kurt Schubert, eds., *Jewish Historiography and Iconography in Early and Medieval Christianity*, vol. 1 (Assen, Netherlands: Fortress Press, 1992), 58.

15. Eusebius, *The Avncient Ecclesiasticall Histories Of The First Six Hundred Years After Christ*, trans. Meredith Hanmer (London, 1577), 37.

16. Ibid., 38.

17. Ibid., 41.

18. Honora Howell Chapman, "'A Myth for the World': Early Christian Reception of Cannibalism in Josephus, *Bellum Judaicum* 6 199–219," *SBL Seminar Papers* (2000): 359–78.

19. For an extensive discussion of the Church Fathers' appropriation of Josephus, see Schreckenberg and Schubert, *Jewish Historiography*, 73–80. Augustine's interpretation of history is discussed at length in: Christopher T. Daly, John Doody, and Kim Paffenroth, eds., *Augustine and History* (Lanham, MD: Lexington Books, 2008); Carol Harrison, *Rethinking Augustine's Early Theology: An Argument for Continuity* (Oxford: Oxford University Press, 2006); Rüdiger Bittner, "Augustine's Philosophy of History," in *The Augustinian Tradition*, ed. Gareth B. Matthews (Berkeley: University of California Press, 1999), 345–60; and F. Smith Fussner, *The Historical Revolution: English Historical Writing and Thought 1580–1640* (London: Routledge, 1962).

20. Pseudo-Hegesippus, *Hegesippi Qui Dicitur Historiae Libri V*, ed. Vincente Ussani, vol. 66 (Vienna: Holder-Pichler-Tempsky, 1932), 296.

21. Stephen Wright, *The Vengeance of the Lord: Medieval Dramatizations of the Destruction of Jerusalem* (Toronto, ON: Pontifical Institute of Mediaeval Studies, 1989), 15.

22. See *The dystruccyon of Iherusalem by Vaspazyan and Tytus* (London, 1513), E2v.

23. Jerusalem's symbolic value for English nationhood is discussed by Alexandra Walsham in *Providence in Early Modern England* (Oxford: Oxford University Press, 2001), and in Achsah Guibbory's study of the influence of Jewish history on seventeenth-century Christian identity *Christian Identity, Jews, and Israel in Seventeenth-Century England* (Oxford: Oxford University Press, 2010).

24. For a study of the cause and motives behind the rise of Christian Hebraism, see G. Lloyd Jones, *The Discovery of Hebrew in Tudor England: A Third Language* (Manchester: Manchester University Press, 1983).

25. William Tyndale, Preface to *The Obedience of a Christian Man* (1528) in *The Works of William Tyndale*, ed. G. E. Duffield (Appleford, Berkshire, UK: Sutton Courtnay Press, 1964), 326. For the distinctive impact of the Hebrew language on early modern English translations of the Bible, see also Naomi Tadmor, *The Social Universe of the Hebrew Bible: Scripture, Society, and Culture in Early Modern England* (Cambridge: Cambridge University Press, 2010).

26. Cited in David Daniell, *William Tyndale: A Biography* (New Haven, CT: Yale University Press, 2001), 379.

27. Hugh Broughton, *A require of agreement to the groundes of divinitie studie* in *The VVorks Of The Great Albionean Divine, Renown'd in Many Nations For rare Skill in Salems and Athens Tongues* (London, 1662), 644.

28. Guibbory, *Christian Identity*, 17.

29. Bishop Joseph Hall, *The Blessings, Sins and Judgments of God's Vineyard* in *The Works of Joseph Hall: Successively Bishop of Exeter and Norwich: With Some Account of his Life and Sufferings*, vol. 5 (Oxford: Talboys, 1837), 321.

30. Paul Knell, *Israel and England Paralelled* (London, 1648), 16. Of course, Knell's jubilation is soon tempered by the fear that England will suffer the dire fate of Israel.

31. Samuel Stollman, "Milton's Dichotomy of 'Judaism' and 'Hebraism,'" *PMLA* 89, no. 1 (1974): 108.

32. Broughton, *VVorks*, 362. In counterpoint, we get Edwin Sandys's description of the Jews as, for the most part, "very honorable and holy." See *A Relation of the State of Religion* (London, 1605), X3r.

33. James Shapiro, *Shakespeare and the Jews* (New York: Columbia University Press, 1996), 174.

34. Walsham, *Providence in Early Modern England*, 285.

35. Adam Hill, *The Crie of England* (London, 1595), 100.

36. William Est, *The Triall Of true teares. Or the Summons to repentance whereby the secure sinner is taught how to escape the terrible Sentence of the Supreme Iudge. Meditated vpon Christes weeping ouer Ierusalem, very necessarie for these present Times* (London, 1613), 78–79.

37. Francis Smith, *Jerusalem's Sins, Jerusalem's Destruction: Or, National Sins the Cause of National Calamities Being a Discourse seasonable for these times* (London, 1691), 12, 20.

38. Groves, *Destruction of Jerusalem*, 29.

39. Ibid., 3, 5–6.

40. Wright, *Vengeance of the Lord*, 15.

41. Groves, *Destruction of Jerusalem*, 31.

42. William Haller, *Foxe's Book of Martyrs and the Elect Nation* (London: Jonathan Cape, 1963), 53. It is worth noting here Guibbory's observation about the "slippage between the idea that England was 'an' elect nation, part of the universal church of God, and 'the' elect nation. Both the New Testament and the Protestant emphasis on election revised but did not dismiss the idea of chosenness and 'chosen people,' as described in the Hebrew Bible." See *Christian Identity*, 13.

43. For important counterarguments to Haller's claims about English exceptionalism, see: Katharine R. Frith, The *Apocalyptic Tradition in Reformation Britain, 1530–1645* (Oxford: Oxford University Press, 1979), 252–54; Michael McGiffert, "Covenant, Crown, and Commons in Elizabethan Puritanism," *The Journal of British Studies* 20, no. 1 (1980): 32–52; Patrick Collinson, *The Birthpangs of Protestant England: Religious and Cultural Change in the Sixteenth and Seventeenth Centuries* (London: Macmillan, 1988), 14–16; Collinson, "Biblical Rhetoric: The English Nation and National Sentiment in the Prophetic Mode," in *Religion and Culture in Renaissance England*, eds. Claire McEachern and Debora Shuger (Cambridge: Cambridge University Press, 1997), 24; Mary Morrissey, "Elect Nations and Prophetic Preaching: *Types* and *Examples* in the Paul's Cross Jeremiad," in *The English Sermon Revised: Religion, Literature and History 1600–1750*, eds. Lori Anne Ferrell and Peter McCullough (Manchester: Manchester University Press, 2000), 43–58; Walsham, *Providence*, 305ff, 290 n56; and Groves, *Destruction*, 17–18.

44. Jesse M. Lander, *Inventing Polemic: Religion, Print, and Literary Culture in Early Modern England* (Cambridge: Cambridge University Press, 2006), 59.

45. Knell, *Israel*, 16.

46. Thomas Becon, *The Flour of Godly Praiers* (London: 1550), Aiii.

47. Stuart Gillespie and Neil Rhodes, eds., *Shakespeare and Elizabethan Popular Culture* (London: Arden Shakespeare, 2006), 9; David Cressy, *Literacy and the Social Order: Reading and Writing in Tudor and Stuart England* (Cambridge: Cambridge University Press, 1980), 42; Adam Fox, *Oral and Literate Culture in England, 1500–1700* (Oxford: Oxford University Press, 2000), 42.

48. Margaret Spufford, *Small Books and Pleasant Histories: Popular Fiction and its Readership in Seventeenth-Century England* (Cambridge: Cambridge University Press, 1981), 27.

49. I follow Ian Green's index of popularity: any title qualifies that was reprinted at least five times over a thirty-year period, which he defines as a figure "low enough to eliminate those works which do not appear to have caught the public imagination sufficiently to warrant more than a couple of editions." See Ian Green, *Print and Protestantism in Early Modern England* (Oxford: Oxford University Press, 2000), 173. For discussions on popularity in early modern England, see also: Peter Burke, *Popular Culture in Early Modern Europe*, 3rd ed. (1978; Farnham, Surrey, UK: Ashgate, 2009); Mary Ellen Lamb, *The Popular Culture of Shakespeare, Spenser and Jonson* (New York: Routledge, 2006); Stephen Purcell, *Popular Shakespeare: Simulation and Subversion on the Modern Stage* (New York: Palgrave Macmillan, 2009); Gary Kelly, Joad Raymond, and Christine Bold, eds., *The Oxford History of Popular Print Culture, Vol. 1: Cheap Print in Britain and Ireland to 1660* (Oxford: Oxford University Press, 2011); and Andy Kesson and Emma Smith, eds., *The Elizabethan Top Ten: Defining Print Popularity in Early Modern England* (Burlington, VT: Ashgate, 2013).

50. Given the popular belief cemented by Morwen's text that the *Josippon* was Josephus's account of the siege that he wrote in his native tongue, it is not a stretch to believe, with Groves, that the preachers, poets, and dramatists who read and referenced the text "were trying to recover a Jewish perspective on Jerusalem's fall." See Groves, *Destruction of Jerusalem*, 65. Certainly, the reprint of Morwen's history with the new title of *The Wonderful and Most Deplorable History of the Latter Times of the Jews* (1652) seemed to regard the *Josippon's* value as being its exclusive attention to "matters as they relate principally to the *Jews* themselves, and the state of their Common-wealth," unlike the "great Volume of *Josephus*," which focused equally on the Romans and other nations (1). All references to *The Wonderful and Most Deplorable History* are to the 1662 edition.

51. John Lightfoot, *The Harmony, Chronicle and Order of the New-Testament* (London, 1655), 178.

52. Ibid., 175.

53. Thomas Hearne, *Ductor Historicus: Or, a Short System of Universal History, and an Introduction to the Study of That Science* (London, 1698), A4r.

54. Groves, *Destruction of Jerusalem*, 35.

55. Lodowick Lloyd, *The Stratagems of Ierusalem With the martiall lawes and militarie discipline, as well of the Iewes as the Gentiles* (London, 1602), 225.

56. John Barker, *Of the horyble and woful destruccion of Jerusalem And of the sygns and tokens that were seene before it was destroied* (London, 1569).

57. Thomas Jackson, *Diverse Sermons with a Short Treatise befitting these Present Times* (Oxford, 1637), 42.

58. John Flavel, *Two Treatises* (London, 1682), 165.

59. Lawrence, *A Golden Trvmpet*, 99.

60. Smith, *Jerusalem's Sins, Jerusalem's Destruction*, A.

61. England became the first European country to officially expel Jews in the thirteenth century after mounting accusations of ritual child murder and host desecration were leveled against them in Norwich, Suffolk, Winchester, Bristol, and London. It would be 366 years before Jews officially returned to England, though some continued to live there incognito. If the motivation for their expulsion was at least partly financial—Edward I first prohibited their practice of usury before exiling them in 1290 and confiscating their property—mercantile as well as religious considerations enabled their eventual return. The years following the Reformation had witnessed a steady rise in Hebraism, and when Oliver Cromwell, urged on by Amsterdam Rabbi Menasseh ben Israel, submitted a formal petition to Parliament to readmit the Jews, he appealed to the belief that they must be brought back and converted to usher in the millennium. Although the specially convened Whitehall Conference (1655) was dissolved by Cromwell before it could reach a decision, Jews began to live openly in England. In 1664, they were formally granted Royal Protection under Charles II.

62. Keith Thomas, *The Perception of the Past in Early Modern England*, Creighton Trust Lecture, University of London (London, 1983), 8.

63. Daniel Woolf, "From Hystories to the Historical: Five Transitions in Thinking about the Past," *The Uses of History in Early Modern England*, ed. Paulina Kewes (San Marina, CA: Huntington Library, 2006), 34.

64. Ibid., 36.

65. Philip J. Ayres's *Classical Culture and the Idea of Rome in Eighteenth-Century England* (Cambridge: Cambridge University Press, 1997) examines the idealized image of republican Rome adopted by aristocracy and gentry in the aftermath of the Glorious Revolution; Freyja Cox Jensen's *Reading the Roman Republic in Early Modern England* (Leiden: Brill, 2012) records the ways in which Roman history was read and absorbed in Tudor and Stuart England. Studies of representations of Rome on the early modern stage include work by Clifford Ronan, *Antike Roman: Power Symbology and the Roman Play in Early Modern England, 1585–1635* (Athens: University of Georgia Press, 1995); and Lisa Hopkins, *The Cultural Uses of the Caesars on the English Renaissance Stage* (Burlington, VT: Ashgate, 2008).

1. Unholy Ghosts

1. John Stockwood, *A very fruitfull and necessarye Sermon of the moste lamemtable destruction of Ierusalem, and the heauy iudgements of God, executed vppon that people for their sinne and dissobedience* (London, 1584), sig. B8r.

2. For Jerusalem as a paradigm for England, see Patrick Collinson, *Religious Publishing in England 1557–1640* in *The Cambridge History of the Book*, Vol. 4, *1557–1695* (Cambridge: Cambridge University Press, 2002), 29–66; Richard L. Greaves, "The Origins and Early Development of English Covenant Thought," *The Historian* 31, no. 1 (1968): 21–35; and Michael McGiffert, "Grace and Works: The Rise and Division of Covenant Divinity in Elizabethan Puritanism," *The Harvard Theological Review* 75, no. 4 (1982): 463–502. For more on the idea of the new covenant in Christ/Christianity after the loss of the Temple, see Mary E. Smallwood, *The Jews Under Roman Rule: From Pompey to Diocletian* (Leiden: Brill, 1976).

3. Peter Morwen, *A compendious and most marueilous Historie of the latter times of the Iewes common weale*, Aiiv (London, 1575). Jugge is mentioned in the 1561, 1567, and 1575 editions. The 1558 edition reads, "Being moued and requested of a certayne honest man prynter of London." All textual references are to the 1575 edition unless otherwise specified.

4. It has been suggested that Jugge may have used Morwen as one of his translators on the project. See Beatrice Groves, *The Destruction of Jerusalem In Early Modern English Literature* (Cambridge: Cambridge University Press, 2015), 41.

5. Morwen, *A compendious and most marueilous Historie*, Aiiiiv

6. Ibid., Aiiv; Aiiir.

7. Jacob Reiner, "The English *Yosippon*," *The Jewish Quarterly Review* 58, no. 2 (1967): 138.

8. Morwen, *A compendious and most marveillous History*, Aiiir, Aiiiiv

9. See also Groves, *Destruction of Jerusalem*, 38.

10. Thomas Lodge, *The Lamentable and Tragicall History of the VVars and Vtter Rvine of the Iewes* in *Famovs and Memorable Workes of Iosephvs*, 555. All references are to the 1620 edition unless otherwise indicated.

11. Lucien Wolf insists that *A compendious and most marueilous Historie* was "a literal version of Munster, although its author pretended to derive it directly from the Hebrew." See Wolf, "'Josippon' in England," *Transactions of the Jewish Historical Society of England, Sessions 1908–1910* (1912): 279–80. Moses Marx and Max Schloesinger concur. See Marx, "Among Recent Acquistions: Joseph ben Gorion Editions," *Studies in Bibliography and Booklore* 6, no. 1 (1962): 39, and Schloesinger, *The Jewish Encyclopedia: A Descriptive Record of the History, Religion, Literature and Customs of the Jewish People from the Earliest Times to the Present Day*, vol. 6 (New York: Funk and Wagnalls, 1912), 60. Jacob Reiner agrees that the first section of Morwen's translation is based on Ibn Daud's work but admits the possibility that Morwen may have used the original Hebrew rather than relying exclusively upon Munster's Latin version (which is, nevertheless, a literal translation of the Hebrew). He also identifies other European editions of the *Yosippon* as potential sources, including the Hebrew text of the Constantinople recension for the later part of Morwen's history. See Reiner, "The English Yosippon," 131.

12. Groves, *Destruction of Jerusalem*, 40. As she observes, "The English translation of the Josippon (like the Slavonic Jewish War), was a text that was at once a continuation

of Jewish history beyond the end of the New Testament, and a witness to the life of Christ. By combining these two roles it presents itself as the perfect companion volume to the Bible" (41). Groves's assertion agrees with James Shapiro's influential thesis that the early modern English looked more and more to Jewish questions to answer English ones, and confirms the pivotal role played by the *Josippon* in this endeavor. See James Shapiro, *Shakespeare and the Jews* (New York: Columbia University Press, 1996), 174.

13. Erin E. Kelly, "Jewish History, Catholic Argument: Thomas Lodge's 'Workes of Josephus' as a Catholic Text," *Sixteenth Century Journal* 34, no. 4 (Winter 2003): 998–99.

14. Groves, *Destruction of Jerusalem*, 167.

15. See Groves's "*Christ's tears over Jerusalem* and maternal cannibalism in early modern London," in *Biblical Women in Early Modern Literary Culture, 1550–1700*, eds. Victoria Brownlee and Laura Gallagher (Manchester: Manchester University Press, 2015), 146–62.

16. Merrall Llewelyn Price, *Consuming Passions: The Uses of Cannibalism in Late Medieval and Early Modern Europe* (New York: Routledge, 2003), 85.

17. See Maggie Kilgour, *From Communion to Cannibalism: An Anatomy of Metaphors of Incorporation* (Princeton, NJ: Princeton University Press, 1990), for a detailed examination of the controversial intersections between cannibalism and the Western Church.

18. Morwen, *A compendious and most marueilous Historie*, Aiiiir.

19. Ibid., 189v; 147v.

20. Ibid., 188r.

21. Ibid., 189v.

22. Ibid., 231r.

23. Ibid., 146v.

24. See Gary Waller, *The Virgin Mary in Late Medieval and Early Modern Literature and Culture* (Cambridge: Cambridge University Press, 2011), 110.

25. Margaret Aston, *Lollards and Reformers: Images and Literacy in Late Medieval Religion* (London: Hambledon, 1984), 325.

26. Joyce Youings, *The Dissolution of the Monasteries* (London: George Allen and Unwin Ltd., 1971), 169.

27. Philip Schwyzer, *Literature, Nationalism and Memory in Early Modern England and Wales* (Cambridge: Cambridge University Press, 2004), 60.

28. Sir John Denham, "Cooper's Hill," in *The Poetical Works of Sir John Denham*, ed. Theodore Banks, 2nd ed. (New Haven, CT: Yale University Press, 1969), 73.

29. William Lambarde, *A perambulation of Kent conteining the description, hystorie, and customes of that shire/written in the yeere 1570* (London: Baldwin, Craddock, and Joy, 1826), 235–36.

30. Morwen, *A compendious and most marueilous Historie*, 230v.

31. Ibid.

32. See Nigel Llewellyn, *Funeral Monuments in Post-Reformation England* (New York: Cambridge University Press, 2000), 20. It is interesting to note that Llewellyn

identifies 1559—the year after Morwen's history was first published—as the date that monumental commemoration stabilized in reformed England.

33. Peter Sherlock, *Monuments and Memory in Early Modern England* (Burlington, VT: Ashgate, 2008), 2.

34. Morwen, *A compendious and most marueilous Historie*, 230v–r.

35. Ibid., 229r.

36. Ibid., 230r.

37. See Nigel Llewellyn, *The Art of Death: Visual Culture in the English Death Ritual, 1500–1800* (London: Reaktion Books, 1991), 17.

38. John Weever, *Ancient Funerall Monvments Within The Vnited Monarchie of Great Britaine, Ireland, and the Islands adiacent* (London, 1631), 18.

39. Jude Jones, "Embodied Shadows: Reading Gender Issues Embedded in Early Modern Tomb Effigies and Mortuary Memorials, 1500–1680," in *Monuments and Monumentality Across Medieval and Early Modern Europe*, ed. Michael Penman (Donington, Lincolnshire, UK: Shaun Tyas, 2013), 80. See also: Peter Marshall, *Beliefs and the Dead in Reformation England* (Oxford: Oxford University Press, 2002), 289–91; Claire Gittings, *Death, Burial and the Individual in Early Modern England* (London: Croom Helm, 1984); and Ralph Houlbrooke, *Death, Religion and the Family in England 1480–1750* (Oxford: Oxford University Press, 1998).

40. See also Jones's discussion of the early modern women who "make their own claims to social memory through the medium of the tomb" in *Monuments and Monumentality*, 85–90.

41. Morwen, *A compendious and most marueilous Historie*, 230r.

42. Llewellyn, citing the case of the Reverend William Evans, who erected a monument in Hereford Church that depicted him (while he was still living) along with his late lamented wife, notes that in post-Reformation England "approximately one third of the funeral monuments erected were intended to commemorate, and thus represent, the living." See *The Art of Death*, 17.

43. Sherlock, *Monuments and Memory*, 3.

44. Morwen, *A compendious and most marueilous Historie*, 230r–231v.

45. Erwin Panofsky, *Tomb Sculpture: Four Lectures on the Changing Aspects from Ancient Egypt to Bernini*, ed. H. W. Janson (New York: H. N. Abrams, 1964).

46. Morwen, *A compendious and most marueilous Historie*, 230r.

47. Ibid., 231v–r.

48. Ibid., 189r.

49. Ibid., 231r.

50. Miles Coverdale, *The Bible that is the holy Scripture of the Olde and New Testament* (London, 1536).

51. See Sarah Duncan, "Princess Elizabeth Travels Across Her Kingdom: In Life, in Text, and on Stage," in *Queens and Power in Medieval and Early Modern England*, eds. Carol Levine and R. O. Bucholz (Lincoln: University of Nebraska Press, 2009), 37.

52. See Jennifer Clement, *Reading Humility in Early Modern England* (Burlington, VT: Ashgate, 2015). See also Carole Levin, *The Heart and Stomach of a King: Elizabeth*

I and the Politics of Sex and Power, 2nd ed. (Philadelphia: University of Pennsylvania Press, 2013), who discusses "Elizabeth's self-presentation as the Virgin Queen, an image she presented to her people as a means to replace the Virgin Mary and help heal the rupture created by the break with the Catholic Church" (26). See additionally Louis Montrose's *The Subject of Elizabeth: Authority, Gender and Representation* (Chicago: University of Chicago Press, 2006), 80–89.

53. Price, *Consuming Passions*, 85.

54. William Heminge, *The Jewes Tragedy* in *The Plays and Poems of William Heminge*, ed. Carol A. Morley (Madison, NJ: Fairleigh Dickinson University Press, 2006), 5.2.51.

55. Kenneth R. Stow, *Alienated Minority: The Jews of Medieval Latin Europe* (Cambridge, MA: Harvard University Press, 1992), 237–38.

56. Heminge, *The Jewes Tragedy*, 5.2.53–55.

57. Thomas Nashe, *Christs Teares over Iervsalem* in *The Works of Thomas Nashe*, ed. Ronald B. McKerrow, vol. 2 (1904; New York: Barnes and Noble, 1966), 16.

58. Ibid., 20.

59. Ibid., 75–76.

60. Ibid., 74.

61. Ibid., 58.

62. See Price, *Consuming Passions*, 84. Marina Warner has also argued that the Virgin belongs in the tradition of "an all-devouring and savage goddess of myth . . . who sacrifices a substitute to the powers of darkness to save herself and then weeps for him." See *Alone of All Her Sex: The Myth and the Cult of the Virgin Mary* (Oxford: Oxford University Press, 1976), 224.

63. *One Hundred Middle English Lyrics*, ed. Robert Stevick, rev. ed. (Urbana: University of Illinois Press, 1994), 144.

64. Alex Mueller, "Corporal Terror: Critiques of Imperialism in the Siege of Jerusalem," *Philological Quarterly* 84, no. 3 (2005): 300.

65. For Aristotle, any individual physical body is made up of its substantial form: its essence, a composite of prime matter and the form that Nature imposes on that prime matter; and its accidents, inherent qualities that, were they to change, would not change the essence of the physical body. See Ross Hamilton, *A Philosophical and Literary History* (Chicago: University of Chicago Press, 2007), 12–13.

66. *Canons and Decrees of the Council of Trent: Original Text with English Translations*, ed. H. J. Schroeder (St. Louis: Herder, 1941), 73.

67. Julia Houston, "Transubstantiation and the Sign: Cranmer's Drama of the Lord's Supper," *Journal of Medieval and Renaissance Studies* 24, no. 1 (1994): 118.

68. Thomas Aquinas, *Summa Theologiae* (London: Blackfriars, 1964–1980), 32.76.1 ad.2; 32.75.5.

69. See note 64 above on "accidents." For an extensive study of the Eucharist and cannibalism, see Miri Rubin, *Corpus Christi: The Eucharist in Late Medieval Culture* (Cambridge: Cambridge University Press, 1991).

70. Aquinas, *Summa Theologiae*, 32.75.5.

71. Ibid. 3a. 75.5.

72. Carolyn Walker Bynum, *The Resurrection of the Body in Western Christianity, 200–1336* (New York: Columbia University Press, 1995), 41.

73. John Calvin, *Institutes of the Christian Religion*, trans. Henry Beveridge, vol. 2 (Grand Rapids, MI: Eerdmans, 1989). Book 4, chapters 14 through 18, express his concerns with the Eucharist. Calvin's objections seem to have developed from a widespread suspicion of hermetic magic. He likened transubstantiation to the magician who manipulated material nature, and equated the words of consecration spoken over the host to magical incantation. Luther too had little use for Rome's "trumpery stuff about transubstantiation, and other metaphysical nonsense without end." See "The Pagan Servitude of the Church: A First Inquiry," in *Reformation Writings of Martin Luther: The Basis of the Protestant Reformation*, trans. with intro and notes from the definitive Weimar, ed. Bertram Lee Woolf, vol. 1 (New York: Philosophical Library, 1953–1956), 226–27. Luther admits real presence but abjures transubstantiation, preferring instead consubstantiation, whereby bread and wine remain along with the body and blood of Christ after the consecration.

74. Kilgour, *From Communion to Cannibalism*, 82–83. See also 83–84.

75. Calvin, *Institutes*, 607.

76. George Hoffman, "Anatomy of the Mass: Montaigne's 'Cannibals,'" *PMLA* 117, no. 2 (2002): 210.

77. Huldrych Zwingli, *Commentary on True and False Religion*, ed. Samuel Macauley Jackson and Clarence Nevin Heller (Eugene, OR: Wipf & Stock, 2015), 216.

78. Jean de Léry, *History of a Voyage to the Land of Brazil*, trans. Janet Whatley (Berkeley: University of California Press, 1992), 40–41.

79. Thomas Cranmer, *Writings and Disputations of Thomas Cranmer, Archbishop of Canterbury, Martyr, 1556, Relative to the Sacrament of the Lord's Supper*, ed. John Edmund Cox (Cambridge: Cambridge University Press, 1844), 42. Italics mine.

80. See *The Early Works of Thomas Becon*, The Parker Society, vol. 10 (New York: Johnson, 1968), 418.

81. Thomas Becon, *Prayers and Other Pieces of Thomas Becon*, ed. John Ayre, vol. 4 (Cambridge: Cambridge University Press, 1844), 364.

82. Quoted in Louise Noble, *Medicinal Cannibalism in Early Modern English Literature and Culture* (New York: Palgrave Macmillan, 2011), 103.

83. For Puritan resistance to Roman Catholicism, see Achsah Guibbory, *Ceremony and Community from Herbert to Milton: Literature, Religion, and Cultural Conflict in Seventeenth-Century England* (Cambridge: Cambridge University Press, 1998), 35–37.

84. Edward Taylor, *God's Determinations and Preparatory Meditations: A Critical Edition*, ed. Daniel Patterson (Kent, OH: The Kent State University Press, 2003), 406.

85. *De Doctrina Christiana*, trans. John Carey and ed. Maurice Kelley, in *Complete Prose Works of John Milton*, gen. ed. Don M. Wolfe, vol. 6 (New Haven, CT: Yale University Press, 1953–1983), 559–60.

86. Ibid., 6:553. As J. B. Broadbent argues, Milton's thought and the language in which it is couched is "away from the incarnate and towards the ideate." See "The

Nativity Ode," in *The Living Milton: Essays by Various Hands*, ed. Frank Kermode (London: Routledge, 1960), 23.

87. Gary Taylor, "Gender, Hunger, Horror: The History and Significance of *The Bloody Banquet*," *Journal of Early Modern Cultural Studies* 1, no. 1 (2001): 32.

88. Morwen, *A compendious and most marueilous Historie*, 231r–232v.

89. Nashe, *Works*, 115.

90. Miri Rubin, "The Person in the Form: Medieval Challenges to Bodily Order," *Framing Medieval Bodies*, eds. Sarah Kay and Miri Rubin (Manchester: Manchester University Press, 1994), 108.

91. It is noteworthy that the Feast of Corpus Christi was formally instituted around this time, courtesy of Pope Urban IV.

92. For instance, a Jew of Cologne described in a sixteenth-century sermon spits out the host he has consumed to find that it had turned into a small child, smiling at him. See R. Po-Chia Hsia, *The Myth of Ritual Murder: Jews and Magic in Reformation Germany* (New Haven, CT: Yale University Press, 1988), 55.

93. Price, *Consuming Passions*, 32. See also *The Minor Poems of the Vernon Ms.*, eds. C. Hortsmann and F. J. Furnivall, vol. 2 (London: EETS, 1892–1901), 197–98.

94. See Rubin "The Person in the Form," 191, 136–40.

95. Francesca Matteoni, "The Jew, the Blood and the Body in Late Medieval and Early Modern Europe," *Folklore* 119, no. 2 (2008): 188. For extensive commentary on the transference of Christian anxiety about transubstantiation and the host fantasized as a child, see Marcel Simon, *Verus Israel: A Study of the Relations Between Christians and Jews In the Roman Empire 135–425* (New York: Published for the Littman Library by Oxford University Press, 1986), 205–21, 470n16; Rosemary Ruether, *Faith and Fratricide: The Theological Roots of Anti-Semitism* (New York: Seabury Press, 1974), 117–82; Gavin Langmuir, *Toward a Definition of Antisemitism* (Berkeley: University of California Press, 1990), 263–81; Hsia, *The Myth of Ritual Murder*; Alan Dundes, *The Blood Libel Legend: A Casebook In Anti-Semitic Folklore* (Madison, WI: University of Wisconsin Press, 1991); Miri Rubin, *Gentile Tales: The Narrative Assault On Late Medieval Jews* (New Haven, CT: Yale University Press, 1999).

96. Shapiro, *Shakespeare and the Jews*, 107.

97. See Chrysostom's *Homilies Against the Jews*, trans. C. Merwyn Maxwell (PhD diss., University of Chicago, 1966), 28. These lines occur in the first part, "Proof that Demons inhabit the Jews." Chrysostom's language echoes Josephus's description of the seditionists and is, in turn, echoed by texts such as the *Polychronicon*—a significant source for the medieval *Siege of Jerusalem*.

98. Hermann L. Strack, *The Jew and Human Sacrifice: Human Blood and Jewish Ritual, an Historical and Sociological Inquiry* (New York: Blom, 1971), 190.

99. Lodge's translation of Josephus, on the other hand, contained *Against Apion*, the first translation in English of a rebuttal of the blood libel. For a brief discussion on this topic, see Groves, *Destruction of Jerusalem*, 141.

100. Nashe, *Works*, 15.

101. Ibid., 9.

102. See Richard Sugg, *Mummies, Cannibals and Vampires: The History of Corpse Medicine from the Renaissance to the Victorians* (Oxford: Routledge, 2011).

103. Cited in ibid., 21.

104. Lanfranc, *A Most Excellent and Learned Work of Chirurgery*, trans. John Hall (London, 1565), 72–73.

105. For the most part, corpse medicine seems to have been promoted by surgeons rather than by physicians. But there was high demand for corpse pharmacology practiced by unlicensed practitioners, as Deborah E. Harkness illustrates in *The Jewel House: Elizabethan London and the Scientific Revolution* (New Haven, CT: Yale, 2007).

106. Gabriel Harvey, *A New Letter of Notable Contents* (London, 1593), ix.

107. Sugg, *Mummies, Cannibals and Vampires*, 37.

108. As late as 1612, Scottish traveler William Lithgow returned from Jerusalem with a pound weight of earth that he claimed had curative powers and "miraculous . . . vertue." See Lithgow, *The Totall Discourse, of the Rare Adventures, and Painefull Peregrinations of Long Nineteene Yearers Travailes from Scotland, to the Most Famous Kingdomes in Europe, Asia and Affrica* (London, 1640), 278. During mid-seventeenth-century witchcraft trials, earth from Jerusalem was referred to as having medicinal properties. See C. L'Estrange Ewen, *Witchcraft and Demonianism: A Concise Account Derived from Sworn Depositions and Confessions Obtained in the Courts of England and Wales* (London: Heath Cranton, 1933), 331.

109. Groves, *Destruction of Jerusalem*, 251.

110. Nashe, *Works*, 62.

111. Ibid., 58–59.

112. Noble, *Medicinal Cannibalism*, 3.

113. Beatrice Groves, "Laughter in the Time of Plague: A Context for the Unstable Style of Nashe's *Christ's Tears Over Jerusalem,*" *Studies in Philology* 108, no. 2 (2011): 250

114. Daniel Featley, *The Grand Sacrilege of the Church of Rome* (London, 1630), 293–94.

115. Noble, *Medicinal Cannibalism*, 3.

116. Ibid. In Piero Camporesi's words, "The divine flesh, transmitter of abstract, impalpable powers that put the soul into communication with the ineffable, was also widely perceived as a mysterious, superhuman nourishment, a sort of divine marrow that would mete out both health and salvation (the two are indistinguishable in the single, ambiguous term *salus*). It was seen as a heavenly manna and balsam, a super-natural *pharmakon*—the 'salubrious elixir vitae of His blood.'" See "The Consecrated Host: A Wondrous Excess," in *Fragments for a History of the Human Body*, eds. Michael Feher, Ramona Nadaff, and Nadia Tazi, vol. 1 (New York: Urzone Inc., 1989), 221. To quote Elaine Scarry, "In the Last Supper and in the communion [Christ] enters the food chain, allowing himself to be taken in . . . as an object of sustenance." See *The Body in Pain: The Making and Unmaking of the World* (New York: Oxford University Press, 1985), 216. The link between the salvific and nutritional aspects of the Eucharist was memorably made by Tertullian: "The flesh is the hinge of salvation . . . The flesh is fed

on the Body and Blood of Christ, so that the soul may grow fat on God." See *De Resurrectione Mortuorum* 8. 2 as quoted in Noble, *Medicinal Cannibalism*, 98.

117. Noble, *Medicinal Cannibalism*, 90.

118. Ibid., 116.

119. Karen Gordon-Grube, "Anthropophagy in Post-Renaissance Europe: The Tradition of Medicinal Cannibalism," *American Anthropologist* 90, no. 2 (1988): 408. See also Scott Dudley, "Conferring with the Dead: Necrophilia and Nostalgia in the Seventeenth Century," *ELH* 66, no. 2 (1999): 277–94.

120. As Gordon-Grube queries: "Why was he [Taylor] squeamish with regard to the flesh and blood of Christ? Did he consider it more 'barbarous' to eat God, in the Sacrament, than man? Or for that matter, did he consider it less 'barbarous' to eat man, as mummy, than God?" See "Evidence of Medicinal Cannibalism in Puritan New England: 'Mummy and Related Remedies in Edward Taylor's 'Dispensatory,'" *Early American Literature* 28, no. 3 (1993): 207.

121. Daniel Featley, *Transubstantiation Exploded* (London, 1638), 83–85.

122. Sugg, *Mummies, Cannibals and Vampires*, 46.

123. Noble, *Medicinal Cannibalism*, 290.

124. There was a popular rumor of an annual Jewish ritual murder wherein the victim was imprisoned, killed, and then eaten to hide all evidence. See Shapiro, *Shakespeare and the Jews*, 104–5.

125. Noble argues that Jack's precarious situation as Dr. Zachary's next dissection victim is undermined by "the rhetoric of corpse pharmacology that positions Jack's body in a much larger medical corpse economy—a very Protestant English economy." See *Medicinal Cannibalism*, 71.

126. See "Jack Wilton and the Jews: The Ambivalence of Anti-Semitism in Nashe's *The Unfortunate Traveller*," *The Mysterious and the Foreign in Early Modern England*, eds. Helen Ostovich, Mary V. Silcox, and Graham Roebuck (Newark: University of Delaware Press, 2008), 97.

2. Bodies Besieged

1. Charlie Taylor-Kroll, "Scientists Pinpoint DNA of Bacteria that Caused Great Plague of 1665," *The Telegraph*, September 8, 2016.

2. I do not mean to suggest that no scientific reasons were advanced for the plague. On the contrary, there were many medical tracts such as William Bullein's *Dialogue against Fever Pestilence* that gave excellent accounts of the unhealthy conditions that provoke plague and supplied useful home remedies for its prevention and treatment. Superior scholarship has already been done on the tension between supernatural and scientific understandings of the plague. My chapter focuses on texts that largely understand plague in times of divine displeasure.

3. W. E. A. Axon, ed., "Documents relating to the plague in Manchester, 1605," *Chetham Miscellanies*, new series, vol. 3 (Manchester: Printed for the Chetham Society, 1915), viii. Axon includes the 1596 edition.

4. J. W. Blench, *Preaching in England in the Fifteenth and Sixteenth Centuries* (Oxford: Blackwell, 1964), 307.

5. Philip G. Caraman, *Henry Morse, priest of the plague* (London: Longman, 1957), 93.

6. Alan D. Dyer, "The Influence of Bubonic Plague in England 1500–1667," *Medical History* 22 (1978): 322.

7. E. P. Wilson, "Richard Leake's Plague Sermons, 1599," *Transactions of the Cumberland and Westmoreland Antiquarian Society* 75 (1975): 153.

8. Ernest B. Gilman, *Plague Writing in Early Modern England* (Chicago: University of Chicago Press, 2009), 42–43.

9. Francis White, *London's VVarning, by Jerusalem* (London, 1619), 33, 34.

10. Beatrice Groves, *The Destruction of Jerusalem In Early Modern English Literature* (Cambridge: Cambridge University Press, 2015), 170. Groves also notes the popularity of the trope of sacked Jerusalem during the plague and ascribes it to the "cohesion" that Josephus's history "with its combination of terrifying admonition and memorably grotesque stories" promoted in society "fracturing under the pressure of a contagious disease." Specifically, she focuses on the way the "perception of Protestant England as a nation likewise vulnerable to (Roman) invasion promoted identification with the besieged Jews" (5). For Groves's fullest work linking the siege with plague, see "Laughter in the Time of Plague: A Context for the Unstable Style of Nashe's *Christ's Tears over Jerusalem*," *Studies in Philology* 108, no. 2 (2011): 238–60.

11. *An Homily concerning the Justice of God in punishing of impenitent sinners and of his mercies towards all such as in their afflictions unfeignedly turn unto him. Appointed to be read in time of sickness* in *The Plague in Print: Essential Elizabethan Sources, 1558–1603*, ed. Rebecca Totaro (Pittsburgh: Duquesne University Press, 2010), 38.

12. Ibid., 36.

13. Ibid., 47, 35.

14. Thomas Lodge, *Famovs and Memorable Workes of Iosephus, a Man of Much Honour and Learning Among the Iewes* (London: Printed for Thomas Adams, 1620), 738.

15. George Wither, *Britains Remembrancer* (1628), Vol. 2 (Manchester: The Spenser Society, 1880), 547–50.

16. *Christs Teares over Jerusalem, Or, a Caveat for England to Call to God for Mercy* (London, 1640).

17. Thomas Dekker, *The Plague Pamphlets of Thomas Dekker*, ed. F. P. Wilson (Oxford: Clarendon Press, 1925), 142.

18. Richard Milton, *London's Misery: The Country's Cruelty with God's Mercy Explained by remarkable observations of each of them during this last Visitation* (1625), in *The Plague Epic in Early Modern England: Heroic Measures, 1603–1721*, ed. Rebecca Totaro (Burlington, VT: Ashgate, 2012).

19. Thomas Nashe, *The Works of Thomas Nashe*, ed. Ronald B. McKerrow, vol. 2 (New York: Barnes and Noble, 1966), 44.

20. Totaro, *Plague in Print*, 54.

21. Totaro, *Plague Epic*, 110.

22. Ibid., 163.

23. Dekker, *Plague Pamphlets*, 141.

24. René Girard, *"To Double Business Bound": Essays on Literature, Mimesis, and Anthropology* (Baltimore: Johns Hopkins University Press, 1978), 138.

25. Girard would have been dismayed to learn of the outbreak of bubonic and pneumonic plague in India in 1994 that resulted in fifty-six deaths out of 693 infected cases. I can well recall the mass exodus from Surat in Western India, where 300,000 people left the city in two days.

26. Thomas Wilson, *Christs Farewell to Jerusalem* (London, 1614), B3r.

27. Michael Neill, *Issues of Death: Mortality and Identity in English Renaissance Tragedy* (Oxford: Clarendon Press, 1997), 15.

28. Gilman, *Plague Writing*, 35.

29. Dekker, *Plague Pamphlets*, 159–60.

30. Ambroise Paré, *A treatise of the plague contayning the causes, signes, symptomes, prognosticks, and cure thereof. Together with sundry other remarkable passages (for the prevention of, and preservation from the pestilence) never yet published by any man.* (London, 1630), 65.

31. Totaro, *Plague in Print*, 98.

32. Gilman, *Plague Writing*, 45.

33. Totaro, *Plague Epic*, 113.

34. William Gouge, *Gods Three Arrovves: Plague, Famine, Svvord, In three Treatises* (London, 1631), 86, 87.

35. Cited in Gilman, *Plague Writing*, 46.

36. Dekker, *Plague Pamphlets*, 90.

37. Nashe, *Works*, 20.

38. Ibid., 63, 35, 36.

39. Ibid., 51.

40. Lancelot Dawes, *Gods Mercies and Iervsalems Miseries* (London, 1609), A5v–r.

41. Ibid., A6v.

42. For extended studies of the body politic in Shakespeare's plays, see David George Hale, *The Body Politic: A Political Metaphor in Renaissance English Literature* (Paris: Mouton, 1971); Leonard Barkan, *Nature's Work of Art: The Human Body as Image of the World* (New Haven, CT: Yale University Press, 1977); Jonathan Gil Harris, *Foreign Bodies and the Body Politic: Discourses of Social Pathology in Early Modern England* (New York: Cambridge University Press, 1998); Gil Harris, *Sick Economies: Drama, Mercantilism, and Disease In Shakespeare's England* (Philadelphia: University of Pennsylvania Press, 2004); Andrew Hadfield, *Shakespeare and Renaissance Politics* (London: Arden Shakespeare, 2004); Hadfield, *Shakespeare and Republicanism* (Cambridge: Cambridge University Press, 2005); Gail Kern Paster, *Humoring the Body: Emotions and the Shakespeare Stage* (Chicago: University of Chicago Press, 2004); and Martha Kalman Diede, *Shakespeare's Knowledgeable Body* (New York: Peter Lang,

2008). Notable essays on the abovementioned plays include Zvi Jagendorf, "Corio-lanus: Body Politic and Private Parts," *Shakespeare Quarterly* Vol. 41, no. 4 (1990): 455–69; Gail Kern Paster, "Nervous Tension: Networks of Blood and Spirit in the Early Modern Body" in *The Body in Parts: Fantasies of Corporeality in Early Modern Europe*, eds. David Hillman and Carla Mazzio (New York: Routledge, 1997), 107–28; Delphine Lemonnier-Texier, "The Analogy of the Body Politic in Shakespeare's Coriolanus: From the Organic Metaphor of Society to the Monstrous Body of the Multitude," *Moreana* 43–44, no. 168–70 (2006): 107–131; Benjamin Bertram, "Fal-staff's Body, The Body Politic and the Body of Trade," *Exemplaria* 21, no. 3 (2009): 296–318; and Laurie McKee, "Giving and Serving in Timon of Athens," *Early Modern Literary Studies* 16, no. 3 (2013): 1–22.

43. Thomas Elyot, *The Boke Named the Governor* (London, 1540), Aii. Gil Harris suggests that for some early modern English "the body politic was not simply a heuris-tic device," but rather one "imbued with cosmic significance." See *Foreign Bodies*, 2.

44. See Nicholas Barbon, *An Apology for the Builder: Or, a Discourse shewing the Cause and Effects of the Increase of Building* (London: Cave Pullen, 1685), 30.

45. Peter Heylyn, *Cosmographie in Four Bookes* [...] (London, 1652), 270. The idea of cities as greedy consumers assumed an ominous aspect during times of plague when the body count in urban spaces far exceeded that in the countryside—so much so that pamphlets were composed mocking the propensity of the privileged to flee their homes, thereby abandoning their less fortunate neighbors to the plague's relent-less march.

46. Paul Slack, *The Impact of Plague in Tudor and Stuart England* (Oxford: Claren-don Press, 1985), 187. See also "Perceptions of the Metropolis in Seventeenth-Century England," in *Civil Histories: Essays Presented to Sir Keith Thomas*, eds. Peter Burke, Brian Harrison, and Paul Slack (Oxford: Oxford University Press, 2000) for Slack's study of the imagery of hearts and spleens.

47. Margaret Healy: *Fictions of Disease in Early Modern England: Bodies, Plagues and Politics* (New York: Palgrave, 2001), 16–17.

48. William Bullein, *Bulwarke of Defense* (London, 1562), C2v.

49. Dekker, *Plague Pamphlets*, 89, 33, 38, 33.

50. Nashe, *Works*, 20.

51. Dekker, *Plague Pamphlets*, 31.

52. Dawes, *Gods mercies*, I5v.

53. Ibid., I6r

54. Dekker, *Plague Pamphlets*, 140.

55. Totaro, *Plague Epic*, 151.

56. Ibid., 106.

57. Ibid., 158.

58. Ibid., 163.

59. Ibid., 182.

60. Ibid., 106.

61. Cited in Slack, *Impact of Plague*, 57.

62. Ibid; Dyer, "Influence of Bubonic Plague," 319.

63. William Cupper, *Certaine Sermons concerning God's late visitation* (London, 1592) 112.

64. Dekker, *Plague Pamphlets*, 155. Dekker exhorts his readers to show pity, for "How can wee expect mercy from [God], when wee expresse such cruelty one towards another? When the Brother defies the Brother, what hope is there for a Londoner to receiue comfort from Strangers?" (156).

65. *Wills and Inventories from Bury St. Edmunds*, ed. Samuel Tymms, 1st series, vol. 49 (London: Camden Society, 1850), 172–73.

66. *Diary of Samuel Pepys*, eds. Robert Latham and William Matthews, vol. 6 (London: G. Bell, 1972), 212.

67. Dekker, *Plague Pamphlets*, 28–29.

68. Healy, *Fictions of Disease*, 62.

69. Dekker, *Plague Pamphlets*, 34. I am indebted to Rebecca Hassler for alerting me to this passage.

70. Peter Morwen, *A compendious and most marueilous Historie* (London, 1575), 146v–147r.

71. Thomas Dekker, *Newes from Hell brought by the Diuells Carrier* (London, 1606), C4v.

72. Totaro, *Plague Epic*, 58.

73. Morwen, *A compendious and most marveilous History*, 188r. Lodge's translation confirms the cruel dastardy of zealots such as Simon who, "hauing gathered together a multitude of seditious people, robbed and spoiled all" (644).

74. Ibid., 692.

75. Dekker, *Plague Pamphlets*, 33.

76. John Stockwood, *A very fruitfull and necessarye Sermon of the moste lamemtable destruction of Ierusalem, and the heauy iudgements of God, executed vppon that people for their sinne and dissobedience* (London, 1584), C2r; Nashe, *Works*, 66.

77. Dekker, *Plague Pamphlets*, 34, 90, 97.

78. Neill, *Issues of Death*, 15.

79. Dekker, *Plague Pamphlets*, 26–27.

80. Morwen, *A compendious and most marueilous Historie*, 146v–r.

81. Totaro, *Plague Epic*, 101.

82. Morwen, *A compendious and most marueilous Historie*, 151r–152v.

83. Lodge, *Famovs and Memorable Workes*, 721.

84. T. D., *Canaan's Calamitie* (London, 1677), C1r.

85. Thomas Clarke, *Meditations in my confinement, when my house was visited with the sickness: in April, May and June, 1666*, vol. 2 (London, 1666), 262–63.

86. Totaro, *Plague Epic*, 19.

87. *A Warning or lanthorn to London* (London, 1658); Totaro, *Plague Epic*, 150.

88. Morwen, *A compendious and most marueilous Historie*, 151r.

89. Lodge, *Famovs and Memorable Workes*, 721.

90. Thomas Dekker, *The Dead Tearme* (London, 1608), 77.

91. Dekker, *Plague Pamphlets*, 26.

92. Ibid., 176.

93. Ibid., 80.

94. Totaro, *Plague in Print*, 107.

95. Groves, *Destruction of Jerusalem*, 169.

96. Oxford MS Gough Eccl. Top. 7, Bodleian Library. Cited in Dyer, "The Influence of Bubonic Plague," 322.

3. Jerusalem in Jamestown

1. Mark Nicholls, "George Percy's '*Trewe Relacyon*': A Primary Source for the Jamestown Settlement," *The Virginia Magazine of History and Biography* 113, no. 3 (2005): 248.

2. Ibid., 249.

3. Composed sometime around 1625, Percy's *A Trewe Relacyon* was privately circulated for years and maintained in family archives until 1922, when it was first published in its entirety in *Tyler's Quarterly Magazine*.

4. Nicholls, "George Percy's '*Trewe Relacyon*,'" 242–43.

5. George Percy, *Observations gathered out of "A Discourse of the Plantation of the Southern Colony in Virginia by the English, 1606,"* ed. David B. Quinn (Charlottesville: The University Press of Virginia, 1967), 2.

6. Columbus was guilty of misnaming; he thought he had found Cathay. Soon, he would be equally convinced that the people he had encountered were related to "The Great Khan." This same imprecision characterized the early modern application of the word "cannibal," which was bandied about broadly and vaguely and, more often than not, for dramatic effect. In the earliest records it was applied to any intransigent peoples encountered in the New World who resisted the overtures of European traders and settlers.

7. See Andrew McGowan, "Eating People: Accusations of Cannibalism against Christians in the Second Century," *Journal of Early Christian Studies* 2 (1994): 413–42, and James Rives, "Human Sacrifice among Pagans and Christians," *Journal of Roman Studies* 85 (1995): 72–73.

8. Nicholls, "George Percy's '*Trewe Relacyon*,'" 249.

9. John Smith, *The Generall Historie of Virginia, New England & the Summer Isles, together with The true travels, adventures and observations, and A sea grammar* (Glasgow: J. MacLehose, 1907), 205.

10. Claude Levi-Strauss, *The Naked Man*, trans. J and D. Weightman (London: Jonathan Cape, 1981), 141.

11. The Church Fathers used the scene of Mary's cannibalism in Book 6 of the *Jewish War* as incontrovertible evidence of divine punishment for the Jews' sinfulness. Eusebius, bishop of Caesarea, who presents the Jewish nation as the prototype for all recalcitrant peoples, expounds upon Mary's cannibalism "in order that those

who study this work may have some partial knowledge how the punishment of God followed close after them for their crime against the Christ of God." Though Eusebius acknowledges the tragic nature of Josephus's account, his interest is in cannibalism as punishment for impiety that takes the form of "crimes against the Christ of God." See *Ecclesiastical History*, trans. Kirsopp Lake (London: Aeterna Press, 2015), 3.5.7. Eusebius, like St. John Chrysostom after, is also interested in the cannibal episode as a fulfillment of Christ's prophecy in Matthew 24:19–21 and marvels at the "foreknowledge and . . . foretelling of our Savior," when he exhorted the women of Jerusalem to weep for themselves and their children. See also *Ecclestiastical History* 3.7.6. Basil in his *Homilia Dicta Tempore Famis et Siccitatis* likewise excoriates the mother who, after having "given birth to a child from her belly, received it back into her belly in evil fashion." Like Eusebius, he sees the "tragedy" of Mary's cannibalism and the "terrible sufferings" of the Jews as "just penalty for their impiety against the Lord." Chrysostom, for his part, specifically mentions the Josephus account of "paidophagian," in *Homilia 76, In Mattheum*, noting how the horror of the Jewish war surpassed all tragedy. For more on the reception of Josephus among the Church Fathers, see Honora Howell Chapman, "A Myth for the World": Early Christian Reception of Infanticide and Cannibalism in Josephus, *Bellum Judaicum* 6. 199–219," *SBL 2000 Seminar Papers* (2000): 359–78.

12. Jer. 19.9 reads, "And I will cause them to eat the flesh of their sons and the flesh of their daughters, and they shall eat every one the flesh of his friend in the siege and straitness, wherewith their enemies, and they that seek their lives, shall straiten them." Lam. 2.20 exhorts, "Behold, O Lord, and consider to whom thou hast done this. Shall the women eat their fruit, and children of a span long? shall the priest and the prophet be slain in the sanctuary of the Lord?" Ezek. 5. 9–10 threatens a terrible and unprecedented reckoning, "And I will do in thee that which I have not done, and whereunto I will not do any more the like, because of all thine abominations. Therefore the fathers shall eat the sons in the midst of thee, and the sons shall eat their fathers; and I will execute judgments in thee, and the whole remnant of thee will I scatter into all the winds."

13. Though it is unclear when exactly Lodge converted, he would almost certainly have come under Catholic influence during his days as a student at Trinity College, Oxford (1573–1578) when it was a haven for recusants. That he was later called before the Privy Council and denied a Master of Arts degree in 1581 suggests that he may already have been suspected of harboring papist sympathies. Lodge did eventually get his medical degree from the University of Avignon, in 1598, where he was required to take an oath of allegiance to the Pope. There is no indication that he kept his Catholic sympathies private upon his return to England. His first solo published work was *The Flowers of Lodowicke of Granado* (1601), an English translation of a devotional tract by a well-known Spanish Catholic writer. Lodge's marriage in 1602 was to a Catholic woman by the name of Joan Aldred, and when, after being denied a medical license from the College of Physicians he relocated to the Continent, it was Catholics who were most prominent among his list of patients. On the subject of Lodge's shifting religious loyalties and professional interests, see Beatrice Groves, "'They repented at

the preachyng of Ionas: and beholde, a greater then Ionas is here': *A Looking Glass for London and England,* Hosea and the destruction of Jerusalem" in *Early Modern Drama and the Bible: Context and Readings, 1570–1625,* ed. Adrian Streete (Basingstoke, UK: Palgrave Macmillan, 2012), 139–55.

14. Peter Morwen, *A compendious and most marueilous Historie* (London, 1575), 155v. For a brief study of Morwen's emphasis on unity as opposed to Lodge's focus on conflict see Beatrice Groves, *The Destruction of Jerusalem in Early Modern English Literature* (Cambridge: Cambridge University Press, 2015), 157.

15. So appalled is Josephus that it is only out of fear that posterity will castigate him as a liar for "not fully recounting all accidents of them that are dead" that he brings himself to narrate the macabre crime. See Thomas Lodge, *The Famous and Memorable Workes of Iosephus, a Man of Much Honour and Learning Among the Iewes* (London, 1620), 734.

16. Louis Feldman persuasively shows Josephus's indebtedness to Greek literature in his discussion of how the description of the Aqedah in the *Antiquities* is derived from Euripides's *Iphigenia.* See "The Influence of the Greek Tragedians on Josephus," in *The Howard Gilman International Conferences I: Hellenic and Jewish Arts,* ed. A. Ovadiah (Tel Aviv: RAMOT Publishing House, 1998), 51–80. Honora Howell Chapman likewise argues that Josephus, in Book 2 of the *Jewish War,* stages a dramatic scene at the Temple with the priests and Levites begging the people not to anger the Romans that distinctly echoes Priam's agonized pleading before Achilles in the *Iliad.* See Chapman, "'By the Waters of Babylon': Josephus and Greek Poetry," in *Josephus and Jewish History in Flavian Rome and Beyond,* eds. Joseph Sievers and Gaia Lembi (Leiden: Brill, 2005), 129–30.

17. Lodge, *Famovs and Memorable Workes,* 734.

18. Ibid.

19. For more on Josephus's indebtedness to Euripides, see Chapman, "'By the Waters of Babylon'"; Chapman, "Spectacle and Theater in Josephus' *Bellum Judaicum*" (PhD diss., Stanford University, 1998); and Chapman, "'A Myth for the World': Early Christian Reception of Infanticide and Cannibalism in Josephus, *Bellum Judaicum* 6 199–219," *SBL 2000 Seminar Papers* (2000): 359–78.

20. See Pseudo-Hegessipus, *De Excidio* 5. 40. 2. Pseudo-Hegessipus seems to have relied on his readership's awareness of the parallels with Euripides when he makes his Mary address the dismembered limbs of the son she has just killed. For other Christian writers who read the infanticide scene in the *Jewish War* as straight out of Euripides, see Chapman, "A Myth for the World," 370–78.

21. Lodge, *Famovs and Memorable Workes,* 734. Chapman rightly notes that the idea of the child's unfortunate story being told for all posterity hearkens back to the role of the tragic child in Greek drama for which Hector's unfortunate son, Astyanax, who is thrown from the battlements of Troy by Greek soldiers, is the model. See Chapman, "Spectacle and Theater," 423.

22. Lodge, *Famovs and Memorable Workes,* 734.

23. Ibid.

24. Origen, *Werke*, Vol. 3, Frag. 105, ed. E. Klosterman (Berlin: GSC, 1983), 273.

25. Elisa Narin Van Court, who writes on the medieval poem *The Siege of Jerusalem*, which is notorious for its virulent anti-Judaic sentiments, observes that Mary's (or Maria's) cannibalism, in particular, is rendered as an act of desperation in a sympathetic account that invites sorrow and sympathy rather than disgust. In the *Siege* poem, the mother is a "mild wyf" (1077) who addresses her child with "rewful wordes" (1079), a "worthi wyf" who confesses that she roasted her son out of "wode hunger" (1089). Rather than castigate her, the townspeople "alway they went for wo, wepyng echone" (1093), lamenting that it is better to die in battle than live in abject misery. See Van Court, "'The Siege of Jerusalem' and Augustinian Historians: Writing about Jews in Fourteenth-Century England," *The Chaucer Review* 29, vol. 3 (1995): 227–48.

26. See Chrysostom's *Homilies Against the Jews*, trans. C. Merwyn Maxwell (PhD diss., University of Chicago, 1966), 28.

27. A notable exception is Ranulf Higden's *Polychronicon* (a source for the medieval *Siege* poem), where Titus, in a rant akin to Chrysostom's, thunders that the Romans "fiyeth ayenst bestes" though even beasts "spareth her owne kynde, be they nevere so needy . . . but these men devoureth here owne children." See Higden, *Polychronicon, Together with the English Translation of John of Trevisa and an Unknown Writer of the Fifteenth-Century*, eds. Churchill Babbington and Joseph R. Lumby, Rolls Series, vol. 4 (London: Longman, Green, 1865–66), 446–47.

28. See Chapman, "Spectacle and Theater," 105.

29. At the same time, Morwen's translation retains the prejudice memorable in *Polychronicon*: Titus excoriates the Jews for being "fierce and cruel beastes" even as he laments that this "mischiefe is come nowe so farre, that a woman hath eaten her owne fleshe, being driuen thereunto by most extreame necessitie" (*A compendious and most marueilous Historie*, 232r).

30. John Stockwood, *A very fruitfull and necessarye Sermon of the moste lamemtable destruction of Ierusalem, and the heauy iudgements of God, executed vppon that people for their sinne and dissobedience* (London, 1584), C4v–r.

31. Thomas Nashe, *The Works of Thomas Nashe*, ed. Ronald B. McKerrow, vol. 2 (New York: Barnes and Noble, 1966), 71.

32. Ibid.,72.

33. See also Catherine Cox, "Voices of Prophecy and Prayer in Thomas Nashe's *Christs Teares over Jerusalem*," in *Renaissance Papers 2000*, eds. T. H. Howard-Hill and Philip Rollinson (New York: Camden House, 2000), 51–69.

34. Nashe, *Works*, 71.

35. Cox, "Prophecy and Prayer," 63.

36. Nashe, *Works*, 80.

37. James I, *A Booke of Proclamations* (London, 1609), 186.

38. Thomas Dekker, *VVork for Armourers: Or, The Peace is Broken open warres likely to happen this Yeare 1609* (London, 1609), C3r

39. Gina Hens-Piazza, *Nameless, Blameless, and Without Shame: Two Cannibal Mothers Before a King* (Collegeville, MN: Liturgical Press, 2003), 86–87, and Julie Faith Parker, *Valuable and Vulnerable: Children in the Hebrew Bible, Especially the Elisha Cycle* (Providence, RI: Brown Judaic Studies, 2013), 185–86.

40. Caryn A. Reeder, "Pity the Women and Children: Punishment by Siege in Josephus's Jewish War," *Journal for the Study of Judaism* 44, vol. 2 (2013),190.

41. It would seem that the narrative logic of the *topos* of cannibalism during siege demands that the devastating loss of the city be heightened and exemplified by the destruction of the household. As Reeder also notes, this loss is particularly damning in Jewish culture where, ideally, the entire household kept the Covenant together, worshipping in communion with one another, and passing on those traditions to their offspring. The great blessing for covenantal obedience was a fruitful womb (Deut. 28:4). Of equal note is the curse for covenantal disobedience, which anticipates sieges in which women are raped, progeny sold into foreign slavery, and parents secretly eat their children rather than share their food (Deut. 28:15–18).

42. Hens-Piazza, *Nameless, Blameless, and Without Shame*, 86–87.

43. Mikhail Bakhtin, *Rabelais and his World*, trans. Hélène Iswolsky (Bloomington: Indiana University Press, 1984), 281.

44. Maggie Kilgour, *From Communion to Cannibalism: An Anatomy of Metaphors of Incorporation* (Princeton, NJ: Princeton University Press, 1990), 6.

45. Georges Bataille, *The Accursed Share: An Essay on Generational Economy*, trans. Robert Hurley, vol. 1 (New York: Zone Books, 1991), 33–34.

46. David B. Goldstein, "The Cook and Cannibal: *Titus Andronicus* and the New World," *Shakespeare Studies* 37 (2009), 99–133.

47. Kilgour, *From Communion to Cannibalism*, 7.

48. Lodge, *Famovs and Memorable Workes*, 556.

49. Ibid.

50. See Merrall Llewelyn Price, *Consuming Passions: The Uses of Cannibalism in Late Medieval and Early Modern Europe* (New York: Routledge, 2003), 150; Reeder, "Pity the Women and Children," 194.

51. See Stephen Greenblatt, *Renaissance Self-Fashioning: From More to Shakespeare* (Chicago: University of Chicago Press, 1980), 115.

52. Thomas Lodge, *The VVovnds of Ciuill War* in *The Complete Works of Thomas Lodge 1580–1623?*, ed. Edmund Grosse, Vol. 3 (Glasgow: Robert Anderson, 1883), 10–11.

53. Ibid., 59.

54. Arthur F. Kinney, *Humanist Poetics: Thought, Rhetoric, and Fiction in Sixteenth-Century England* (Amherst: University of Massachusetts Press, 1986), 363–424.

55. Lodge, *Famovs and Memorable Workes*, 717.

56. Ibid.

57. Giorgio Agamben, *Homo Sacer: Sovereign Power and Bare Life* (Stanford, CA: Stanford University Press, 1998), 8.

58. Lodge, *Famovs and Memorable Workes*, 721.

59. Lodge's description of the suffering caused by the famine is stark and implacable. The Jews, stripped of all dignity, hide up in secret rooms, scrape for bits of corn, snatching it unboiled from the fire to devour it raw. And when the seditonists suspect that food is being kept from them, they break down the doors and extract the food, already half-chewed, from the mouths of the hapless Jews within (ibid., 717).

60. Ibid.

61. Ibid., 697.

62. Ibid., 698.

63. Ibid., 718.

64. Distinguished by marked Semitic features and referred to as "Red Jews" in several medieval German texts, Gog and Magog illustrate the terrifying invasive quality Christendom ascribed to the Jews. Because they were believed to be descendants from Japhet and excluded therefore from the elect people descended from Shem, they functioned as stand-ins for whoever and whatever did not belong to the Chosen People (Chosen People here signifying both the Jews of the Old Testament and the Christians). Ralph Churton's fourth sermon on Matthew 24:8 presents a gruesome image of the rebels Simon and John, who "drank, as it were, to each other the blood of the people; and contending for superiority, were confederate in crime." See Churton, *Eight Sermons on the Prophesies Respecting the Destruction of Jerusalem* (Oxford: Clarendon Press, 1785), 205.

65. The most notable instance of cannibalism in Ovid is in the story of Philomela (Book VI), whose brutal rape at the hands of her insatiable brother-in-law, Tereus, is avenged by his wife Procne, who kills him, cooks him, and serves him to their son, Itys. In the story of Lycaon (Book I), cannibalism is clearly connected to the violation of *pietas*—a theme that emerges again in the briefly mentioned story of Thyestes, who unwittingly eats his sons, as well in the story of Erysichthon, whose self-cannibalism is the final punishment for his *impietas*.

66. See Janet Adelman, "'Anger's my Meat': Feeding, Dependency, and Aggression in *Coriolanus*," in *Representing Shakespeare*, eds. Murray M. Schwart and Coppelia Kahn (Baltimore: Johns Hopkins University Press, 1980), 30. See also Gail Kern Paster, "To Starve with Feeding: The City in Coriolanus," *Shakespeare Studies* 11 (1978): 123–44 for the thematic link between animal imagery, food, and eating.

67. Memorable references to devouring in *Titus Andronicus*, in addition to the famous familial pie Tamora consumes (Act V), include the "fell devouring receptacle," the "blood drinking pit" with a hideous "mouth" into which Titus's sons Quintus and Martius fall in Act II (II. iii. 224–35). In *Timon of Athens*, Apemantus, whose savage cynicism serves as a counterpoint to Timon's faith in Athenian civilization, exposes social and political fellowship as cannibalism. His repudiation of Timon's invitation to dinner with "No, I eat not Lords," (I. i. 204) is followed swiftly by a denigration of the ladies who eat lords and "come by great bellies" (I.i. 206). Both sexual and social

intercourse become forms of grotesque consumption, as men and women feed on one another to advance their interests and desires.

68. See Anthony J. Lewis, "'I Feed on Mother's Flesh': Incest and Eating in *Pericles*," *Essays in Literature* 15, no. 2 (1998): 156.

69. Ibid., 158.

70. Michel de Montaigne, *The Essayes of Michael Lord of Montaigne*, trans. John Florio, introd. Thomas Seccombe, vol. 1 (London: Grant Richards, 1908), 263.

71. The New World cannibals seem to have existed outside the Judeo-Christian mythic framework entirely, and their discovery put considerable strain on the way the peoples of the world were understood as descendants of Ham, Shem, and Japhet. If the natives were none of these, was it possible that they were not descended at all from Adam and Eve? And if that were the case, might they be free from the taint of Original Sin? As George Hoffman suggests, "The possibility, for example, that Amerindians are not descended from Adam and Eve would hold enormous implications for the doctrine of original sin, and this seems the point made by the essay's second anomaly, the oddly utopian description of the natives. . . . If the New World natives are born outside original sin, then it is clear why they do not need a word for 'pardon,' as he notes at the close of this passage, since they do not appear to have experienced the Fall and this still inhabit their paradise. Or, rather, their 'fall' figuratively and literally comes from contact with Christians of the Old World." See Hoffman, "Anatomy of the Mass: Montaigne's 'Cannibals.'" *PMLA* 117, no. 2 (2002): 212.

72. Stephen Greenblatt, *Marvelous Possessions: The Wonder of the New World* (Chicago: University of Chicago Press, 1991), 150.

73. An instance of this would be the cannibal priests in Book VI of Edmund Spenser's *The Faerie Queene*, whose bloody ritual of dismemberment and consumption parodies the Catholic Mass. See chapter 1 for a longer discussion of anti-transubstantiation diatribes in early modern England.

74. Supriya Chaudhuri, "Eating People is Wrong: Cannibalism and Renaissance Culture," in *Writing Over: Medieval to Renaissance*, eds. Supriya Chaudhuri and Sukanta Chaudhuri (Calcutta: Allied Publishers, 1996), 80.

75. See Anthony Pagden, *The Fall of Natural Man: The American Indian and the Origins of Comparative Ethnology* (Cambridge: Cambridge University Press, 1982); Tzvetan Todorov, *The Conquest of America: The Question of the Other*, trans. Richard Howard (New York: Harper and Row, 1984); Peter Hulme, *Colonial Encounters: Europe and the Native Caribbean 1492–1797* (London: Metheun Books,1986); Joseph Campbell, *Historical Atlas of World Mythology: The Way of the Animal Powers: Mythology of the Primitive Hunter and Gatherers*, vol. 1, pts. 1–2 (New York: Harper and Row, 1988); Greenblatt, *Marvelous Possessions*; and Joan-Pau Rubiés,

76. Wes Williams, "'L'Humanite du tout perdue?': Early Modern Monsters, Cannibals and Human Souls," *History and Anthropology* 23, no. 2 (2012): 241.

77. Montaigne, *Essayes*, vol. 2, 143.

78. Ibid., vol. 1, 264.

79. Nicholls, "George Percy's 'Trewe Relacyon,'" 227.

80. Forrest K. Lehmann, "Settled Place, Contested Past: Reconciling George Percy's *A Trewe Relacyon* with John Smith's *Generall Historie*," *Early American Literature* 42, no. 2 (2006): 238.

81. Kathleen Donegan, *Seasons of Misery: Catastrophe and Colonial Settlement in Early America* (Philadelphia: University of Pennsylvania Press, 2014), 92.

82. King of England and Wales James I, *The Order [Banishing Rogues to the New Found Lands]* (London: Robert Baker, 1603). See also Robert Gray, et al., *A Good Speed to Virginia* (London: Printed by Philip Kyngston for William Welbie, 1609).

83. Percy, *Observations*, 8.

84. Ibid., 4, 5, 7, 10, 15.

85. Donegan, *Seasons of Misery*, 80.

86. Ibid..

87. Smith, *Generall Historie*, 91–92.

88. Smith, *A History of the Settlement of Virginia* (New York: E. Maynard, 1890), 22.

89. Lehmann, "Settled Place, Contested Past," 250.

90. I am indebted to Donegan for this reading.

91. See Peter Force, *Tracts and Other Papers, Relating Principally to the Origin, Settlement and Progress of the Colonies in North America, from the Discovery of the Country to the year 1776*, vol. 4 (Washington, D.C.: William Q. Force, 1846), 10–11.

92. Percy, *Observations*, 26.

93. Smith, *Generall Historie*, 123.

94. Julia Kristeva, *Powers of Horror: An Essay on Abjection*, trans. Leon Samuel Roudiez (New York: Columbia University Press, 1982), 4.

95. Don Alonso de Velasco to Philip III, June 14, 1610, in Alexander Brown, *Genesis of the United States: A Narrative of the movement in England, 1605–1616* (New York: Houghton Mifflin & Co., 1890), 392.

96. Nicholls, "George Percy's 'Trewe Relacyon,'" 248–49.

97. Kristeva, *Powers of Horror*, 4.

98. Donegan, *Seasons of Misery*, 88.

99. Nicholls, "George Percy's, 'Trewe Relacyon,'" 250–51; Lodge, *Famovs and Memorable Workes*, 721.

100. Percy, *Observations*, 25.

101. Ibid., 26.

102. Ibid., 2.

103. Donegan, *Seasons of Misery*, 104. Donegan, however, focuses exclusively on Percy's writings and does not read them in conjuction with Lodge's history.

4. From Providence to Politics

1. Virginia Mason Vaughan, *Performing Blackness on English Stages, 1500–1800* (Cambridge: Cambridge University Press, 2005), 121.

2. William Heminge, *The Jewes Tragedy* in *The Plays and Poems of William Heminge*, ed. Carol A. Morley (Madison, NJ: Fairleigh Dickinson University Press, 2006). All references are to this edition and are cited parenthetically.

3. See Beatrice Groves, *The Destruction of Jerusalem in Early Modern English Literature* (Cambridge: Cambridge University Press, 2015), 55. Groves's thesis is supported by Stephen K. Wright's "The Destruction of Jerusalem: An Annotated Checklist of Plays and Performances, Ca. 1350–1620," *Research Opportunities in Renaissance Drama* 41 (2002), 145. See also Frank Marcham, *The King's Office of the Revels, 1610–1622* (London: Frank Marcham, 1925), 14–15.

4. See George M. Logan, ed., *The History of King Richard III: A Reading Edition* (Bloomington: Indiana University Press, 2005), xlvi.

5. Perhaps because it may never have been performed in a public playhouse, *The Jewes Tragedy* barely features in the comprehensive studies of Jews on the early modern stage. A rare mention occurs in Hyman Michelson's *The Jew in Early English Literature*, which describes Heminge as a "younger contemporary of Shakespeare" and notes that, while the Jews are not depicted "with the black colours usually employed for this malicious race," the play "contains no points of traditionally or really Jewish peculiarity." See *The Jew in Early English Literature* (New York: Hermon Press, 1972), 96. James Shapiro merely identifies the date of composition as 1626. Edward Coleman and Edgar Rosenberg's *The Jew in Western Drama* relegates Heminge's play to an appendix entry that also lists a corrupted copy of the play, entitled *The Jewish War Tragedy*. Its modern stage history consists of a single "performance with scripts" at the Globe in August 1998, under the direction of Graham Watts, as part of a series on Shakespeare and the Jews. Maggy Williams, author of the program notes, appears to share in the critical opinion of her scholarly predecessors when she notes elements in the play "which suggest we need not take it entirely seriously," and intimates that the scenes of horror are so overdone as to become parodic and invite laughter (Qtd. in *The Plays and Poems of William Heminge*, 94). Recently, Beatrice Groves discussed the play in relation to the theatrical presentation of Jews in early modern England, citing "the raw emotional power of the native English tradition" on display in the bloody murder of Ananias (4.10.1–35). See *The Destruction of Jerusalem*, 57.

6. Twentieth-century scholarship, quite paltry, is dismissive of the play and its author. Fredson Bowers describes Heminge's literary output as "typical," and derides the "confused account of the capture of Jerusalem." See Bowers, *Elizabethan Revenge Tragedy, 1587–1642* (Princeton: Princeton University Press, 1940), 235. J. W. Hebel offers a withering assessment of Heminge's skills in his 1920 doctoral thesis, "The Plays of William Heminge" (Cornell University, 1920), and denigrates its poor construction and impractical staging (30). Like Heinrich A. Cohn, who produced an edition of *The Jewes Tragedy* in 1913 (Louvain: Bang), Hebel restricts his critical efforts to tracing the play's historical sources and cataloguing the verbal echoes of Shakespeare, Francis Beaumont, and John Fletcher, which are legion. (*The Jewes Tragedy* is notorious

for being the first play to borrow liberally from *Hamlet*'s famous "To be or not to be" speech.) John Quincy Adams, in "William Heminge and Shakespeare," *Modern Philology* 12, no. 1 (1914): 51–64, likewise dusts off *The Jewes Tragedy* to expose Heminge's extensive borrowing from Shakespeare.. See also Irving T. Richards, "The Meaning of Hamlet's Soliloquy," *PMLA* 48, no. 3 (1933), 741–66, and *The Revels History of Drama in English, 1613–1660*, ed. Lois Potter (London: Methuen, 1981), 4:xxx. George Eades Bentley's *The Jacobean and Caroline Stage*, vol. 4 (Oxford: Clarendon Press, 1941–68) offers a brief biography of Heminge but has nothing to say specifically about *The Jewes Tragedy* beyond confirming the date of publication as 1662 (546–47).

7. *The Biographia Dramatica; Or, A Companion to the Playhouse*, vol. 2 (London, 1812), 345.

8. Heminge's extraordinary departure from tradition has attracted scant critical interest, with the exception of Carol Morley who observes briefly in the introduction to her critical edition of *The Jewes Tragedy* that "nowhere does [Heminge] suggest that a righteous Providence is steering the Jewish people to merited disaster." See *Plays and Poems*, 25. Because *The Jewes Tragedy*'s novelty has gone strangely unnoticed by other scholars, there has been no sustained critical examination of the motivations for and the consequences of Heminge's singular non-providential interpretation of Josephus until now.

9. Morley makes a compelling case for Heminge's use of a post-1575 edition of Morwen's text based on the substitution of the word "Jews" for "Judges" in Skimeon's rousing proclamation to the mob in 3.6.59–63, which Heminge lifts verbatim from Morwen. Morley notes that though editions of Morwen from 1558–1575 say "iudges," editions from 1579 onward substitute "Iewes." See *Plays and Poems*, 48–49.

10. Peter Morwen, *A compendious and most maruelous Historie* (London, 1575), Aiiii.

11. Thomas Nashe, *The Works of Thomas Nashe*, ed. Ronald B. McKerrow, vol. 2 (New York: Barnes and Noble, 1966), 21.

12. Ibid., 59.

13. *Canaan's Calamitie*, A3v. All references are to the 1677 edition, which identifies Thomas Dekker as the author.

14. Ronald J. VanderMolen, "Providence as Mystery, Providence as Revelation: Puritan and Anglican Modifications of John Calvin's Doctrine of Providence," *Church History: Studies in Christianity and Culture* 47, no. 1 (1978): 29.

15. Thomas Beard, *The theatre of God's iudgements: or, a collection of histories out of sacred, ecclestiatical, and prophane authours concerning the admirable iudgements of God vpon the transgressours of his commandments* (London, 1597), 41, 40.

16. Eusebius, *The Avncient Ecclesiasticall Histories Of The First Six Hundred Years After Christ*, trans. Meredith Hanmer (London, 1577), 41–42.

17. Thomas Lodge, *The Famous and Memorable Workes of Iosephus, a Man of Much Honour and Learning Among the Iewes* (London, 1620), 739.

18. Walsham, *Providence in Early Modern England*, 116, 141; Groves, *The Destruction of Jerusalem*, 201.

19. Friedrich Nausea, *A Treatise of Blazing Starres in Generall*, trans. Abraham Fleming (London, 1618), E3r.

20. *The Levellers Almanacke: For the Yeare of Wonders, 1652* (London, 1651), 4.

21. Nashe, *Works*, 16.

22. Ibid., 60–61.

23. Ibid., 61.

24. Ibid., 62.

25. John Taylor, *All the Workes of John Taylor the Water-Poet, Bring sixty and three in number* (London, 1630). Taylor elaborates: "O Jerusalem, Jerusalem, / Thou Killst the Prophets, and to death did ding / Those that were sent, thee heav'nly grace to bring . . . / Your houses shall to desolation fall" (12–13).

26. T.D., *Canaan's Calamitie*, Br.

27. Ibid., B3v.

28. Ibid., B2r.

29. Ibid., B3v.

30. For a detailed study of Crowne's depiction of the fall of Jerusalem, see the following chapter.

31. John Crowne, *The Destruction of Jerusalem by Titus Vespasian in Two Parts: as it is acted at the Theatre Royal* (London, 1677). All references are to this edition and are cited parenthetically as part, act, and scene.

32. Thomas Legge's Latin play *Solymitana Clades*, performed at Cambridge, also focused on the complexities of the Jewish rebellion and, like Heminge would later, invokes an explicit parallel between the Roman conquest of Briton and the subjugation of Judaea.

33. For convenience I will call Heminge's character Joseph, to distinguish him from the historical Josephus.

34. Though there is no historical precedent for Ananias's murder at the hands of Zareck (instigated by Eleazar), Morwen does describe the murder of another priest, Amitta, by a servant of Schimeon (as Morwen calls him). As Morley notes, this may have suggested to Heminge a scenario for the murder of Ananias. Morley also speculates that Zareck might have been inspired by Morwen's brief account of one Sarach, who sought refuge in the Roman camp during the siege. In her words, "It is a possible hint for a character in the play (Zareck) whose main trait is treachery." See *Plays and Poems*, 51–52.

35. Bowers, *Elizabethan Revenge Tragedy*, 235.

36. William Hampton, *A Proclamation of Warre from the Lord of Hosts* (London, 1627), 21.

37. William Laud, *Seven Sermons Preached Upon severall occasions* (London, 1651), 103. This sermon is also cited by Groves, who observes that "Preachers who threatened England with the direful example of religious factionalism at the siege of Jerusalem" most often inveighed "against those (Catholics or Puritans) who rejected the Elizabethan religious settlement." See *The Destruction of Jerusalem*, 149.

38. John Spencer, *Kaina Kai Palaia. Things New and Old* (London, 1658), 8.

39. As Morley observes, "It would have been quite possible to write into the play the existence of some early Christians in Jerusalem (or Rome) to include a doctrinal perspective, had he so wished." See *Plays and Poems*, 61.

40. The Duke of Buckingham, the king's favorite and a primary instigator of the war with the Spanish, was also a vocal supporter of the Arminian cause.

41. Nicholas Tyacke, "Puritanism, Arminianism, and Counter-Revolution," in *The Origins of the English Civil War*, ed. Conrad Russell (New York: Barnes and Noble, 1973), 128.

42. Robert F. Lay, ed., *Readings in Historical Theology: Primary Sources of the Christian Faith* (Grand Rapids, MI: Kregel, 2009), 271.

43. See John Calvin, *Institutes of the Christian Religion*, ed. John T. McNeill, trans. Ford Lewis Battles, vol. 1 (Philadelphia: Westminster Press, 1960), 201.

44. Ibid. 1.16.4–9.

45. John Calvin, *Two Godly and Notable Sermons preached by the excellent and famous clarke, Master Iohn Caluyne, in the yere. 1555* (London, 1560).

46. George Hakewill, *An Answere to a Treatise Written by D. Carrier* (London, 1616), 30.

47. George Hakewill, *An Apologie of the Power and Providence of God in the Government of the World* (Oxford, 1627), 295.

48. See VanderMolen, "Providence as Mystery," 38.

49. Qtd. in Reid Barbour, *English Epicures and Stoics: Ancient Legacies in Early Stuart Culture* (Boston: University of Massachusetts Press, 1998), 96.

50. The scholarly controversy was not just whether or how consensus broke down but who established and maintained it, and for how long. Part of the problem is that "Puritanism," "Calvinism," "Arminianism," and "Laudianism" are complex shifting labels. To quote Peter Lake, "In using the terms Calvinism and Arminianism, Tyacke was talking about rival versions of the theology of grace, different sets of opinions about predestination. But were the opinions he was calling Calvinism really derived from Calvin and his immediate followers? Were indeed the tenets he was calling Arminianism derived from Arminus?" In brief, Lake questions whether Tyacke's terms are adequate to the task of accurately characterizing "the range of opinions on these questions to be found among theologically literate English people during the period." See Lake, "Introduction: Puritanism, Arminianism and Nicholas Tyacke," in *Religious Politics in Post-Reformation England*, eds. Kenneth Fincham and Peter Lake (Woodbridge, Suffolk, UK: Boydell Press, 2006), 13–14.

51. Barbour, *English Epicures and Stoics*, 78.

52. Peter White, *Predestination, Policy and Polemic: Conflict and Consensus in the English Church from the Reformation to the Civil War* (Cambridge: Cambridge University Press, 1992), 256–71.

53. Thomas Jackson, *The Works of Thomas Jackson*, vol. 5 (Oxford: Oxford University Press, 1844), 100.

54. Barbour, *English Epicures and Stoics*, 96. See Jackson, *Works*, 361. For further discussion on Thomas Jackson's engagement with providence, see also William E. Burns, "Signs of the Times: Thomas Jackson and the Controversy over Prodigies in the Reign of Charles I," *Seventeenth Century* 11, no. 1 (1996): 21–33.

55. See Barbara Donagan's discussion of chance and contingency in "Providence, Chance and Explanation: Some Paradoxical Aspects of Puritan Views of Causation," *Journal of Religious History* 1, no. 1 (1981): 385–403.

56. Thomas Gataker, *Of the Nature and Use of Lots: A Treatise Historicall and Theologicall* (London, 1627).

57. For an extensive study on the relationship between luck and divine providence, see Norman Jones, *God and the Moneylenders: Usury and Law in Early Modern England* (Oxford: Blackwell, 1989), and Brian Cummings, *Mortal Thoughts: Religion, Secularity and Identity in Early Modern Culture* (Oxford: Oxford University Press, 2013). See also Eric Watkins, *The Divine Order, The Human Order, and the Order of Nature: Historical Perspectives* (New York: Oxford University Press, 2013).

58. Keith Thomas, *Religion and the Decline of Magic* (New York: Scribner, 1971), 122. For a brief discussion on William Ames's providentially inflected interpretation of lots, see Reid Barbour, *Literature and Religious Culture in Seventeenth-Century England* (Cambridge: Cambridge University Press, 2004), 215–16.

59. Walsham, *Providence in Early Modern England*, 220. Laura Lunger Knoppers argues that while dissenters, in their jeremiads on the plague and the Great Fire, "found a powerful mode to interpret and appropriate a spectacle of misery, to posit divine punishment of the newly royalized nation," the established clergy—especially with the fire—deployed the jeremiad mode to argue against the sin not of royalism but of rebellion. See Knoppers, *Historicizing Milton: Spectacle, Power, and Poetry in Restoration England* (Athens: University of Georgia Press, 1994), 142. The upshot, as Margery Kingsley notes in "Interpreting Providence: The Politics of Jeremiad in Restoration Polemic," in *Wonders, Marvels, and Monsters in Early Modern Culture*, ed. Peter G. Platt (Newark: University of Delaware Press, 1999), 251–67, was that prophecy was rendered suspect "through the accusation that it was more accurate after the fact than before" and that the "predictions . . . were themselves originally motivated not by divine inspiration but by transparent political interest" (257).

60. See Michael Witmore, *Culture of Accidents: Unexpected Knowledges in Early Modern England* (Stanford, CA: Stanford University Press, 2001), 132–33.

61. Walsham, *Providence in Early Modern England*, 221.

62. Paul Boyer, *When Time Shall Be No More: Prophecy Belief in Modern American Culture* (Cambridge, MA: Harvard University Press, 1992), 65.

63. Jonathan Rogers, "'We Saw a New Created Day': Restoration Revisions of Civil War Apocalypse," in *The English Civil Wars in the Literary Imagination*, eds. Claude J. Summers and Ted-Larry Pebworth (Columbia: University of Missouri Press, 1999), 193.

64. Abraham Cowley, *The Complete Works in Verse and Prose of Abraham Cowley*, ed. Alexander B. Grosart, vol. 1 (Edinburgh: Edinburgh University Press, 1881).

65. Abraham Cowley, *Ode on the Majesties Restauration and Return* (London, 1660), 103–4, 114–16, 137–38.

66. Anonymous, *Vox Populi* (1660), B2v.

67. See Steven N. Zwicker, "Israel, England, and the Triumph of Roman Virtue," in *Millenarianism and Messianism in English Literature and Thought, 1650–1800*, ed. Richard H. Popkin (Leiden: Brill, 1988), 39–40.

68. Jessica Munns, Laura Lunger Knoppers ,and Achsah Guibbory have convincingly shown its application throughout the early 1660s. See Munns, "Accounting for Providence: Contemporary Descriptions of the Restoration of Charles II," in *Recording and Reordering: Essays on the Seventeenth-and Eighteenth-Century Diary and Journal*, eds. Dan Doll and Jessica Munns (Cranbury, NJ: Rosemont, 2006), 102–21, for a detailed examination of providentialist rhetoric in Clarendon's *History*, and the diaries of John Evelyn, Samuel Pepys, and Ralph Josselin.

69. John Dryden, *Astraea Redux: A Poem on the Happy Restoration and Return of His Sacred Majesty Charles the Second* (London, 1660), 7.

70. *By The King A Proclamation Setting Apart a Day of Solemn and Publick Thanksgiving* (London, 1660).

71. Edward Waterhouse, *A Short Narrative of the late Dreadful Fire in London* (London, 1667).

72. Margery Kingsley reminds us that these texts were not disinterested quests for religious truth and that they can almost never be disassociated from party politics and factionalism. As she argues, these narratives were not just a way of understanding misfortune but also politically powerful polemic. For the dissenters, the plague and the Great Fire were proof of divine rejection of the monarchy; for the royalists, however, the same events—especially the fire—were perceived as cleansing the state of the last vestiges of civil insurrection and thereby creating space for a new beginning. See Kingsley, "Interpreting Providence," 254–55.

73. Achsah Guibbory discusses Dryden's attempts to balance providentialism with political awareness in Astraea Redux and in his heroic drama in *The Map of Time: Seventeenth-Century English Literature and Ideas of Pattern in History* (Urbana: University of Illinois Press, 1986), 213–53.

74. Edward, Earl of Clarendon, *The History of the Rebellion and Civil Wars in England*, ed. Duncan Macray, vol. 5 (Oxford: Clarendon Press, 1888), 274.

75. Munns, "Accounting for Providence," 107.

76. *John Evelyn: The Diary*, ed. John Howard Davies (Brighton: Book Guild, 2009).

77. Daniel Woolf, "From Hystories to the Historical: Five Transitions in Thinking about the Past, 1500–1700," *The Uses of History in Early Modern England*, ed. Paulina Kewes (San Marino: University of California Press, 2006), 45.

78. Rabbi Menasseh Ben Israel in the Netherlands exploited this belief in his plea to Oliver Cromwell and the Rump Parliament to readmit the Jews into England, stating that "the opinion of many Christians and mine do concur herein, that we both believe that the restoring time of our Nation into their native country is very near at hand."

See Menasseh Ben Israel, "A Declaration to the Commonwealth of England by Rabbi Menasseh Ben Israel, Showing the Motives of his Coming to England," in *Male and Female Voices in Early Modern England: An Anthology of Renaissance Writing*, eds. Anne Lake Prescott and Betty Travitsky (New York: Columbia University Press, 2000), 53.

79. David Katz, *The Jews in the History of England, 1485–1850* (Oxford: Oxford University Press, 1994), 137.

80. For a further discussion of tolerance toward Jews in early modern England, see John Marshall, *John Locke, Toleration and Early Enlightenment Culture* (Cambridge: Cambridge University Press, 2006); Alan Levine, *Early Modern Skepticism and the Origins of Toleration* (Lanham, MD: Lexington Books, 1996); and Cary J. Nederman and John Christian Lauersen, eds., *Difference and Dissent: Theories of Tolerance in Medieval and Early Modern Europe* (Lanham, MD: Rowman and Littlefield, 1996).

5. Exile and Restoration

1. Simone Weil, *The Need for Roots: Prelude to a Declaration of Duties Toward Mankind* (New York: Routledge, 2002), 43.

2. Walter Brueggemann, *The Land: Place as Gift, Promise and Challenge in Biblical Faith* (Minneapolis: Fortress Press, 2002), 15. Brueggeman argues that land given or promised by God is the central organizing principle of Old Testament theology. For him "land is a central, if not *the central theme* of biblical faith," illustrated in the numerous movements to and away from land: the gift of Eden, the expulsion of Adam, the exile of Cain, the promise to Abraham, and the very movement from slavery (Exodus) to liberation (Deuteronomy), which is also a movement from landlessness to a covenanted relationship with God.

3. See Chaim Milikowsky, "Notions of Exile, Subjugation, and Return in Rabbinic Literature," *Exile: Old Testament, Jewish, and Christian Conceptions*, ed. James M. Scott (Leiden: Brill, 1997), 265–96. Milikowsky's claim that in Tannaitic sources of the second and third centuries CE, the term "exile" connoted political subjugation rather than expulsion from the land is consistent with Israel J. Yuval's careful analysis of the myth of Jewish exile after the destruction of the Second Temple in both Jewish and Christian iterations. See Yuval, "The Myth of the Jewish Exile from the Land of Israel: A Demonstration of Irenic Scholarship," *Common Knowledge* 12, no. 1 (2006): 16–33. For the role of exile in the Jewish historical consciousness, see also Yitzhak F. Baer, *Exile*, trans. Robert Warshaw (New York: Schocken, 1947).

4. Yuval, "The Myth of the Jewish Exile," 21.

5. Ibid., 23.

6. James Pilkington, *Aggeus and Abdias Prophetes, the one corrected, the other newly added and both at large declared* (London, 1562).

7. John Greene, *Nehemiah's teares for the affliction of Jerusalem* (1644), 8. The Presbyterian Edmund Calamy employs the trope somewhat differently when he compares the English who had become complacent under Archbishop Laud to those Jews who were reluctant to return from Babylonian exile: they were like "the *Israelites*

in *Babylon*, that liked their habitations in *Babylon* so well, that when *Cyrus* gave them leave to goe to *Jerusalem*, they would not leave *Babylon*." See Calamy, *Gods free Mercy to England. Presented as a Pretious and Powerfull motive to Humiliation: In a Sermon before the Honourable House of Commons, at their late solemne Faste, Feb. 23, 1641* (London, 1642), 44–45.

8. [Thomas Cranmer], *The Lame[n]tacion of England* (London, 1558), 6–7. See Edwin Sandys, *Sermons made by the most reuerend Father in God, Edwin, Archbishop of Yorke, primate of England and metropolitane* (1585), 310. For a detailed study of tropes regarding biblical exile in early modern England, see Hannibal Hamlin, "Strangers in Strange Lands: Biblical Models of Exile in Early Modern England," *Reformation* 15, no. 1 (2010): 63–81; and Christopher Highley, "Exile and Religious Identity in Early Modern England," *Reformation* 15, no. 1 (2010): 51–61.

9. See Theophilus Cibber, *The Lives of the Poets of Great Britain and Ireland*, vol. 3 (1753; Teddington: Echo Library, 2007), 69.

10. See Stuart Gillespie and David Hopkins, *The Oxford History of Literary Translation in English: 1660–1790* (Oxford: Oxford University Press, 2005), 321.

11. John Downes, *Roscius Anglicanus, or An Historical Review of the Stage*, ed. Montague Summers (Bronx, NY: Benjamin Blom, 1928), 13, 135.

12. *The Destruction of Jerusalem* was offered initially to the Duke's Company who were unwilling to produce it, no doubt because it had already produced Otway's *Titus and Berenice*. Crowne's defection to the King's Company while still under contract to the Duke's Company required the King's to buy Crowne's contract. It is recorded that Mr. Crowne "being under the like agreemt with the Dukes house writ a play call'd the *Destruction of Jerusalem*, and being forced by their refuseall of it to bring it to us, the said Company compell'd us after the studying of it, & a vast expence in Scenes and Cloathes to buy off their clayme, by paying all the pension he had received from them Amounting to one hundred and twelve pounds paid by the Kings Company, Besides neare forty pound he the said Mr. Crowne paid out of his owne Pocket." See James M. Osborn, *John Dryden: Some Biographical Facts and Problems*, rev. ed. (Gainesville: University Press of Florida, 1965), 204–5.

13. Thomas Otway, *The Works of Thomas Otway*, ed. J. C. Ghosh, 2 vols. (1932; Oxford: Oxford University Press, 1968). All references are to this edition and are cited parenthetically as act, scene, and line.

14. Adolphus William Ward and A. R. Waller, eds., *The Cambridge History of English Literature*, vol. 8 (Cambridge: Cambridge University Press, 1912), 190.

15. See Arthur Franklin White, *John Crowne: His Life and Dramatic Works* (Cleveland: Western Reserve University Press, 1922), 93, 180.

16. See John Wilmot Rochester, *The Works of the Earl of Rochester, Roscommon, and Dorset*, vol. 2 (London, 1731), 218.

17. J. Maidment and W. H. Logan, ed., *The Dramatic Works of John Crowne*, vol. 2 (Edinburgh: William Patterson, 1873), 219.

18. White, *John Crowne*, 98.

19. Robert Hume, *The Development of English Drama in the Late Seventeenth Century* (Oxford: Clarendon Press, 1976), 312–13.

20. Don-John Dugas, "Elkanah Settle, John Crowne, and Nahum Tate," *A Companion to Restoration Drama*, ed. Susan J. Owen (Malden, MA: Blackwell Publishers, 2001), 387.

21. See Richard Capwell, *A Biographical and Critical Study of John Crowne* (PhD diss., Duke University, 1964), 214.

22. John B. Rollins, "Judaeo-Christian Apocalyptic Literature and John Crowne's *The Destruction of Jerusalem*," *Comparative Drama* 35, no. 2 (2001): 209. For a brief reading of Crowne's depiction of apocalypse as the estrangement between humanity and God, and the relevance of this episode of Jewish history to contemporary English politics, see also Derek Hughes, *English Drama 1660–1700* (Oxford: Clarendon Press, 1996), 240–42.

23. Joseph ben Gorion, *The Wonderful and Most Deplorable History of the Latter Times of the Jews with the Destruction of the City of Jerusalem . . . moreover, there is a parallel of the late times, and crimes in London, with those in Jerusalem*. All references are to the 1662 edition.

24. Ibid., A2r–v.

25. Ibid., A2r–A3v.

26. Ibid., A4r.

27. Ibid. B3v.

28. Eva Scott, *The King In Exile: The Wanderings of Charles II. From June 1646 to July 1654* (New York: E. P. Dutton and Company [Edinburgh printed], 1905), 1.

29. Paul Hardacre, "The Royalists in Exile During the Puritan Revolution, 1642–1660," *Huntington Library Quarterly* 16, no. 4 (1953): 353.

30. Geoffrey Smith, *The Cavaliers In Exile, 1640–1660* (Basingstoke, Hampshire, UK: Palgrave Macmillan, 2003), 208.

31. John Stoye, *English Travellers Abroad 1604–1667* (New York: Octagon Books, 1952), 458.

32. Edward Chaney, *The Grand Tour and the Great Rebellion: Richard Lassels and "The Voyage of Italy" in the Seventeenth Century* (Geneva: Slatkine, 1985), 354–55; Philip Major, *Literatures of Exile in the English Revolution and its Aftermath, 1640–1690* (Burlington, VT: Ashgate, 2010), 11.

33. James II, *The Memoirs of James II; His Campaigns as Duke of York, 1652–1660*, eds. J. S. Clark and A. Lytton Sells (London: Chatto and Windus, 1962), 57.

34. See *State Papers Collected by Edward, Earl of Clarendon*, eds. R. Scrope and T. Monkhouse, vol. 3 (Oxford: Clarendon, 1786), 179.

35. Smith, *Cavaliers in Exile*, 195.

36. *Calendar of State Papers, Domestic Series 1640–1641*, ed. M. A. E. Green, (London: Longman & Co. and Trübner & Co., 1876–1886), 299–300, 314, 435.

37. Margaret Cavendish, *The Cavalier in Exile: Being the Lives of the First Dvke and Dvchess of Newcastle* (New York: C. Scribner's Sons, 1903), 232.

38. Edward Niles Hooker and H. T. Swedenborg Jr., ed., *The Works of John Dryden: Poems 1649–1680*, vol. 1 (Berkeley: University of California Press, 1961), 72. All references are to this edition and are cited parenthetically in the text.

39. Smith, *Cavaliers in Exile*, 98.

40. Isaac Basire, *The Correspondence of Isaac Basire, D.D.*, ed. Edward Chaney (London: John Murray, 1831), iv.

41. Ibid., 79–84, 105–6, 115–20, 127–31.

42. Richard Flecknoe, *Pourtrait of His Majesty, Made a Little before His Happy Restauration* (London, 1660), 24.

43. See David R. Evans, "Charles II's 'Grand Tour': Restoration Panegyric and the Rhetoric of Travel Literature," *Philogical Quarterly* 720, no. 10 (1993): 53–71.

44. Edward Said, *Reflections on Exile and Other Essays* (Cambridge, MA: Harvard University Press, 2002), 173, 174.

45. Moses Finley, *The World of Odysseus* (New York: The New York Review of Books, 1982), 56.

46. Said, *Reflections on Exile*, 177, 173.

47. Ibid., 177.

48. Hughes, *English Drama*, 242.

49. Melvin Seeman, "On the Meaning of Alienation," *American Sociological Review* 24, no. 6 (1959): 783–91.

50. Michèle Longino's study of Racine's *Bérénice*, *Orientalism in French Classical Drama* (Cambridge: Cambridge University Press, 2002), discerns in Antiochus's lovesickness an essentializing discourse that Eastern men are melancholic, aimless, defeated, and emasculated. In the same way, Bérénice's lament in 4.1.955–56 sums up the directionless frenzy of the Orient as a whole: "I'm agitated, I run, languishing, worn out / Strength abandons me, and rest kills me." Here, she comes close to echoing the lamentations of the truly exiled figure, Antiochus, whose restless activity Longino pronounces "worthless" since "no value" can be "assigned to or gleaned" from it (175).

51. Thomas Wyatt, *Sir Thomas Wyatt: Collected Poems*, ed. Joost Daalder (Oxford: Oxford University Press, 1975), 28.

52. See Jane Kingsley-Smith, "That One Word 'Banishèd': Linguistic Crisis in *Romeo and Juliet*" in *Shakespeare's Drama of Exile* (Basingstoke, Hampshire, UK: Palgrave Macmillan, 2003), 31–55.

53. See J. Hannah, ed., *The Courtly Poets from Raleigh to Montrose* (London: Elibron Classics Series, 2006), 154: "The sollitarie woodes my Cittie shall become / The darkest den shal be my lodge, whereto noe light shall come / Of heban blacke my boorde, the wormes my feast shal be / Wherewith my Carcasse shal be fed, till they doe feede on mee / My wine of Niobe, my bedd the cragie rocke."

54. See Rollins, "Judaeo-Christian Apocalyptic Literature," 209–24.

55. Andrew Crome, *The Restoration of the Jews: Early Modern Hermeneutics, Eschatology, and National Identity in the Works of Thomas Brightman* (Cham, Switzerland: Springer, 2014), 3. Richard Muller notes that the promise of the restored Jewish

kingdom emphasizes "more pointedly than any other class of texts, the problem of literal meaning, future referents, and ultimate intended implication of a text." See Muller, "The Hermeneutic of Promise and Fulfillment in Calvin's Exegesis of the Old Testament Prophecies of the Kingdom," in *The Bible in the Sixteenth Century*, ed. David Steinmetz (London: Duke University Press, 1990), 70.

56. For a compelling study of the growing seventeenth-century desire to understand ancient works in their own historical contexts, see Kevin Killeen, *Biblical Scholarship, Science and Politics in Early Modern England* (Aldershot: Ashgate, 2009).

57. Thomas Brightman, *A Revelation of the Revelation* (Amsterdam, 1615), B3r.

58. See also Cecil Roth, "The Resettlement of the Jews in England in 1656," in *Three Centuries of Anglo-Jewish History*, ed. V. D. Lipman (London: Jewish Historical Society, 1961); David Katz, *Philo-Semitism and the Readmission of the Jews to England, 1603–1655* (Oxford: Oxford University Press, 1982); Richard Henry Popkin, ed., *Millenarianism and Messianism in English Literature and Thought, 1650–1800* (Leiden: Brill, 1988); James Shapiro, *Shakespeare and the Jews* (New York: Columbia University Press, 1996); and D. R. Woolf, *Reading History in Early Modern England* (Cambridge: Cambridge University Press, 2000).

59. Menasseh Ben Israel, "A Declaration to the Commonwealth of England by Rabbi Menasseh Ben Israel, Showing the Motives of his Coming to England," in *Male and Female Voices in Early Modern England: An Anthology of Renaissance Writing*, eds. Anne Lake Prescott and Betty Travitsky (New York: Columbia University Press, 2000), 53.

60. For a full transcript of the translated letter, see Cecil Roth, "New Light on the Resettlement," *Transactions (Jewish Historical Society of England)* 11 (1924–1927): 116–17.

61. Henry Jessey, *A Narrative of the late Proceeds at White-Hall, Concerning the Jews* (London, 1656), 6. For Beatrice Groves's discussion of seventeenth-century philosemitism, see her conclusion in *The Destruction of Jerusalem in Early Modern English Literature* (Cambridge: Cambridge University Press, 2015), 219–31

62. David Katz, *The Jews in the History of England, 1485–1850* (Oxford: Oxford University Press, 1994), 137.

63. Bagshaw was more interested in matters of ritual and praxis in which he hoped for the license to deviate from the Church of England. In response, Locke argued that the ritual aspects of Judaism as well as of Islam were an essential part of the maintenance of their faith. Locke cites the scrupulousness of the God of Israel, who "descended to the lowest actions and most trivial utensils, not leaving out the very snuffers and firepans of the sanctuary." See *Two Tracts on Government* (Cambridge: Cambridge University Press, 1967), 133. Locke suggests that one might try and use persuasion to convert the Jews, but an external and autocratic imposition of the Christian faith would achieve nothing. That said, there were so few Jews and they were so little inclined to proselytize that they there were not as great a threat as the dissenters who were copious in number and strident in voice.

64. For a discussion of tolerance toward Jews in early modern England, see John Marshall, *John Locke, Toleration and Early Enlightenment Culture* (Cambridge: Cambridge University Press, 2006); Alan Levine, *Early Modern Skepticism and the Origins of Toleration* (Lanham, MD: Lexington Books, 1999); and Cary J. Nederman and John Christian Lauersen, eds., *Difference and Dissent: Theories of Tolerance in Medieval and Early Modern Europe* (Lanham, MD: Rowman and Littlefield, 1996).

65. Locke, *Political Thought*, ed. David Wooton (Indianapolis: Hackett, 1993), 190.

66. Peter Morwen, *A compendious and most marueilous Historie* (London, 1575), Aiiii.

67. "The Returne of the renowned Cauliero Pasquill" (1589) in Thomas Nashe, *The Works of Thomas Nashe*, ed. Ronald B. McKerrow, vol. 1 (New York: Barnes and Noble, 1966), 76.

68. See *The Subjects Sorrow: Or, Lamentations Upon the Death of Britains Josiah, KING CHARLES* (London, 1649), 30.

69. [John Gauden and Charles I], *Eikon Basilike: The Pourtraicture of His Sacred Maiestie in His Solitudes and Sufferings* (London: s.n., 1648), 224. For a commentary on the way that Milton's *Eikonoklastes* contests this view, and for his employment of the siege trope, see Groves, *The Destruction of Jerusalem*, 187–218.

70. See Harold Love, "Restoration and Early Eighteenth-Century Drama," in *The Cambridge History of English Literature, 1660–1780*, ed. John J. Richetti (Cambridge: Cambridge University Press, 2005), 117. See also Hughes, *English Drama*, 240–41.

71. Crowne, whose Epistle Dedicatory to the Duchess of Portsmouth identifies "Beauty" as "the fairest visible Image of Divinity in the world," and imagines his patroness's image fixed "at this Jewish Temple Gate, to render the building sacred," naturally had little sympathy for the icon-smashing fervor displayed by John and the other rebels.

72. Rollins, "Judaeo-Christian Apocalyptic Literature," 211.

73. Ibid., 215.

74. For the role of heroic drama in reconstructing royalist values, see J. Douglas Canfield, "The Significance of the Restoration Rhymed Heroic Play," *Eighteenth Century Studies* 13, no.1 (1979): 49–62, and David R. Evans, "'Private Greatness': The Feminine Ideal in Dryden's Early Heroic Drama," *Restoration* 16, no. 1 (1992): 2–19.

75. Evans, "Charles II's 'Grand Tour,'" 55–56.

76. Gerald MacLean, *Time's Witness: Historical Representation in English Poetry, 1603–1660* (Madison, WI: University of Wisconsin Press, 1990), 259.

Epilogue

1. Although Beatrice Groves maintains that the destruction depicted could have been either Babylonian or Roman or perhaps even a combination of both (*The Destruction of Jerusalem in Early Modern English Literature* [Cambridge: Cambridge University Press, 2015], 115), Martin Wiggins and Catherine Teresa Richardson identify the siege as Roman in *British Drama, 1533–1642: A Catalogue, Vol. V: 1603–1608* (Oxford: Oxford University Press, 2015), 34.

2. Thomas Crosfield, *The Diary of Thomas Crosfield*, ed. Fredrick S. Boas (London: Oxford University Press, 1935), 71, 79.

3. See also George Speaight, *The History of the English Puppet Theatre* (New York: J. de Graff, 1955), 325.

4. Cited in Thomas Roebuck, "'Great Expectation Among the Learned': Edward Bernard's Josephus in Restoration Oxford," *International Journal of the Classical Tradition* 23, no. 3 (2016): 308.

5. Ibid.

6. Cited in ibid., 309.

7. MS Royal Library of Copenhagen, NKS 1675, 2, No. 10. Cited in Roebuck, "'Great Expectation,'" 312.

8. Ibid.

9. Daniel Woolf, *Reading History in Early Modern England* (Cambridge: Cambridge University Press, 2000), 7.

10. Laurence Price, *Englands Golden Legacy: or, A brief description of the manifold mercies and blessings which the Lord hath bestowed upon our sinful nation.* (London, 1657), 3.

11. Ibid., 11.

12. Ibid., 13. 15.

13. R.D., *The Strange and Prodigious Religions, Customs, and Manners of Sundry Nations. The second edition. By R.D.* (London, 1688), A2r, B1v.

14. Ibid, 132.

15. John Flavel, *Two Treatises* (London: Robert Boulter, 1682), 164, 165–66.

16. Gilbert Burnet, *A Sermon Preached at Bow-Church, before the Court of Aldermen, on March 12, 1689/90* (London, 1690), 15.

17. John Cockburn, *Fifteen Sermons Preach'd Upon Several Occasions, and on Various Subjects* (London, 1697), 150, 153.

18. Ibid., 154 (italics mine).

Bibliography

Achinstein, Sharon. "John Foxe and the Jews." *Renaissance Quarterly* 54, no. 1 (2001): 86–120.

Adams, H. M. *Catalogue of Books Printed on the Continent of Europe, 1501–1600 in Cambridge Libraries.* Vol. 1. London: Cambridge University Press, 1967; repr. Cambridge: Cambridge University Press, 1990.

Adams, John Quincy. "William Heminge and Shakespeare." *Modern Philology* 12, no .1 (1914): 51–64.

Agamben, Giorgio, and Daniel Heller-Roazen. *Homo Sacer: Sovereign Power and Bare Life.* Stanford, CA: Stanford University Press, 1998.

Anon. *The dystruccyon of Iherusalem by Vaspazian and Tytus.* Enprynted at London : In flete strete at the sygne of the sonne by Wynkyn de Word. London, 1510.

Anon. *Christs teares over Jerusalem, Or, A caveat for England, to call to God for mercy, lest we be plagued for our contempt and wickednesse. To the tune of The merchants.* London: 1640.

Anon. *Londons Lamentation, Or, A Fit Admonishment for City and Countrey: Wherein Is Described Certaine Causes of This Affliction and Visitation of the Plague, Yeare 1641, Which the Lord Hath Been Pleased to Inflict Upon Us: and Withall What Meanes Must Be Used to the Lord to Gaine His Mercy and Favor : with an Excellent Spirituall Medicine to Be Used for the Preservative Both of Body and Soule.* London: Printed by E. P. for Iohn Wright, Junior, 1641.

Anon. *The Subjects Sorrow: or, Lamentations upon the Death of Britains Josiah King Charles most unjustly and cruelly put to death by his owne people, before his royall palace White-Hall, January the 30, 1648. Expressed in a sermon upon Lam. 4. 20. Wherein the divine and royall prerogatives, personall virtues, and theologicall graces of His late Majesty are briefly delivered: and that His Majesty was taken away in Gods mercy unto himselfe and for the certaine punishment of these kingdomes, from the parallel is clearly proved.* London : [s.n.], printed in the yeare, 1649.

Anon. *The Levellers Almanacke: For the Yeare of Wonders, 1652.* London, 1651.

Anon. *Warning Or lanthorn to London, by the Doleful Destruction of Faire Jerusalem Whose Misery and Unspeakable Plague Doth Most Justly Declare Gods Heavy Wrath and Judgement for the Sinns and Wickedness of the People, Except by Repentance We Call to God for Mercy: To the Tune of Brigandary. Of the horyble and woful destruccion of Jerusalem, and the Signes and Tokens That Were Seen before it Was Destroyed, Which Destruction Was After Christs Ascension Xlii Years: to the Tune of The Queens Almaine.* London: Printed for F. Coles, J. VVright, Tho. Vere, and VV. Gilbertson, 1658.

Anon. *Great Britain's Warning-piece: Or, Christ's Tears Over Jerusalem.* [London]: Printed for W. Thackery at the Angel in Duck Lane, 1688.

Aquinas, Thomas. *Summa Theologiae: Latin Text and English Translation, Introductions, Notes, Appendices, and Glossaries.* Cambridge: Blackfriars, 1964.

Aston, Margaret. *Lollards and Reformers: Images and Literacy in Late Medieval Religion.* London: Hambledon, 1984.

Auger, Peter. "Playing Josephus on the English Stage." *International Journal of the Classical Tradition* 26, no. 3 (2016): 326–32.

Axon, W. E. A. "Documents relating to the plague in Manchester, 1605." *Chetham Miscellanies.* New Series Vol. 3. Manchester: Chetham Society, 1915.

Ayres, Philip. *Classical Culture and the Idea of Rome In Eighteenth-Century England.* Cambridge: Cambridge University Press, 1997.

Baer, Yitzhak F., and Robert Warshaw. *Exile.* New York: Schocken, 1947.

Baker, David Erskine, Stephen Jones, and Isaac Reed. *Biographia Dramatica, Or, A Companion to the Playhouse: Containing Historical and Critical Memoirs and Original Anecdotes of British and Irish Dramatic Writers From the Commencement of Our Theatrical Exhibitions . . . Together with an Introductory View of the Rise and Progress of the British Stage.* London: Printed by Longman, Hurst, Rees, Orme, and Brown [etc.], 1812.

Bakhtin, M. M. *Rabelais and His World.* Bloomington: Indiana University Press, 1984.

Barbon, Nicholas. *An Apology for the Builder, Or, A Discourse Shewing the Cause and Effects of the Increase of Building.* London: Printed by Cave Pullen . . . , 1685.

Barbour, Philip L. *The Jamestown Voyages Under the First Charter, 1606–1609: Documents Relating to the Foundation of Jamestown and the History of the Jamestown Colony Up to the Departure of Captain John Smith, Last President of the Council In Virginia Under the First Charter, Early In October 1609.* London: published for the Hakluyt Society [by] Cambridge University Press, 1969.

Barbour, Reid. *English Epicures and Stoics: Ancient Legacies In Early Stuart Culture.* Amherst: University of Massachusetts Press, 1998.

———. *Literature and Religious Culture In Seventeenth-Century England.* Cambridge: Cambridge University Press, 2002.

Barker, John. *Of the horyble and woful destruccion of Jerusalem: And of the Sygnes and Tokens That Were Seene before it Was Destroied: Which Distruction Was After Christes Assension. Xlii. Yeares. To the Tune of the Queenes Almayne.* Imprinted at London: In Fleetestreate beneath the Conduit, at the signe of S. Iohn Euangelist, by Thomas Colwell, 1569.

Barkan, Leonard. *Nature's Work of Art: The Human Body As Image of the World*. New Haven, CT: Yale University Press, 1975.

Barnard, John, D. F McKenzie, and Maureen Bell. *The Cambridge History of the Book in Britain. Vol. 4: 1557–1695*. Cambridge: Cambridge University Press, 2008.

Basire, Isaac, and W. N Darnell. *The Correspondence of Isaac Basire, D.D., Archdeacon of Northumberland and Prebendary of Durham, In the Reigns of Charles I. and Charles II: With a Memoir of His Life, by W. N. Darnell*. London: John Murray, 1831.

Bataille, Georges. *The Accursed Share: An Essay On General Economy*. New York: Zone Books, 1991.

Beard, Thomas. *The theatre of God's iudgements: or, a collection of histories out of sacred, ecclestiatical, and prophane authours concerning the admirable iudgements of God vpon the transgressours of his commandments*. London: Printed by . . . . ? 1597.

Becon, Thomas. *The Flour of Godly Praiers: Most Worthy to Be Vsed In These Our Daies for the Sauegard, Health, and Comforte of All Degrees, and Estates*. Imprinted at London: By Ihon Day, dwelling ouer Aldersgate, a lytle beneth S. Martins, these bokes are to be solde at hys shop by the lytle cunduite in Chepesyde, 1550.

Becon, Thomas, and John Ayre. *Prayers and Other Pieces of Thomas Becon*. Cambridge: Cambridge University Press, 1844.

Becon, Thomas, and John Ayre. *The Early Works of Thomas Becon: Being the Treatises Published by Him In the Reign of King Henry VIII*. New York: Johnson Reprint Corp., 1968.

ben Gorion, Joseph. *The Wonderful and Most Deplorable History of the Latter Times of the Jews: With the Destruction of the City of Jerusalem: Which History Begins Where the Holy Scriptures Do End*. London: Printed for Christopher Eccleston . . . , 1662.

Bentley, Gerald Eades. *The Jacobean and Caroline Stage*. Oxford: Clarendon Press, 1941–68.

Bertram, Benjamin. "Falstaff's Body, the Body Politic, and the Body of Trade." *Exemplaria* 21, no. 3 (2009): 296–318.

Blench, J. W. *Preaching In England In the Late Fifteenth and Sixteenth Centuries: A Study of English Sermons 1450-C. 1600*. Oxford: Blackwell, 1964.

Bowers, Fredson. *Elizabethan Revenge Tragedy, 1587–1642*. Princeton, NJ: Princeton University Press, 1940.

Boyer, Paul S. *When Time Shall Be No More: Prophecy Belief In Modern American Culture*. Cambridge, MA: Belknap Press of Harvard University Press, 1992.

Brightman, Thomas. *A Revelation of the Reuelation that is The Revelation of St. John opened clearly with a logicall Resolution and Exposition. Wherein the Sense is cleared, out of Scripture, the euent also of things foretold is Discussed out of Church-Historyes*. Amsterdam, 1615.

Brinsley, John. *Tears for Ieruvsalem, Or, The Compassionate Lamentation of a tender hearted Saviour over a rebellious and Obdurate People: A Subject Entered Upon On the Late Day of Solemn Humiliation, December 6, 1655, Afterwards Prosecuted, and*

Now Published As Useful At All Times, but Very Seasonable for the Present. London: Printed by J.L. for Tho. Newberry, 1656.

Broughton, Hugh, John Lightfoot, W. Primroes, and James Speght. *The Vvorks of the Great Albionean Divine, Renown'd In Many Nations For rare Skill In Salems & Athens Tongues, and Familiar Acquaintance with All Rabbinical Learning, Mr. Hugh Broughton: Collected Into One Volume and Digested Into Four Tomes*. London: Printed for Nath. Ekins, 1662.

Brown, Alexander. *Genesis of the United States: A Narrative of the movement in England, 1605–1616*. New York: Houghton Mifflin & Co., 1890.

Brownlee, Victoria, and Laura Gallagher. *Biblical Women In Early Modern Literary Culture, 1550–1700*. Manchester: Manchester University Press, 2015.

Brueggemann, Walter. *The Land: Place As Gift, Promise, and Challenge In Biblical Faith*. 2nd ed. Minneapolis: Fortress Press, 2002.

Bullein, William. *Bulleins Bulwarke of defense against all sicknesse, soarenesse, and vvoundes that doe dayly assaulte mankinde: which bulwarke is kept with Hilarius the gardener, [and] Health the phisicion, with the chirurgian, to helpe the wounded sol-diours. Gathered and practised from the most worthy learned, both olde and new: to the great comfort of mankinde: by VVilliam Bullein, Doctor of Phisicke*. London: Thomas Marshe, 1562.

Burke, Peter. *Popular Culture In Early Modern Europe*. London: T. Smith, 1978.

Burke, Peter, Brian Howard Harrison, Paul Slack, and Keith Thomas. *Civil Histories: Essays Presented to Sir Keith Thomas*. Oxford: Oxford University Press, 2000.

Burnet, Gilbert. *A Sermon Preached At Bow-Church, before the Court of Aldermen, On March 12. 1689/90: Being the Fast-Day Appointed by Their Majesties*. London: Printed for Richard Chiswell, at the Rose and Crown in St. Paul's church-yard, 1690.

Burns, William E. "Signs of the Times: Thomas Jackson and the Controversy over Prodigies in the reign of Charles I." *Seventeenth Century* 11, no. 1 (1996): 21–33.

Bynum, Carolyn Walker. *The Resurrection of the Body in Western Christianity, 200–1336*. New York: Columbia University Press, 1995.

Calamy, Edmund. *Gods Free Mercy to England: Presented As a Pretious and Powerfull Motive to Humiliation : In a Sermon Preached before the Honourable House of Commons At Their Late Solemne Fast, Feb. 23, 1641*. London: Printed for Christopher Meredith . . . , 1642.

Calvin, Jean. *Tvvo Godly and Notable Sermons Preached by the Excellent and Famous Clarke, Master Iohn Caluyne, In the Yere. 1555: The One Concernynge Pacience In Aduersitie: The Other Touchyng the Most Comfortable Assurance of Oure Saluation In Chryste. Iesu. Translated Out of Frenche Into Englyshe*. [Imprynted at London: By VVyllyam Seres dvveling at the vvest ende of Paules churche at the sygne of the hedgehogge, 1560.

Calvin, John. *Institutes of the Christian Religion*. Edited by Henry Beveridge. Grand Rapids, MI: Eerdmans, 1989.

Campbell, Joseph. *Historical Atlas of World Mythology*. New York: Harper and Row, 1988.

Canfield, Douglas J. "The Significance of the Restoration Rhymed Heroic Play." *Eighteenth Century Studies* 13, no. 1 (1979): 49–62.

Capwell, Richard. *A Biographical and Critical Study of John Crowne*. PhD diss., Duke University, 1964.

Caraman, Philip G. *Henry Morse, priest of the plague*. London: Longman, 1957.

Carroll, James. *Constantine's Sword: The Church and the Jews: A History*. Boston: Houghton Mifflin, 2001.

Cavendish, Margaret. *The Cavalier in Exile: Being the Lives of the First Dvke and Dvchess of Newcastle*. New York: C. Scribner's Sons, 1903.

Chapman, Honora Howell. "Spectacle and Theater in Josephus' *Bellum Judaicum*." PhD diss., Stanford University, 1998.

———. "'A Myth for the World': Early Christian Reception of Infanticide and Cannibalism in Josephus, *Bellum Judaicum* 6 199–219." *SBL 2000 Seminar Papers* (2000): 359–78.

Charles I. *By the King. A Proclamation for Setting Apart a Day of Solemn and Publick Thanksgiving Throughout the Whole Kingdom*. London: Printed by Christopher Barker and John Bill . . . , 1660.

Charles I and John Gauden. *Eikōn Basilikē: The Pourtraicture of His Sacred Maiestie In His Solitudes and Sufferings*. London: s.n., 1648.

Chaudhuri, Supriya, and Sukanta Chaudhuri. *Writing Over: Medieval to Renaissance*. Calcutta: Allied Publishers, 1996.

Chrysostom, John. *Homilies Against the Jews: An English Translation*. Translated by C. Merwyn Maxwell. PhD diss., University of Chicago, 1966.

Churton, Ralph. *Eight sermons on the prophecies respecting the destruction of Jerusalem, preached before the University of Oxford in the year 1785, at the lecture founded by the late Rev. John Bampton*. Oxford: Clarendon, 1785.

Cibber, Theophilus. *The Lives of the Poets of Great Britain and Ireland*. 5 vols. London, 1753; repr. Teddington: Echo Library, 2007.

Clarendon, Edward Hyde. *The History of the Rebellion and Civil Wars In England Begun In the Year 1641*. Edited by William Dunn Macray. Oxford: Clarendon Press, 1888.

Clarke, Thomas. *Meditations In My Confinement, When My House Was Visited with the Sickness: In April, May and June, 1666, In Which Time I Buried Two Children, and Had Three More of My Family Sick*. London: Printed by W.G. for the use of the author, 1666.

Clement, Jennifer. *Reading Humility in Early Modern England*. Burlington, VT: Ashgate, 2015.

Cockburn, John. *Fifteen Sermons Preach'd Upon Several Occasions, and on Various Subjects*. London: William Keblewhite, 1697.

Cogan, Thomas. *The Haven of health: Chiefly Gathered for the Comfort of Students, and Consequently of All Those That Have a Care of Their Health, Amplified Upon Five*

Words of Hippocrates, Written Epid. 6. Labour, Cibus, Potio, Somnus, Venus. Here-unto Is Added a Preservation From the Pestilence, with a Short Censure of the Late Sicknes At Oxford. By Thomas Coghan Master of Arts, and Batcheler of Physicke. The fourth edition, London: Printed by Anne Griffin, for Roger Ball, and are to be sold at his, [sic] shop without Temple-barre, at the Golden Anchor next the Nags-head Taverne, 1636.

Cohn, Heinrich. *"The Jewes Tragedy" von William Hemings.* Louvain: Bang, 1913.

Coleman, Edward Davidson, Joshua Bloch, and Edgar Rosenberg. *The Jew In English Drama: An Annotated Bibliography.* New York: New York Public Library, 1970.

Collinson, Patrick. *The Birthpangs of Protestant England: Religious and Cultural Change in the Sixteenth and Seventeenth Centuries.* London: Macmillan, 1988.

Cooper, Thomas. *Certaine Sermons vvherin Is Contained the Defense of the Gospell Nowe Preached: Against Such Cauils and False Accusations, As Are Obiected Both Against the Doctrine it Selfe, and the Preachers and Professors Thereof, by the Friendes and Fauourers of the Church of Rome. Preached of Late by Thomas by Gods Sufferance Byshop of Lincolne.* Imprinted at Londo[n]: By Ralphe Newbery dwelling in Fleet street, 1580.

Cowley, Abraham. *The Complete Works In Verse and Prose of Abraham Cowley: Now for the First Time Collected and Edited: with Memorial Introduction and Notes and Illustrations, Portraits, Etc.* Edited by Alexander Balloch Grosart. [Edinburgh: T. and A. Constable] Printed for private circulation, 1881.

Cox Jensen, Freyja. *Reading the Roman Republic In Early Modern England.* Leiden: Brill, 2012.

Cranmer, Thomas. *Writings and Disputations of Thomas Cranmer, Archbishop of Canterbury, Martyr, 1556, Relative to the Sacrament of the Lord's Supper.* Edited by John Edmund Fox. Cambridge: Cambridge University Press, 1844.

Cressy, David. *Literacy and the Social Order: Reading and Writing In Tudor and Stuart England.* Cambridge: Cambridge University Press, 1980.

Crome, Andrew. *The Restoration of the Jews: Early Modern Hermeneutics, Eschatology, and National Identity In the Works of Thomas Brightman.* Cham, Switzerland: Springer, 2014.

Crosfield, Thomas. *The Diary of Thomas Crosfield.* Edited by Samuel Boas. London: Oxford University Press, 1935.

Crown, John. *The Destruction of Jerusalem by Titus Vespasian.* London: Printed for James Magnes and Richard Bently in Russel-street, near the piazza's, and the Post-house in Covent-Garden, 1677.

Cummings, Brian. *Mortal Thoughts: Religion, Secularity, & Identity In Shakespeare and Early Modern Culture.* Oxford: Oxford University Press, 2013.

Cupper, William. *Certaine Sermons Concerning Gods Late Visitation In the Citie of London and Other Parts of the Land: Teaching All Men to Make Vse Thereof That Meane to Profit by Gods Fatherly Chastisements. Preached At Alphages Chuch Neare Creplegate 1592. By William Cupper.* Imprinted at London: [By R. Field] for

Robert Dexter, and are to be sold at the Brasen serpent in Paules Church yard, 1592.

Daly, Christopher T., John Doody, and Kim Paffenroth. *Augustine and History*. Lanham, MD: Lexington Books, 2008.

Daniell, David. *William Tyndale: A Biography*. New Haven, CT: Yale University Press, 2001.

Dawes, Lancelot. *Gods Mercies and Iervsalems Miseries: A Sermon Preached At Pauls Crosse, the 25. of Iune. 1609. By Lancelot Dawes, Master of Arts and Fellow of Queenes Colledge In Oxford*. [London]: Printed [by John Windet] for Cle. Knight, 1609.

de Léry, Jean. *History of a Voyage to the Land of Brazil*. Translated and introduction by Janet Whately. Berkeley: University of California Press, 1992.

Dekker, Thomas, *Nevves From Hell: Brought by the Diuells Carrier. Tho: Dekker*. London: Printed by R. B[lower, S. Stafford, and Valentine Simmes] for VV. Ferebrand, and are to be sold at his shop in Popes head Alley, neere vnto the Royall Exchaunge, 1606.

———. *The Dead Tearme. Or, VVestminsters Complaint for Long Vacations and Short Termes: Written In Manner of a Dialogue Betweene the Two Cityes London and Westminster. The Contentes of This Discourse Is In the Page Following. By T. Dekker*. London: Printed [by W. Jaggard] and are to be sold by Iohn Hodgets at his house in Pauls Churchyard, 1608.

———. *Canaan's Calamitie, Jerusalems Misery, and England's Mirror: The Doleful Destruction of Fair Jerusalem, by Titus, the Son of Vespasian, Emperour of Rome, In the Year of Chirst's [sic] Incarnation 74 : Wherein Is Shewed the Wonderful Miseries Which God Brought Upon That City for Sin, Being Utterly Overthrown and Destroyed by Sword, Pestilence, and Famine : Briefly Gathered Into This Small Volume, for the Benefit of All Well-Disposed Persons, Wherein They Shall Find Many Strange and Notable Things, Worthy to Be Regarded and Had In Remembrance*. London: Printed by Tho. James for Edward Thomas . . . , 1677.

Dekker, Thomas. *The Plague Pamphlets of Thomas Dekker*. Edited by F. P Wilson. Oxford: Clarendon Press, 1925.

Denham, John. *The Poetical Works of Sir John Denham*, 2nd ed. Edited, with notes and introduction by, Theodore Howard Banks. New Haven: Yale University Press, 1969.

Diede, Martha Kalnin. *Shakespeare's Knowledgeable Body*. New York: Peter Lang, 2008.

Doll, Dan, and Jessica Munns. *Recording and Reordering: Essays on the Seventeenth- and Eighteenth-Century Diary and Journal*. Lewisburg, PA: Bucknell University Press, 2006.

Donagan, Barbara. "Providence, Chance and Explanation: Some Paradoxical Aspects of Puritan Views of Causation." *Journal of Religious History* 1, no. 1 (1981): 385–403.

Donegan, Kathleen. *Seasons of Misery: Catastrophe and Colonial Settlement In Early America*. Philadelphia: University of Pennsylvania Press, 2014.

Downes, John. *Roscius Anglicanus, or An Historical Review of the Stage.* Edited by Montague Summers. Bronx, NY: Benjamin Blom, 1928.

Dryden, John. *The Works of John Dryden.* Edited by Edward Niles Hooker and H. T. Swedenberg. Berkeley: University of California Press, 1961.

Dudley, Scott. "Conferring with the Dead: Necrophilia and Nostalgia in the Seventeenth Century." *ELH* 66, no. 2 (1999): 277–94.

Dundes, Alan. *The Blood Libel Legend: A Casebook In Anti-Semitic Folklore.* Madison, WI: University of Wisconsin Press, 1991.

Dyer, Alan D. "The Influence Of Bubonic Plague In England, 1500–1667." *Medical History* 22, no. 3 (July 1978): 308–26.

Elyot, Thomas. *The boke named the Gouernour, deuysed by syr Thomas Elyot knight.* London: Thomas Berthelet, 1537.

Est, William. *The Triall of True Teares. Or the Summons to Repentance: Whereby the Secure Sinner Is Taught How to Escape the Terrible Sentence of the Supreame Iudge. Meditated Vpon Christes Weeping Ouer Ierusalem, Very Necessarie for These Present Times. By William Est, Maister of Arts, and Preacher of Gods Word.* London: Printed by Tho. Creede, for Arthur Iohnson, dwelling neere the great north doore of S. Paules Church, at the signe of the white Horse, 1613.

Eusebius and Meredith Hanmer. *The Auncient Ecclesiasticall Histories of the First Six Hundred Yeares After Christ, Wrytten In the Greeke Tongue by Three Learned Historiographers, Eusebius, Socrates, and Euagrius. Eusebius Pamphilus Bishop of Cæsarea In Palæstina Vvrote 10 Bookes. Socrates Scholasticus of Constantinople Vvrote 7 Bookes. Euagrius Scholasticus of Antioch Vvrote 6 Bookes. Vvhereunto Is Annexed Dorotheus Bishop of Tyrus, of the Liues of the Prophetes, Apostles and 70 Disciples. All Which Authors Are Faithfully Translated Out of the Greeke Tongue by Meredith Hanmer, Maister of Arte and Student In Diuinitie. Last of All Herein Is Contayned a Profitable Chronographie Collected by the Sayd Translator, the Title Whereof Is to Be Seene In the Ende of This Volume, with a Copious Index of the Principall Matters Throughout All the Histories.* Imprinted at London: By Thomas Vautroullier dwelling in the Blackefriers by Ludgate, 1577.

Eusebius. *The Ecclesiastical History.* Translated by Kirsopp Lake. London: Aeterna Press, 2015.

Evans, David R. "'Private Greatness': The Feminine Ideal in Dryden's Early Heroic Drama." *Restoration: Studies in English Literary Culture, 1660–1700* 16, no. 1 (1992): 2–19.

———. "Charles II's 'Grand Tour': Restoration Panegyric and the Rhetoric of Travel Literature." *Philological Quarterly* 72, no. 1 (1993): 53–71.

Ewen, C. L'Estrange. *Witchcraft and Demonianism: A Concise Account Derived From Sworn Depositions and Confessions Obtained In the Courts of England and Wales.* London: Heath, Cranton, Limited, 1933.

Featley, Daniel. *The Grand Sacrilege of the Church of Rome, In Taking Away the Sacred Cup From the Laiety At the Lords Table: Detected, and Conuinced: By the Euidence of Holy Scripture, and Testimonies of All Ages Successiuely From the First Propagation of the Catholike Christian Faith to This Present: Together with Two Conferences; the Former At Paris with D. Smith, Now Stiled by the Romanists B of Calcedon; the Later At London with M Euerard, Priest: by Dan. Featly, Doctor In Diuinity.* London: Printed by Felix Kyngston for Robert Milbourne, and are to be sold in Pauls Churchyard at the signe of the Greyhound, 1630.

Featley, Daniel, Christopher Bagshaw, and Richard Smith. *Transubstantiation Exploded: Or An Encounter Vvith Richard the Titularie Bishop of Chalcedon Concerning Christ His Presence At His Holy Table: Faithfully Related In a Letter Sent to D. Smith the Sorbonist, Stiled by the Pope Ordinarie of England and Scotland. By Daniel Featley D.D. Whereunto Is Annexed a Publique and Solemne Disputation Held At Paris with Christopher Bagshaw D. In Theologie, and Rector of Ave Marie Colledge.* London: Printed by G. M[iller] for Nicolas Bourne, at the south entrance of the Royall Exchange, 1638.

Feher, Michel, Ramona Naddaff, and Nadia Tazi. *Fragments for a History of the Human Body.* New York: Urzone, Inc., 1989.

Feldman, Louis. "The Influence of the Greek Tragedians on Josephus." *The Howard Gilman International Conferences I: Hellenic and Jewish Arts.* Edited by A. Ovadiah. Tel Aviv University: RAMOT Publishing House, 1998.

Feldman, Louis H., and Gōhei Hata. *Josephus, Judaism, and Christianity.* Detroit: Wayne State University Press, 1987.

Fincham, Kenneth, and Peter Lake. *Religious Politics In Post-Reformation England: Essays In Honour of Nicholas Tyacke.* Woodbridge, Suffolk, UK: Boydell Press, 2006.

Finley, M. I. *The World of Odysseus.* New York: New York Review Books, 2002.

Firth, Katharine R. *The Apocalyptic Tradition In Reformation Britain, 1530–1645.* Oxford: Oxford University Press, 1979.

Flavel, John. *Two Treatises: The First of Fear, From Isa. 8, V. 12, 13, and Part of the 14 : the Second, The Righteous Man's Refuge In the Evil Day, From Isaiah 26, Verse 20.* London: Printed by H.H. for Robert Boulter, 1682.

Flecknoe, Richard. *Pourtrait of His Majesty, Made a Little before His Happy Restauration.* London, 1660.

Force, Peter. *Tracts and Other Papers, Relating Principally to the Origin, Settlement and Progress of the Colonies in North America, from the Discovery of the Country to the year 1776,* vol. 4. Washington, D.C.: William Q. Force, 1846.

Fox, Adam. *Oral and Literate Culture In England, 1500–1700.* Oxford: Clarendon Press, 2000.

France, Peter, and Stuart Gillespie. *The Oxford History of Literary Translation In English.* Oxford: Oxford University Press, 2005.

Fussner, F. Smith. *The Historical Revolution: English Historical Writing and Thought, 1580–1640.* London: Routledge, 1962.

Gataker, Thomas, *Of the Nature and Use of Lots: A Treatise Historicall and Theologicall; Written by Thomas Gataker B. of D. Sometime Preacher At Lincolnes Inne, and*

Now Pastor of Rotherhith. The second edition. London: Printed by Iohn Hauiland, 1627.

Gillespie, Stuart, and David Hopkins. *The Oxford History of Literary Translation In English: 1660–1790*. Oxford: Oxford University Press, 2005.

Gillespie, Stuart, and Neil Rhodes. *Shakespeare and Elizabethan Popular Culture*. London: Arden Shakespeare, 2006.

Gilman, Ernest B. *Plague Writing In Early Modern England*. Chicago: University of Chicago Press, 2009.

Girard, René. *"To Double Business Bound": Essays On Literature, Mimesis, and Anthropology*. Baltimore: Johns Hopkins University Press, 1978.

Gittings, Clare. *Death, Burial and the Individual In Early Modern England*. London: Croom Helm, 1984.

Glaser, Eliane. *Judaism without Jews: Philosemitism and Christian Polemic In Early Modern England*. Basingstoke, Hampshire, UK: Palgrave Macmillan, 2007.

Goldstein, David. "The Cook and Cannibal: *Titus Andronicus* and the New World." *Shakespeare Studies* 37 (2009): 99–133.

Goodman, Martin. *The Ruling Class of Judaea: The Origins of the Jewish Revolt Against Rome, A.D. 66–70*. Cambridge: Cambridge University Press, 1987.

Gordon-Grube, Karen. "Anthropophagy in Post-Renaissance Europe: The Tradition of Medicinal Cannibalism." *American Anthropologist* 90, no. 2 (1988): 405–9.

———. "Evidence of Medicinal Cannibalism in Puritan New England: 'Mummy' and Related Remedies in Edward Taylor's 'Dispensatory.'" *Early American Literature* 28, No. 3 (1993): 185–221.

Gouge, William. *Gods Three Arrovves, Plague, Famine, Sword: In Three Treatises, I. A Plaister for the Plague, II. Dearths Death, III. The Churches Conquest Over the Sword*. London: Printed by George Miller for Edward Brewster, and are to be sold at his shop at Fleet-Bridge at the signe of the Bible, 1631.

Gray, Robert, Cyrus Hall McCormick, and Grenville Kane. *A Good Speed to Virginia*. London: Printed by Felix Kyngston for VVilliam Welbie, and are to be sold at his shop at the signe of the Greyhound in Pauls Church-yard, 1609.

Greaves, Richard L. "The Origins and Early Development of English Covenant Thought." *The Historian* 31, no. 1 (1968): 21–35.

Green, I. M. *Print and Protestantism In Early Modern England*. Oxford: Oxford University Press, 2000.

Green, Mary Anne Everett. *Calendar of State Papers, domestic series [of the Commonwealth] . . . preserved in the State Paper Department of Her Majesty's Public Record Office*. London: Longman & Co. and Trübner & Co., 1875–86.

Greenblatt, Stephen. *Renaissance Self-Fashioning: From More to Shakespeare*. Chicago: University of Chicago Press, 1980.

———. *Marvelous Possessions: The Wonder of the New World*. Chicago: University of Chicago Press, 1991.

Greene, John. *Nehemiah's Teares and Prayers for Judah's Affliction: And the Ruines and Repaire of Jerusalem. Delivered In a Sermon In the Church of Margarets Westminster, before the Honourable House of Commons Upon the Day of Their Monethly Humilia-tion, April 24. 1644.* London: Printed by G. M. for Philemon Stephens, and are to be sold at his shop at the golden Lion in Pauls Church-yard, 1644.

Groves, Beatrice. "Laughter in the Time of Plague: A Context for the Unstable Style of Nashe's *Christ's Tears over Jerusalem.*" *Studies in Philology* 108, no. 2 (2011): 238–60.

———. *The Destruction of Jerusalem in Early Modern English Literature.* Cambridge: Cambridge University Press, 2015.

Guibbory, Achsah. *The Map of Time: Seventeenth-Century English Literature and Ideas of Pattern In History.* Urbana: University of Illinois Press, 1986.

———. *Ceremony and Community from Herbert to Milton: Literature, Religion, and Cultural Conflict in Seventeenth-Century England.* Cambridge: Cambridge University Press, 1998.

———. *Christian Identity, Jews, and Israel In Seventeenth-Century England.* Oxford: Oxford University Press, 2010.

Hadfield, Andrew. *Shakespeare and Renaissance Politics.* London: Arden Shakespeare, 2004.

———. *Shakespeare and Republicanism.* Cambridge: Cambridge University Press, 2005.

Hakewill, George. *An Apologie of the Power and Providence of God In the Government of the World,* 3rd ed. Oxford: W. Turner, 1635.

Hakewill, George, and Benjamin Carier. *An Ansvvere to a Treatise Vvritten by Dr. Carier, by Way of a Letter to His Maiestie: Vvherein He Layeth Downe Sundry Poli-tike Considerations; by Which Hee Pretendeth Himselfe Was Moued, and Endeuoureth to Moue Others to Be Reconciled to the Church of Rome, and Imbrace That Religion, Which He Calleth Catholike. By George Hakewil, Doctour of Diuinity, and Chapleine to the Prince His Highnesse.* Imprinted at London: By Iohn Bill, 1616.

Hale, David George. *The Body Politic: A Political Metaphor in Renaissance English Literature.* Paris: Mouton, 1971.

Hall, Joseph. *The Works of Joseph Hall: Successively Bishop of Exeter and Norwich: With Some Account of his Life and Sufferings.* Oxford: Talboys, 1837.

Haller, William. *Foxe's Book of Martyrs and the Elect Nation.* London: Jonathan Cape, 1963.

Hamilton, Ross. *A Philosophical and Literary History.* Chicago: University of Chicago Press, 2007.

Hamlin, Hannibal. "Strangers in Strange Lands: Biblical Models of Exile in Early Modern England." *Reformation* 15, no. 1 (2010): 63–81.

Hampton, William. *A Proclamation of Warre From the Lord of Hosts. Or Englands Warning by Israels Ruine: Shewing the Miseries Like to Ensue Vpon Vs by Reason of Sinne and Securitie. Deliuered In a Sermon At Pauls Crosse Iuly the 23. 1626. By William Hampton Master of Arts, and Preacher of Gods Word.* London: Printed by Iohn Norton for Mathew Lawe and are to be sold for the signe of the Fox in Saint Paules Church-yard, neere Saint Austens Gate, 1627.

Hannah, J. *The Courtly Poets from Raleigh to Montrose*. London: Elibron Classics Series, 2006.

Hardacre, Paul. "The Royalists in Exile During the Puritan Revolution, 1642–1660." *Huntington Library Quarterly* 16, no. 4 (1953): 353–70.

Hardwick, M. E. *Josephus as an Historical Source in Patristic Literature Through Eusebius*. Atlanta: Scholars Press, 1989.

Harkness, Deborah E. *The Jewel House: Elizabethan London and the Scientific Revolution*. New Haven, CT: Yale University Press, 2007.

Harris, Jonathan Gil. *Foreign Bodies and the Body Politic: Discourses of Social Pathology In Early Modern England*. Cambridge: Cambridge University Press, 1998.

———. *Sick Economies: Drama, Mercantilism, and Disease In Shakespeare's England*. Philadelphia: University of Pennsylvania Press, 2004.

Harrison, Carol. *Rethinking Augustine's Early Theology: An Argument for Continuity*. Oxford: Oxford University, 2006.

Harvey, Gabriel. *A Nevv Letter of Notable Contents: With a Straunge Sonet, Intituled Gorgon, Or the Wonderfull Yeare*. London: Printed by Iohn Wolfe, 1593.

Healy, Margaret. *Fictions of Disease In Early Modern England: Bodies, Plagues and Politics*. Houndmills, England: Palgrave, 2001.

Hearne, Thomas, and Vallemont. *Ductor Historicus, Or, A Short System of Universal History and an Introduction to the Study of That Science: Containing a Chronology of the Most Celebrated Persons and Actions From the Creation to This Time, a Compendious History of . . . Transactions . . . of the Ancient Monarchies and Governments of the World, an Account of the Writings of the Most Noted Historians . . . Together with Definitions and Explications of Terms Used In History and Chronology, and General Instructions for the Reading of History*. London: Printed for Tim. Childe . . . , 1698.

Hebel, J. W. *The Plays of William Heminge*. PhD diss., Cornell University, 1920.

Heminge, William. *The Plays and Poems of William Heminge*. Edited by Carol A. Morley. Madison, NJ: Fairleigh Dickinson University Press, 2006.

Hens-Piazza, Gina. *Nameless, Blameless, and Without Shame: Two Cannibal Mothers Before a King*. Collegeville, MN: Liturgical Press, 2003.

Heylyn, Peter. *Cosmographie: In Four Bookes : Containing the Chorographie and Historie of the Whole Vvorld, and All the Principall Kingdomes, Provinces, Seas and Isles Thereof*. London: Printed for Henry Seile . . . , 1652.

Higden, Ranulf. *Polychronicon Ranulphi Higden Monachi Cestrensis: Together with the English Translations of John Trevisa and of an Unknown Writer of the Fifteenth Century*. Including translations by John Trevisa, edited and compiled by William Caxton, John Malverne, Churchill Babington, and J. Rawson Lumby. London: Longman & Co., 1865.

Highley, Christopher. "Exile and Religious Identity in Early Modern England." *Reformation* 15, no. 1 (2010): 51–61.

Hill, Adam. *The Crie of England A Sermon Preached At Paules Crosse In September 1593 by Adam Hill Doctor of Diuinitie, & Published At the Request of the Then Lord*

Maior of the Citie of London, and Others the Aldermen His Brethren. London: Printed by Ed. Allde, for B. Norton, 1595.

Hill, Christopher. "Thomas Nashe's Imitation of Christ." *Prose Studies* 28, no. 2 (2006): 211–21.

Hillman, David, and Carla Mazzio. *The Body In Parts: Fantasies of Corporeality In Early Modern Europe.* New York: Routledge, 1997.

Hoffman, George. "Anatomy of the Mass: Montaigne's 'Cannibals.'" *PMLA* 117, no. 2 (2002): 207–21.

Hopkins, Lisa. *The Cultural Uses of the Caesars On the English Renaissance Stage.* Aldershot, Hampshire, UK: Ashgate, 2008.

Horstmann, Carl, and Frederick James Furnivall, eds. *The Minor Poems of the Vernon Ms. ..: (with a Few From the Digby Mss. 2 and 86)* . . . London: Pub. by K. Paul, Trench, Trübner & Co., for the Early English Text Society, 1892.

Houlbrooke, Ralph A. *Death, Religion, and the Family In England, 1480–1750.* Oxford: Clarendon Press, 1998.

Houston, Julia. "Transubstantiation and the Sign: Cranmer's Drama of the Lord's Supper." *Journal of Medieval and Renaissance Studies* 24, no. 1 (1994): 113–30.

Howard-Hill, T. H., Philip Rollinson. *Renaissance Papers 2000.* New York: Camden House, 2000.

Hsia, R. Po-chia. *The Myth of Ritual Murder: Jews and Magic In Reformation Germany.* New Haven, CT: Yale University Press, 1988.

Hughes, Derek. *English Drama, 1660–1700.* Oxford: Clarendon Press, 1996.

Hulme, Peter. *Colonial Encounters: Europe and the Native Caribbean, 1492–1797.* London: Methuen, 1986.

Hume, Robert D. *The Development of English Drama In the Late Seventeenth Century.* Oxford: Clarendon Press, 1976.

Jackson, Thomas. *Diverse Sermons: With a Short Treatise Befitting These Present Times, Now First Published by Thomas Iackson, Dr In Divinity, Chaplaine In Ordinary to His Majestie, and President of Corpus Christi Colledge In Oxford. . . .* Oxford: Printed by Leonard Lichfield, 1637.

———. *The Works of Thomas Jackson,* 12 vols. Oxford: Oxford University Press, 1844.

Jagendorf, Zvi. "Coriolanus: Body Politic and Private Parts." *Shakespeare Quarterly* 41, no. 4 (1990): 455–69.

James I. *The Order [Banishing Rogues to the New Found Lands].* London: Robert Barker, 1603.

———. *A Booke of Proclamations Published Since the Beginning of His Maiesties Most Happy Reigne Ouer England, &c., Untill This Present Moneth of Febr. 3. Anno Dom. 1609.* Imprinted at London: By Robert Barker . . . , 1609.

James II. *The Memoirs of James II: His Campaigns As Duke of York, 1652–1660,* edited by J. S. Clark and A. Lytton Sells. London: Chatto & Windus, 1962.

Jessey, Henry, and Menasseh ben Israel. *A Narrative of the Late Proceeds At White-Hall, Concerning the Jews: Who Had Desired by R. Manasses an Agent for Them,*

That They Might Return Into England, and Worship the God of Their Fathers Here In Their Synagogues, &c. . . . London: Printed for L. Chapman, 1656.

Jones, G. Lloyd. *The Discovery of Hebrew In Tudor England: A Third Language*. Manchester: Manchester University Press, 1983.

Jones, Norman L. *God and the Moneylenders: Usury and the Law In Early Modern England*. Oxford: Blackwell, 1989.

Josephus, Flavius, and Thomas Lodge. *The Famous and Memorable Workes of Iosephus, a Man of Much Honour and Learning Among the Iewes*. London: Printed for Thomas Adams, 1620.

Katz, David S. *Philo-Semitism and the Readmission of the Jews to England, 1603–1655*. Oxford: Clarendon Press, 1982.

———. *The Jews In the History of England, 1485–1850*. Oxford: Clarendon Press, 1994.

Kay, Sarah, and Miri Rubin. *Framing Medieval Bodies*. Manchester: Manchester University Press, 1994.

Kelly, Erin E. "Jewish History, Catholic Argument: Thomas Lodge's 'Workes of Josephus' as a Catholic Text." *Sixteenth Century Journal* 34, no. 4 (Winter 2003): 993–1010.

Kelly, Gary, Joad Raymond, and Christine Bold. *The Oxford History of Popular Print Culture*. Oxford: Oxford University Press, 2011.

Kermode, Frank. *The Living Milton: Essays by Various Hands*. London: Routledge, 1960.

Kesson, Andy, and Emma Smith. *The Elizabethan Top Ten: Defining Print Popularity In Early Modern England*. Burlington, VT: Ashgate, 2013.

Kewes, Paulina. *The Uses of History In Early Modern England*. San Marino, CA: Huntington Library, 2006.

Kilgour, Maggie. *From Communion to Cannibalism: An Anatomy of Metaphors of Incorporation*. Princeton, NJ: Princeton University Press, 1990.

Killeen, Kevin. *Biblical Scholarship, Science and Politics In Early Modern England: Thomas Browne and the Thorny Place of Knowledge*. Farnham, Surrey, UK: Ashgate, 2009.

Kingsley-Smith, Jane. *Shakespeare's Drama of Exile*. Basingstoke, Hampshire, UK: Palgrave Macmillan, 2003.

Kinney, Arthur F. *Humanist Poetics: Thought, Rhetoric, and Fiction In Sixteenth-Century England*. Amherst: University of Massachusetts Press, 1986.

Knell, Paul. *Israel and England Paralelled: In a Sermon Preached before the Honourable Society of Grayes-Inne, Upon Sunday In the Afternoon, April 16. 1648. By Paul Knell, Master In Arts of Clare-Hall In Cambridge. Sometimes Chaplain to a Regiment of Curasiers In His Majesties Army*. London: [s.n.], 1648.

Knoppers, Laura Lunger. *Historicizing Milton: Spectacle, Power, and Poetry In Restoration England*. Athens: University of Georgia Press, 1994.

Kristeva, Julia, and Leon Samuel Roudiez. *Powers of Horror: An Essay On Abjection*. New York: Columbia University Press, 1982.

Lamb, Mary Ellen. *The Popular Culture of Shakespeare, Spenser and Jonson*. New York: Routledge, 2006.

Lambarde, William, *A Perambulation of Kent: Conteining the Description, Hystorie, and Customes of That Shire*. London: Baldwin, Cradock, and Joy, 1826.

Lander, Jesse M. *Inventing Polemic: Religion, Print, and Literary Culture In Early Modern England*. Cambridge: Cambridge University Press, 2006.

Lanfranc of Milan and John Hall. *A Most Excellent and Learned Work of Chirurgery*. London, 1565.

Langmuir, Gavin I. *Toward a Definition of Antisemitism*. Berkeley: University of California Press, 1990.

Lassels, Richard. *The Grand Tour and the Great Rebellion: Richard Lassels and "the Voyage of Italy" In the Seventeenth Century*. Geneva: Slatkine, 1985.

Laud, William. *Seven Sermons Preached Upon Several Occasions*. London: Printed for R. Lowndes, 1651.

Lawrence, John, *A Golden Trvmpet, to Rowse Vp a Drowsie Magistrate: Or, A Patterne for a Governors Practise: Drawne From Christs Comming To, Beholding Of, and Weeping Ouer Hierusalem. As it Was Founded At Pauls Crosse the 1. of Aprill, 1624. By Iohn Lawrence Preacher of the Word of God In the Citie of London*. London: Printed by Iohn Haviland, 1624.

Lay, Robert F. *Readings in Historical Theology: Primary Sources of the Christian Faith*. Grand Rapids, MI: Kregel, 2009.

Leech, Clifford, T. W Craik, and Lois Potter. *The Revels History of Drama In English*. London: Methuen, 1975.

Legge, Thomas, Robert Ketterer and Robert Joseph Lordi. *Richardus Tertius; Solymitana Clades*. Hildesheim, Germany: Georg Olms Verlag, 1989.

Lehmann, Forrest K. "Settled Place, Contested Past: Reconciling George Percy's *A Trewe Relacyon* with John Smith's *Generall Historie*." *Early American Literature* 42, no. 2 (2006): 235–61.

Lemonnier-Texier, Delphine. "The Analogy of the Body Politic in Shakespeare's *Coriolanus*: From the Organic Metaphor of Society to the Monstrous Body of the Multitude." *Moreana* 43–44, no. 168–70 (2006): 107–31.

Levi-Strauss, Claude. *The Naked Man*. Translated by J and D. Weightman. London: Jonathan Cape, 1981.

Levin, Carole, and R. O. Bucholz. *Queens & Power In Medieval and Early Modern England*. Lincoln: University of Nebraska Press, 2009.

Levine, Alan. *Early Modern Skepticism and the Origins of Toleration*. Lanham, MD: Lexington Books, 1999.

Levine, Carol. *The Heart and Stomach of a King': Elizabeth I and the Politics of Gender and Power*, 2nd ed. Philadelphia: University of Pennsylvania Press, 2013.

Lewis, Anthony J. "'I Feed on Mother's Flesh': Incest and Eating in *Pericles*." *Essays in Literature* 15, no. 2 (1998): 147–63.

Lightfoot, John. *The Harmony, Chronicle and Order of the New Testament: The Text of the Four Evangelists Methodized, Story of the Acts of the Apostles Analyzed, Order of the Epistles Manifested, Times of the Revelation Observed : All Illustrated, with Variety of Observations Upon the Chiefest Difficulties Textuall & Talmudicall, for Clearing of Their Sense and Language : with an Additional Discourse Concerning the Fall of Jerusalem and the Condition of the Jews In That Land Afterward*. London: Printed by A.M. for Simon Miller . . . , 1655.

Lipman, V. D. *Three Centuries of Anglo-Jewish History: A Volume of Essays*. Cambridge: Published for the Jewish Historical Society of England by W. Heffer, 1961.

Lithgow, William. *The Totall Discourse, of the Rare Adventures, and Painefull Peregrinations of Long Nineteene Yeares Travailes From Scotland, to the Most Famous Kingdomes In Europe, Asia, and Affrica: Perfited by Three Deare Bought Voyages, In Surveying of Forty Eight Kingdomes Ancient and Modern; Twenty One Rei-Publicks, Ten Absolute Principalities, with Two Hundred Islands. . . . Divided Into Three Bookes: Being Newly Corrected, and Augmented In Many Severall Places, with the Addition of a Table Thereunto Annexed of All the Chiefe Heads. Wherein Is Contayed an Exact Relation of the Lawes, Religions, Policies and Governments of All Their Princes, Potentates and People. Together with the Grievous Tortures He Suffered by the Inquisition of Malaga In Spaine . . . And of His Last and Late Returne From the Northern Isles, and Other Places Adjacent. By William Lithgow*. Imprinted at London: By I. Okes, 1640.

Llewellyn, Nigel. *Funeral Monuments in Post-Reformation England*. Cambridge: Cambridge University Press, 2000.

———. *The Art of Death: Visual Culture in the English Death Ritual, 1500–1800*. London: Reaktion Books, 1991.

Lloyd, Lodowick. *The Stratagems of Ierusalem: VVith the Martiall Lavves and Militarie Discipline, As Well of the Iewes, As of the Gentiles. By Lodowick Lloyd Esquier, One of Her Maiesties Serieants At Armes*. London: Printed by Thomas Creede, 1602.

Locke, John. *Two Tracts On Government*. Edited by Philip Abrams. London: Cambridge University Press, 1967.

Locke, John. *Political Writings*. Edited with introduction by David Wooton. Cambridge: Hackett Publishing, 1993.

Lodge, Thomas. *The Complete Works of Thomas Lodge 1580–1623*. Edited by Edmund Gosse. Glasgow: Robert Anderson, 1883.

Logan, George M. *The History of King Richard the Third: A Reading Edition*. Bloomington: Indiana University Press, 2005.

Longino, Michèle. *Orientalism In French Classical Drama*. Cambridge: Cambridge University Press, 2002.

MacLean, Gerald M. *Time's Witness: Historical Representation In English Poetry, 1603–1660*. Madison, WI: University of Wisconsin Press, 1990.

Maden, Richard. *Christs Love and Affection Towards Jerusalem: Delivered In Sundry Sermons Out of His Words and Carriage When He Came Unto Her, As They Are*

Recorded, Luke 19. 41,42. Wherein Are Handled, 1 Christs Teares Which He Shed for Ierusalem, and the Matter of Singular Observation In Them. . . . 6 The Sin and Misery of Those Who Live Under the Meanes, and Have the Things of Christ and the Gospell Hid From Them. By Richard Maden B.D. Preacher of the Word of God At St. Helens London, and Late Fellow of Magdalen Colledge In Cambridge. London: Printed by M[iles] F[lesher] for John Clark, and are to be sold at his shop under S. Peters Church in Cornhill, 1637.

Maidment, James, and W. H Logan. *The Dramatic Works of John Crowne.* Edinburgh: William Paterson, 1873.

Major, Philip. *Literatures of Exile In the English Revolution and Its Aftermath, 1640–1690.* Burlington VT: Ashgate, 2010.

Marcham, Frank. *The King's Office of the Revels, 1610–1622: Fragments of Documents In the Department of Manuscripts, British Museum.* London: Frank Marcham, 1925.

Marshall, Peter. *Beliefs and the Dead In Reformation England.* Oxford: Oxford University Press, 2002.

Marshall, John. *John Locke, Toleration and Early Enlightenment Culture: Religious Intolerance and Arguments for Religious Toleration In Early Modern and 'Early Enlightenment' Europe.* Cambridge: Cambridge University Press, 2006.

Marx, Moses. "Among Recent Acquisitions: Joseph ben Gorion Editions." *Studies in Bibliography and Booklore* 6, no. 1 (1962): 38–42.

Matar, N. I. *Islam In Britain, 1558–1685.* Cambridge: Cambridge University Press, 1998.

Matteoni, Francesca. "The Jew, the Blood and the Body in Late Medieval and Early Modern Europe." *Folklore* 119, no. 2 (2008): 182–200.

Matthews, Gareth B., *The Augustinian Tradition.* Berkeley: University of California Press, 1999.

McCullough, Peter E., and Lori Anne Ferrell. *The English Sermon Revised: Religion, Literature and History 1600–1750.* Manchester: Manchester University Press, 2000.

McEachern, Claire, and Debora K. Shuger. *Religion and Culture In Renaissance England.* Cambridge: Cambridge University Press, 1997.

McGiffert, Michael. "Grace and Works: The Rise and Division of Covenant Divinity in Elizabethan Puritanism." *The Harvard Theological Review* 75, no. 4 (1982): 463–502.

———. "Covenant, Crown, and Commons in Elizabethan Puritanism." *The Journal of British Studies* 20, no. 1 (1980): 32–52.

McGowan, Andrew. "Eating People: Accusations of Cannibalism against Christians in the Second Century." *Journal of Early Christian Studies* 2, no. 4 (1994): 413–42.

McKee, Laurie. "Giving and Serving in *Timon of Athens.*" *Early Modern Literary Studies* 16, no. 3 (2013): 1–22.

Michelson, Hyman. *The Jew in Early English Literature.* New York: Hermon Press, 1972.

Milton, John. *Complete Prose Works of John Milton.* Don M. Wolfe, General Editor. New Haven, CT: Yale University Press, 1953–83.

Milton, Richard. *Londons Miserie, the Countryes Crueltie: With Gods Mercie. Explained by Remarkeable Obseruations of Each of Them, During This Last Visitation. Vvritten by Richard Milton.* London: Printed by Nicholas Okes, 1625.

Montaigne, Michel de. *The Essayes of Michael Lord of Montaigne.* Translated by John Florio, with and introduction by Thomas Seccombe. London: G. Richards, 1908.

Montrose, Louis. *The Subject of Elizabeth: Authority, Gender and Representation.* Chicago: University of Chicago Press, 2006.

Morwen, Peter, Abraham ben David Ibn Daud, and Joseph ben Gorion. *A compendious and most marueilous Historie of the latter times of the Iewes common weale: begynnyng where the Bible Or Scriptures leaue, and continuing to the vtter subuertion and last destruction of that countrey and people. Written In Hebrue by Ioseph Ben Gorion, a Noble Man of the Same Countrey, Who Saw the Most Thinges Him Selfe, and Was Aucthor and Doer of a Great Part of the Same. Translated Into Englishe by Peter Morwyng, of Magdalen Colledge In Oxforde.* And nowe newely corrected and amended by the sayde translatour. [Imprinted at London: By Newgate marget [sic] next vnto Christes Churche, by Richarde Iugge, printer to the Queenes Maiestie], 1575.

Mueller, Alex. "Corporal Terror: Critiques of Imperialism in the Siege of Jerusalem." *Philological Quarterly* 84, no. 3 (2005): 287–310.

Nashe, Thomas. *The Works of Thomas Nashe.* Edited by Ronald B. McKerrow. New York: Barnes and Noble, 1966.

Nausea, Freidrich, and Abraham Fleming. *A Treatise of Blazing Starres in Generall.* London, 1618.

Nederman, Cary J., and John Christian Laursen. *Difference and Dissent: Theories of Toleration In Medieval and Early Modern Europe.* Lanham, MD: Rowman & Littlefield, 1997.

Neill, Michael. *Issues of Death: Mortality and Identity In English Renaissance Tragedy.* Oxford: Clarendon Press, 1997.

Nicholls, Mark. "George Percy's 'Trewe Relacyon:' A Primary Source for the Jamestown Settlement." *The Virginia Magazine of History and Biography* 113, no. 3 (2005): 212–75.

Noble, Louise Christine. *Medicinal Cannibalism In Early Modern English Literature and Culture.* New York: Palgrave Macmillan, 2011.

Origen. *Origenes Werke.* Edited by Erich Klostermann. Berlin: GSC, 1983.

Osborn, James M. *John Dryden: Some Biographical Facts and Problems,* rev. ed. Gainesville: University of Florida Press, 1965.

Ostovich, Helen, Mary V Silcox, and Graham Roebuck. *The Mysterious and the Foreign In Early Modern England.* Newark: University of Delaware Press, 2008.

Otway, Thomas. *The Works of Thomas Otway: Plays, Poems, and Love-Letters.* Edited by J. C Ghosh. Oxford: Clarendon, 1968.

Ovadiah, A. *The Howard Gilman International Conferences I: Hellenic and Jewish Arts.* Tel Aviv University: RAMOT Publishing House, 1998.

Owen, Susan J. *A Companion to Restoration Drama*. Oxford: Blackwell Publishers, 2001.

Pagden, Anthony. *The Fall of Natural Man: The American Indian and the Origins of Comparative Ethnology*. Cambridge: Cambridge University Press, 1982.

Panofsky, Erwin. *Tomb Sculpture: Four Lectures on The Changing Aspects from Ancient Egypt to Bernini*. New York: H. N. Abrams, 1964.

Paré, Ambroise. *A Treatise of the Plague: Contayning the Causes, Signes, Symptomes, Prognosticks, and Cure Thereof : Together with Sundry Other Remarkable Passages (for the Prevention Of, and Preservation From the Pestilence) Never Yet Published by Anie Man*. London: Printed by R.Y. and R.C. and are sold by Mich. Sparke, in the green Arbor Court in little Old Bailey, at the blew Bible, 1630.

Parker, Julie Faith. *Valuable and Vulnerable: Children in the Hebrew Bible, Especially the Elisha Cycle*. Providence, RI: Brown Judaic Studies, 2013.

Paster, Gail Kern. "To Starve with Feeding" The City in *Coriolanus*." *Shakespeare Studies* 11 (1978): 123–44.

———. *Humoring the Body: Emotions and the Shakespearean Stage*. Chicago: University of Chicago Press, 2004.

Penman, Michael. *Monuments and Monumentality Across Medieval and Early Modern Europe*. Donington, Lincolnshire, UK: Shaun Tyas, 2013.

Pepys, Samuel. *The Diary of Samuel Pepys*. Edited by Robert Latham and William Matthews. Berkeley: University of California Press, 1972.

Percy, George. *Observations gathered out of "A Discourse of the Plantation of the Southern Colony in Virginia by the English, 1606."* Edited by David B. Quinn. Charlottesville: The University Press of Virginia, 1967.

Pilkington, James, *Aggeus and Abdias Prophetes: The One Corrected, the Other Newly Added, and Both At Large Declared*. Imprinted at London: By Willyam Seres, 1562.

Platt, Peter G. *Wonders, Marvels, and Monsters In Early Modern Culture*. Newark: University of Delaware Press, 1999.

Po-Chia Hsia, R. *The Myth of Ritual Murder: Jews and Magic in Reformation Germany*. New Haven, CT: Yale University Press, 1988.

Popkin, Richard H. *Millenarianism and Messianism In English Literature and Thought, 1650–1800: Clark Library Lectures, 1981–1982*. Leiden: Brill, 1988.

Potter, Lois. *The Revels History of Drama in English, 1613–1660*. London: Methuen, 1981.

Prescott, Anne Lake, and Betty Travitsky. *Female & Male Voices In Early Modern England: An Anthology of Renaissance Writing*. New York: Columbia University Press, 2000.

Price, Laurence. *Englands Golden Legacy: or, A brief description of the manifold mercies and blessings which the Lord hath bestowed upon our sinful nation. Set forth to the end that all people that reads or hears it, may repent them of their sins, and be thankful to the Lord for his benefits. Here is also a brief description of Jerusalems sorrows and tronbles, [sic] which is worthy to be kept in memory*. London: Theo Jenkins, 1657.

Price, Merrall Llewelyn. *Consuming Passions: The Uses of Cannibalism in Late Medieval and Early Modern Europe*. New York: Routledge, 2003.

Pseudo-Hegesippus. *Hegesippi Qui Dicitur Historiae Libri V. Corpus Scriptorum Ecclesiasticorum Latinorum*. Edited by Vincenzo Ussani. Vienna: Holder-Pichler-Tempsky, 1932.

Purcell, Stephen. *Popular Shakespeare: Simulation and Subversion On the Modern Stage*. Basingstoke, Hampshire, UK: Palgrave Macmillan, 2009.

R.D. *The Strange and Prodigious Religions, Customs, and Manners, of Sundry Nations Containing, I. Their ridiculous rites and ceremonies in the worship of their several deities. II. The various changes of the Jewish religion, and the state it is now in; with the final destruction of Jerusalem under Titus. III. The rise and growth of Mahometanism, with the life of that great imposter. IV. The schisms and heresies in the Christian church; being an account of those grand hereticks the Adamites, Muggletonians, &c. All intermingled with pleasant relations of the fantastical rites both of the ancients and moderns in the celebration of their marriages, and solemnization of their funerals, &c. Faithfully collected from ancient and modern authors; and adorned with divers pictures of several remarkable passages therein. The second edition. By R.D.* London: Hen. Rodes, 1688.

Reeder, Caryn A. "Pity the Women and Children: Punishment by Siege in Josephus's *Jewish War*." *Journal for the Study of Judaism* 44, no. 2 (2013): 174–94.

Reiner, Jacob. "The English *Yosippon*." *The Jewish Quarterly Review* 58, no. 2 (1967): 126–42.

Richards, Irving T. "The Meaning of Hamlet's Soliloquy." *PMLA* 48, no. 3 (1933): 741–66.

Richetti, John J. *The Cambridge History of English Literature, 1660–1780*. Cambridge: Cambridge University Press, 2005.

Rives, James. "Human Sacrifice among Pagans and Christians." *Journal of Roman Studies* 85 (1995): 65–85.

Rochester, John Wilmot. *The Works of the Earls of Rochester, Roscommon, and Dorset: The Dukes of Devonshire, Buckinghamshire, &c. with Memoirs of Their Lives. In Two Volumes. Adorned with Cuts*. London: printed in the year, 1731.

Roebuck, Thomas. "'Great Expectation Among the Learned': Edward Bernard's Josephus in Restoration Oxford." *International Journal of the Classical Tradition* 23, no. 3 (2016): 307–25.

Rollins, John B. "Judaeo-Christian Apocalyptic Literature and John Crowne's *The Destruction of Jerusalem*." *Comparative Drama* 35, no. 2 (2001): 209–24.

Ronan, Clifford. *Antike Roman: Power Symbology and the Roman Play In Early Modern England, 1585–1635*. Athens: University of Georgia Press, 1995.

Roth, Cecil. "New Light on the Resettlement." *Transactions (Jewish Historical Society of England)* 11 (1924–27): 112–42.

Rubiés, Joan-Pau. *Travellers and Cosmographers: Studies In the History of Early Modern Travel and Ethnology*. Aldershot, Hampshire, UK: Ashgate, 2007.

Rubin, Miri. *Corpus Christi: The Eucharist In Late Medieval Culture*. Cambridge: Cambridge University Press, 1991.

———. *Gentile Tales: The Narrative Assault On Late Medieval Jews.* New Haven, CT: Yale University Press, 1999.

Ruether, Rosemary Radford. *Faith and Fratricide: The Theological Roots of Anti-Semitism.* New York: Seabury Press, 1974.

Russell, Conrad. *The Origins of the English Civil War.* London: Macmillan, 1973.

Said, Edward W. *Reflections On Exile and Other Essays.* Cambridge, MA: Harvard University Press, 2002.

Sandys, Edwin. *Sermons Made by the Most Reuerende Father In God, Edwin, Archbishop of Yorke, Primate of England and Metropolitane.* At London: Printed by Henrie Midleton, for Thomas Charde, 1585.

———. *A Relation of the State of Religion: And with What Hopes and Pollicies it Hath Beene Framed, and Is Maintained In the Severall States of These Westerne Parts of the World.* London: Printed for Simon Waterson dwelling in Paules Churchyard at the signe of the Crowne, 1605.

Scarry, Elaine. *The Body In Pain: The Making and Unmaking of the World.* New York: Oxford University Press, 1985.

Schloesinger, Max. *The Jewish Encyclopedia: A Descriptive Record of the History, Religion, Literature and Customs of the Jewish People from the Earliest Times to the Present Day*, Vol. 6. New York: Funk and Wagnalls, 1912.

Schreb, Victor I. "Assimilating Giants: The Appropriation of Gog and Magog in Medieval and Early Modern England." *Journal of Medieval and Early Modern Studies* 32, no.1 (2002): 59–84.

Schreckenberg, Heinz, and Kurt Schubert. *Jewish Historiography and Iconography In Early and Medieval Christianity.* Assen, Netherlands: Van Gorcum, 1992.

Schroeder, H. J. *Canons and Decrees of the Council of Trent: Original Text with English Translations.* St. Louis: Herder, 1941.

Schwartz, Murray M., and Coppélia Kahn. *Representing Shakespeare: New Psychoanalytic Essays.* Baltimore: Johns Hopkins University Press, 1980.

Schwyzer, Philip. *Literature, Nationalism and Memory in Early Modern England and Wales.* Cambridge: Cambridge University Press, 2004.

Scott, Eva. *The King In Exile: The Wanderings of Charles II. From June 1646 to July 1654.* New York: E. P. Dutton and Company, 1905.

Scott, James M. *Exile: Old Testament, Jewish, and Christian Conceptions.* Leiden: Brill, 1997.

Scrope, R., and T. Monkhouse. *State Papers Collected by Edward, Earl of Clarendon: Commencing From the Year MDCXXI. Containing the Materials From Which His History of the Great Rebellion Was Composed, and the Authorities On Which the Truth of His Relation Is Founded.* Oxford: At the Clarendon Printing-House, 1767–86.

Seeman, Melvin. "On the Meaning of Alienation." *American Sociological Review* 24, no. 6 (1959): 783–91.

Shapiro, James. *Shakespeare and the Jews.* New York: Columbia University Press, 1996.

Sherlock, Peter. *Monuments and Memory in Early Modern England.* Burlington, VT: Ashgate, 2008.

Sievers, Joseph, and Gaia Lembi. *Josephus and Jewish History In Flavian Rome and Beyond.* Leiden: Brill, 2005.

Simon, Marcel. *Verus Israel: A Study of the Relations Between Christians and Jews In the Roman Empire (135–425).* New York: Published for the Littman Library by Oxford University Press, 1986.

Slack, Paul. *The Impact of Plague In Tudor and Stuart England.* London: Routledge & K. Paul, 1985.

Smallwood, Mary E. *The Jews Under Roman Rule: From Pompey to Diocletian.* Leiden: Brill, 1976.

Smith, Geoffrey. *The Cavaliers In Exile, 1640–1660.* Basingstoke, Hampshire, UK: Palgrave Macmillan, 2003.

Smith, John. *A History of the Settlement of Virginia.* New York: E. Maynard, 1890.

———. *The Generall Historie of Virginia, New England & the Summer Isles: Together With, The True Travels, Adventures and Observations ; And, A Sea Grammar.* Glasgow: J. MacLehose and Sons, 1907.

Smith, Francis. *Jerusalem's Sins, Jerusalem's Destruction: Or, National Sins the Cause of National Calamities: Being a Discourse Seasonable for These Times : Preached In the Parish-Church of Tottenham High-Cross In Middlesex.* London: Printed by J.B. and are to be sold by Henry Bonwick, 1691.

Speaight, George. *The History of the English Puppet Theatre.* New York: J. de Graff, 1955.

Spencer, John, and Thomas Fuller. *Kaina Kai Palaia: Things New and Old, Or, A Store-House of Similies, Sentences, Allegories, Apophthegms, Adagies, Apologues, Divine, Morall, Politicall, &c. : with Their Severall Applications.* London: Printed by W. Wilson and J. Streater, for John Spencer . . . , 1658.

Spufford, Margaret. *Small Books and Pleasant Histories: Popular Fiction and its Readership in Seventeenth-Century England.* Cambridge: Cambridge University Press, 1981.

Steinmetz, David Curtis. *The Bible In the Sixteenth Century.* Durham, NC: Duke University Press, 1990.

Stevick, Robert. *One Hundred Middle English Lyric,* rev. ed. Urbana: University of Illinois Press, 1994.

Stockwood, John. *A Very fruitfull and necessarye Sermon of the Moste Lamemtable [sic] Destruction of Ierusalem, and the Heauy Iudgementes of God, Executed Vppon That People for Their Sinne and Dissobedience: Published At This Time to the Wakening and Stirring Vp of All Such, As Bee Lulled Asleepe In the Cradle of Securitie Or Carelesnesse, That They Maye At Length Repente Them of Their Harde Hartednes, and Contempt of God His Word, Least They Taste of the Like Plagues for Their Rebellion and Vnrepentance, Not Knowing with the Wilfull Inhabitants of Ierusalem, the Daye of Their Visitation. By Iohn Stockwood, Schoolemaister of Tunbridge.* Imprinted at London: By Thomas Dawson, 1584.

Stollman, Samuel. "Milton's Dichotomy of 'Judaism' and 'Hebraism.'" *PMLA* 89, no. 1 (1974): 105–12.

Stow, Kenneth R. *Alienated Minority: The Jews of Medieval Latin Europe*. Cambridge: Harvard University Press, 1992.

Stoye, John. *English Travellers Abroad, 1604–1667: Their Influence In English Society and Politics*. London: Cape, 1952.

Strack, Hermann Leberecht. *The Jew and Human Sacrifice: Human Blood and Jewish Ritual, an Historical and Sociological Inquiry*. New York: B. Blom, 1971.

Streete, Adrian. *Early Modern Drama and the Bible: Contexts and Readings, 1570–1625*. Houndmills, Basingstoke, Hampshire: Palgrave Macmillan, 2012.

Sugg, Richard. *Mummies, Cannibals, and Vampires: The History of Corpse Medicine From the Renaissance to the Victorians*. Oxford: Routledge, 2011.

Summers, Claude J., and Ted-Larry Pebworth. *The English Civil Wars In the Literary Imagination*. Columbia: University of Missouri Press, 1999.

Tadmor, Naomi. *The Social Universe of the English Bible: Scripture, Society, and Culture In Early Modern England*. Cambridge: Cambridge University Press, 2010.

Taylor, Edward. *God's Determinations and Preparatory Meditations: A Critical Edition*. Edited, and with an introduction by Daniel Patterson. Kent, OH: The Kent State University Press, 2003.

Taylor, Gary. "Gender, Hunger, Horror: The History and Significance of *The Bloody Banquet*." *Journal for Early Modern Cultural Studies* 1, no. 1 (2001): 1–45.

Taylor, John, Thomas Pearson, William Curtis, and Grenville Kane. *All the Workes of Iohn Taylor the Water-Poet: Beeing Sixty and Three In Number*. At London: Printed by I.B. for Iames Boler . . . , 1630.

Thomas, Keith. *Religion and the Decline of Magic*. New York: Scribner, 1971.

———. *The Perception of the Past in Early Modern England*, Creighton Trust Lecture. London: University of London, 1983.

Todorov, Tzvetan. *The Conquest of America: The Question of the Other*. New York: Harper & Row, 1984.

Totaro, Rebecca Carol Noel. *The Plague Epic In Early Modern England: Heroic Measures, 1603–1721*. Burlington, VT: Ashgate, 2012.

———. *The Plague In Print: Essential Elizabethan Sources, 1558–1603*. Pittsburgh: Duquesne University Press, 2010.

Tymms, Samuel. *Wills and Inventories From the Registers of the Commissary of Bury St. Edmunds and the Archdeacon of Sudbury*. London: Printed for the Camden Society, 1850.

Tyndale, William. *The Work of William Tyndale*. Edited by G. E Duffield. Appleford, Berkshire, UK: Sutton Courtenay Press, 1964.

Van Court, Elisa Narin. "'The Siege of Jerusalem' and Augustinian Historians: Writing about Jews in Fourteenth-Century England." *The Chaucer Review* 29, no. 3 (1995): 227–48.

VanderMolen, Ronald. "Providence as Mystery, Providence as Revelation: Puritan and Anglican Modifications of John Calvin's Doctrine of Providence." *Church History: Studies in Christianity and Culture* 47, no. 1 (1978): 27–47.

Vaughan, Virginia Mason. *Performing Blackness On English Stages, 1500–1800*. Cambridge: Cambridge University Press, 2005.

Waller, Gary. *The Virgin Mary in Late Medieval and Early Modern Literature and Culture*. Cambridge: Cambridge University Press, 2011.

Walsham, Alexandra. *Providence in Early Modern England*. Oxford: Oxford University Press, 1999.

Ward, Adolphus William, and A. R Waller. *The Cambridge History of English Literature*, Vol. 8. Cambridge: Cambridge University Press, 1912.

Warner, Marina. *Alone of All Her Sex: The Myth and the Cult of the Virgin Mary*. Oxford: Oxford University Press, 1976.

Waterhouse, Edward. *A Short Narrative of the Late Dreadful Fire In London: Together with Certain Considerations Remarkable Therein, and Deducible Therefrom* . . . London: Printed by W.G. for R. Thrale [etc.], 1667.

Watkins, Eric. *The Divine Order, the Human Order, and the Order of Nature: Historical Perspectives*. New York: Oxford University Press, 2013.

Weever, John, and Thomas Cecil. *Ancient Funerall Monvments Within the Vnited Monarchie of Great Britaine, Ireland, and the Islands Adiacent: With the Dissolued Monasteries Therein Contained: Their Founders, and What Eminent Persons Haue Beene In the Same Interred. As Also the Death and Buriall of Certaine of the Bloud Royall; the Nobilitie and Gentrie of These Kingdomes Entombed In Forraine Nations. A Worke Reuiuing the Dead Memory of the Royall Progenie, the Nobilitie, Gentrie, and Communaltie, of These His Maiesties Dominions. Intermixed and Illustrated with Variety of Historicall Obseruations, Annotations, and Briefe Notes, Extracted Out of Approued Authors* . . . *Whereunto Is Prefixed a Discourse of Funerall Monuments* . . . *Composed by the Studie and Trauels of Iohn Weeuer*. London: Printed by Thomas Harper. 1631. And are to be sold by Laurence Sadler at the signe of the Golden Lion in little Britaine, 1631.

Weil, Simone. *The Need for Roots: Prelude to a Declaration of Duties Towards Mankind*. New York: Routledge, 2002.

White, Arthur Franklin. *John Crowne: His Life and Dramatic Works*. Cleveland: Western Reserve University Press, 1922.

White, Francis. *Londons VVarning, by Ierusalem: A Sermon Preached At Pauls Crosse On Mid-Lent Sunday Last. By Francis White, Mr. of Arts, and Sometime of Magdalene Colledge In Oxford*. London: Printed by George Purslowe, for Richard Flemming: and are to be sold at his shop at the signe of the three Flower-de-Luces, in Saint Pauls Alley, neere Saint Gregories Church, 1619.

White, Peter. *Predestination, Policy and Polemic: Conflict and Consensus in the English Church from the Reformation to the Civil War*. Cambridge: Cambridge University Press, 1992.

Wiggins, Martin, and Catherine Teresa Richardson. *British Drama 1533–1642: A Catalogue. Volume V: 1603–1608*. Oxford: Oxford University Press, 2015.

Wilken, Robert Louis. *The Land Called Holy: Palestine In Christian History and Thought*. New Haven, CT: Yale University Press, 1992.

Williams, Wes. "'L'Humanite du tout perdue?' Early Modern Monsters, Cannibals and Human Souls." *History and Anthropology* 23, no. 2 (2012): 235–56.

Wilson, E. P. "Richard Leake's Plague Sermons, 1599." *Transactions of the Cumberland and Westmoreland Antiquarian Society* 75 (1975): 150–73.

Wilson, Thomas. *Christs Farewell to Jerusalem, and Last Prophesie: A Sermon Preached In the Quier of the Cathedrall Church of Canterburie, At the Funerall of That Reuerend and Worthy Man, Mr. Doctor Colfe, Vice-Deane of the Said Church. Octob. 12. 1613. By Thomas Wilson, Minister of Gods Word*. London: Printed [by T. Snodham] for Francis Burton, and are to bee sould at the signe of the greene Dragon in Paules Church-yard, 1614.

Wither, George. *Britains Remembrancer* (1628), 2 Vols. Manchester: The Spenser Society, 1880.

Witmore, Michael. *Culture of Accidents: Unexpected Knowledges In Early Modern England*. Stanford, CA: Stanford University Press, 2001.

Wolf, Lucien. "'Josippon' in England." *Transactions of the Jewish Historical Society of England, Sessions 1908–1910* (1912): 277–81.

Woolf, Bertram Lee. *Reformation Writings of Martin Luther: The Basis of the Protestant Reformation*. New York: Philosophical Library, 1953–56.

Woolf, D. R. *Reading History In Early Modern England*. Cambridge: Cambridge University Press, 2000.

Wright, Stephen K. *The Vengeance of Our Lord: Medieval Dramatizations of the Destruction of Jerusalem*. Toronto: Pontifical Institute of Mediaeval Studies, 1989.

———. "The Destruction of Jerusalem: An Annotated Checklist of Plays and Performances, Ca. 1350–1620." *Research Opportunities in Renaissance Drama* 41 (2002): 131–56.

Wyatt, Thomas. *Collected Poems*. Edited, with an introduction by Joost Daalder. London: Oxford University Press, 1975.

Youings, Joyce. *The Dissolution of the Monasteries*. London: George Allen and Unwin Ltd., 1971.

Yuval, Israel J. "The Myth of the Jewish Exile from the Land of Israel: A Demonstration of Irenic Scholarship." *Common Knowledge* 12, no.1 (2006): 16–33.

Zwingli, Huldrych. *Commentary on True and False Religion*. Edited by Samuel Macauley Jackson and Clarence Nevin Heller. Eugene, OR: Wipf & Stock, 2015.

Index